DATE DUE

OCT 19 1989		
NOV 0 9 1989		
OCT 8 1990		
NOV 0 6 1990		
NOV 2 6 1990		
MAY 1 3 1991		
NOV 2 1992		
DEC 1 1 1993		
FEB 1 7 1994		

Pelican Books

The Apartheid Handbook

Roger Omond was born in East London, South Africa, in 1944. His first political memory is of the 1948 election victory of the National Party, which implemented apartheid. Educated at Grey High School, Port Elizabeth, and Rhodes University, Grahamstown, where he graduated in history and politics in 1966, he joined the *Daily Dispatch*, with Donald Woods as editor, in 1967. He became successively political correspondent, head of the office in South Africa's first African 'homeland' of Transkei, features editor, leader writer and night editor. When he left the *Dispatch* in 1978 he was assistant editor. While in South Africa he wrote for the *New Statesman*, *Observer* and Gemini News Service. He joined the *Guardian* in 1978 and is now chief sub-editor in the foreign department. He is married and lives in London.

Publisher's Note

This book describes the system of racial discrimination in South Africa today: it is an anatomy of apartheid. Although headlines about South Africa change daily, the system of apartheid remains essentially intact.

Roger Omond

The Apartheid Handbook

Second edition

PENGUIN BOOKS

Penguin Books Ltd, Harmondsworth, Middlesex, England
Viking Penguin Inc., 40 West 23rd Street, New York, New York 10010, U.S.A.
Penguin Books Australia Ltd, Ringwood, Victoria, Australia
Penguin Books Canada Limited, 2801 John Street, Markham, Ontario, Canada L3R 1B4
Penguin Books (N.Z.) Ltd, 182–190 Wairau Road, Auckland 10, New Zealand

First published as a Penguin Special 1985
Reprinted 1985 (twice)
Second edition Published in Pelican Books 1986

Made and printed in Great Britain by
Richard Clay (The Chaucer Press) Ltd,
Bungay, Suffolk

Filmset in Monophoto Photina

Contents

South Africa and the Homelands

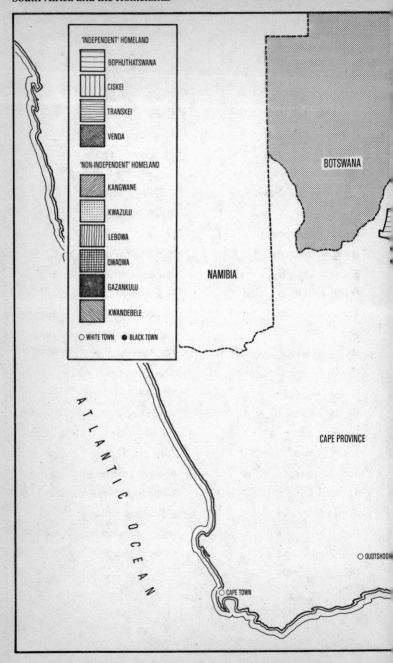

'INDEPENDENT' HOMELAND

BOPHUTHATSWANA

CISKEI

TRANSKEI

VENDA

'NON-INDEPENDENT' HOMELAND

KANGWANE

KWAZULU

LEBOWA

QWAQWA

GAZANKULU

KWANDEBELE

○ WHITE TOWN ● BLACK TOWN

BOTSWANA

NAMIBIA

CAPE PROVINCE

A T L A N T I C   O C E A N

○ OUDTSHOORN

○ CAPE TOWN

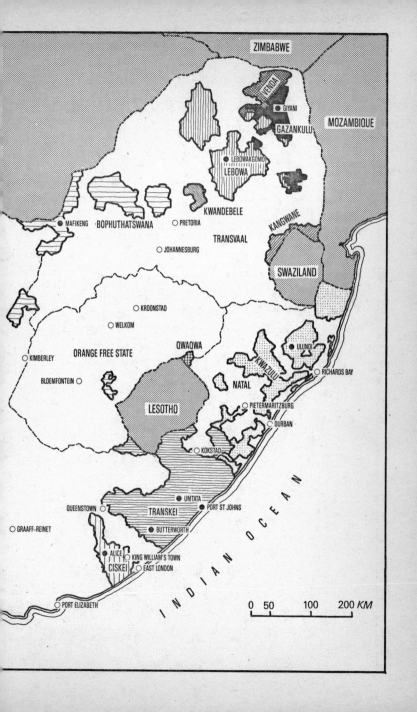

Acknowledgements

This book would have been almost impossible to write were it not for two organizations: the South African Institute of Race Relations and South African Pressclips. The former's annual *Survey of Race Relations* is invaluable for anybody interested in South Africa, containing as it does a mass of objective and carefully documented facts, often based on newspaper reports and information given to Parliament. Many of the newspaper reports are duplicated in *SA Pressclips*. When there has been duplication, for convenience' sake and because the *Surveys* are more easily available, I have credited a particular *Survey*. *SA Pressclips* is a weekly digest of cuttings from South African newspapers sent on subscription by Barry Streek, 36 Woodside Road, Tamboerskloof, Cape Town, and is essential for keeping up to date with South Africa throughout the year. Two books published by the Institute of Race Relations, *Laws Affecting Race Relations in South Africa 1948–1976* and *Race Relations as Regulated by Law in South Africa 1948–1979*, have been indispensable in understanding much of the legislation described in the following pages.

The BBC's Summary of World Broadcasts, which daily monitors South African radio and television and the South African Press Association (Sapa), also proved valuable in getting quick and ready access to South African news, particularly for the second edition of this book.

Several people with detailed knowledge of South Africa read through the manuscript while it was in preparation: Tony Kleu of the *Guardian* and Sarah Christie of Rhodes University's Law Faculty both made useful suggestions; Barry Streek added to these, and put much time and effort into supplying late information. He also allowed me the use of his extensive library of cuttings, the basis for his *SA Pressclips*.

Professor John Dugard of the University of the Witwatersrand's Centre for Applied Legal Studies pointed the way towards several sources, particularly on security laws. A number of other academics and friends in South Africa also gave useful help.

Any mistakes in the book are, of course, mine.

Peter Mayer of Penguin Books, whose idea this book was, made some valuable points while we went through a long debate on its format and style. Geraldine Cooke, who first approached me to write the book, and Martin Soames, both of Penguin, suggested some changes.

Annie Pike, who copy-edited the book, deserves special thanks for her painstaking checking, re-phrasing of questions and answers, restructuring, and patience with a complicated and changing manuscript. It would have been a far poorer book without her help.

Liz Bland and Keith Taylor, also of Penguin, were helpful and accommodating in the preparation of this second edition.

Finally, thanks to my wife, Mary, for all the help during the long months of researching, writing and re-writing.

Introduction

Apartheid has made South Africa what a government-supporting news-paper, *Die Burger*, called 'the polecat of the world'. The word itself means literally 'apart-ness'. The policy has been given a variety of names: *baasskap* ('domination'), 'white leadership', 'separate development', 'parallel development', 'multi-national development', and, most recently, by the State President, P. W. Botha, 'co-operative co-existence'. Its op-ponents, too, use a number of descriptions: 'institutionalized racism' is one which is frequently employed.

Just what the policy is or should be often depends on the observer's viewpoint and, if South African, standing in the racial/social hierarchy. The government claims, as the phrase 'co-operative co-existence' implies, that the policy is misunderstood, that the days of white *baasskap* are over, and that there are equal opportunities for every South African regardless of race. Because of the complex racial make-up of South African society, unique solutions have to be found for a unique situation. Integration of all races in a common society will not guarantee peace, freedom and prosperity for all: the solution lies in 'apart-ness'.

Opponents of apartheid say that the policy has little to do with 'co-operative co-existence' and more to do with the government's intention to maintain white political and economic power at the expense of the majority of South Africans. They see the new constitutional dispensation, introduced in late 1984, which for the first time gives Coloured and Indians their own parliaments and some say in central government, as an ill-disguised way of bolstering white control, giving the illusion of power-sharing without any real substance. They note that Africans are still excluded from the levers of power, their political future confined to self-governing and 'independent' homelands with a small consultative voice sometime in the future.

Supporters of apartheid have claimed that all the policy does is to give customary racial segregation a legislative base. Yet it is that very body of legislation that has made South Africa 'the polecat of the world'. This book explores the laws underpinning apartheid: legislation that says all South Africans must be classified by race and, following on from that, how their lives are regulated. The laws dictate where they are allowed to live and work, and often under what conditions; where and how they are educated; and where and how they are governed.

Along with this legislation based on race has come a mass of laws that curtail the civil liberties of all South Africans: what political beliefs they can express; what organizations they can join; what political meetings they can attend; and what penalties – legal and extra-legal – are attached to contravention.

The government says that these 'security' laws are needed against what it calls the 'total onslaught' against South Africa. Opponents say that security legislation is used to stifle criticism of apartheid and that racially based legislation goes hand in hand with a highly authoritarian state.

Both apartheid and 'security' laws are examined in the book, together with some of the structures of the state – Parliament, homeland governments, the Defence Force and the police, among others – that need to be understood for an appreciation of the apartheid state.

A number of examples are given of how people have been affected by South African legislation. Both statistics and individual cases are cited. In some areas, however, government statistics have not been furnished, even under parliamentary questioning. In others, as a number of observers of the South African scene have pointed out, the statistics are misleading because they exclude the millions of people in the 'independent' homelands, whose governments often do not have the facilities, or the desire, to fill in the gaps left by the central South African authorities. In a number of cases figures have been supplied by private organizations and individuals who do painstaking work that the government has tried to ignore.

Many examples of how South Africans are touched by the country's laws are drawn from press reports, themselves sometimes based on the work of individuals and organizations. Looking at the statistics and the personal examples together with the legislation, a picture of the apartheid society takes shape.

It is not a picture that will be readily accepted by all South Africans. There is controversy about the origins of apartheid, about the present state of play, and about the future.

The origins of apartheid are linked to a dispute on who arrived where and when in South Africa. White mythology is that Europeans and Africans arrived roughly at the same time: this leads some whites to claim that territorial segregation, one of the main planks of latter-day apartheid, is justified. In reality, the Africans arrived in South Africa much earlier than the first Dutch settlers, who reached Cape Town in 1652. Radiocarbon dating, says the liberal historian T. R. H. Davenport, 'has produced evidence of negroid iron age settlement in the trans-Vaal as early as the fifth century AD'.[1]

When the Dutch settled at the Cape they did not encounter any Africans. They did, however, come across earlier settlers: the Khoi-khoi (Hottentots) and San (Bushmen). Often competing for the same natural resources as the whites, many died, killed by white hunting parties, in wars, and by smallpox. The Khoi-khoi, particularly, lost their identity and inter-married with slaves from the East Indies and East Africa to form the basis of what today is called the Coloured community.

The Coloureds – the term is often resented but there is no other generally accepted name and it is enshrined in law – also have white blood. Just how much is a matter of acrimonious dispute. The leader of the right-wing Conservative Party, Dr Andries Treurnicht, contends that any 'white' blood among the Coloureds came from visiting sailors and that 'never since the establishment of the [Afrikaner] nation were the Coloured groups allowed into the Afrikaner ranks or accepted as part of the white community'.[2]

However, historical evidence does point to a problem. The first 'Immorality Act' curtailing sexual liaison across the colour line came in 1685, when marriage between whites and full-blooded blacks was forbidden, although marriage between whites and half-castes was still allowed.[3] The Coloured poet-philosopher Adam Small said recently: 'We have blackness and whiteness in our families. There are some of us who are as black as pitch and some as white as snow. That is what being Coloured is all about. We are the past and the future of South Africa.'[4]

The white community soon began to move away from Cape Town. Known as the *Trekboers* and described by the novelist André Brink as 'a ruggedly independent race of individuals',[5] they were stock farmers. Restlessly in search of new grazing, they moved north and east, encountering the Khoi-khoi, then the San, and then Africans – all competing for land.

By the end of the eighteenth century many of the Boers were in what is now called the Eastern Cape. They were pushing east, the Africans west. Into this conflict came the British government, whose permanent occupation of the Cape began in 1806. London, or its local administrators, felt the only way to maintain control in the colony was through large-scale immigration. In 1820 just over 5,000 Britons came to farm around Grahamstown. With these settlers came a more efficient system of government and some liberal thinking. Ordinance 50 of 1828 repealed the pass laws and established the principle of equality with whites of 'all persons of colour'. Slavery was abolished in 1834. Missionaries from London cast what the Boers called 'unjustifiable odium' on their treatment of blacks. In addition, an attempt was made to suppress the Dutch language. A new war with the Africans broke out and land became scarcer.

The Boers responded to these pressures by moving on again: the Great

Trek – a 'major intimation of national unity', as Brink calls it – had begun. The Trek has been important in Afrikaner folklore: the centenary re-enactment, in which wagons from many parts of the country converged on Pretoria, gave some impetus to the rise of the National Party and its election victory in May 1948.

The first Trekkers went initially to Natal around 1836, leaving again after a series of bloody wars with the Zulus and when, more importantly, the British followed them there. Their next havens were the Transvaal (called the South African Republic) and the Orange Free State. In these two republics the Boers enshrined the principle of 'no equality in church or state', a theme that, according to critics, was to form the basis of *baasskap* apartheid legislation nearly a century later.

The self-governing Cape Colony, largely controlled by the descendants of the 1820 settlers, began on a different political path. In Cecil Rhodes's phrase, the policy was 'equal rights for all civilized men'. In the Cape there was a non-racial qualified franchise from 1853 for all Her Majesty's subjects, 'without distinction to class or colour'. In the 1870s, however, Rhodes raised the franchise qualifications to exclude 'red blanket' Africans – unwesternized peasants.

The political development of Natal, very much an English colony with fewer Afrikaners than the Cape, was different again. After 1860 it saw an influx of Indians imported as indentured labourers to work on the sugar plantations. This became a political issue among the white voters of Natal, which supposedly also had a non-racial franchise, and a law was passed denying the vote to anybody whose country of origin did not have 'representative institutions founded on the parliamentary franchise'. In 1896 India, of course, did not have these; and the measure also disqualified the Africans.

The four states of South Africa – the Cape, Natal, the South African Republic and the Orange Free State – co-existed uneasily for decades. All attempts at national unity were aborted. However, when diamonds and then gold were discovered, the economy began to move away from its old agricultural base. Led by people like Rhodes, the British began to enter the South African Republic in greater numbers with the twin aims of making money and extending the Empire. What the Afrikaners (as they were calling themselves) thought of as their freedom from British rule came to an end with their defeat in the Anglo-Boer War of 1899–1902.

After the war, talk of unity revived. In 1910 the Union of South Africa was formed from the four colonies. Their different racial policies nearly sank the union before it was established; only a compromise averted the collapse of the National Convention of the colonies which set up the Union.

The compromise involved accepting all four colonies' franchise policies, rather than imposing a general system over the country. Blacks were therefore permanently barred from voting in the Transvaal (as it had reverted to being called) and the Orange Free State. The Cape's non-racial franchise was allowed to continue. By that stage 15 per cent of the electorate was black, with two Coloureds for every African. Natal's token non-racialism, with less than one per cent of the voters' roll black, also continued. Parliamentary seats in the new House of Assembly and Senate were, however, reserved exclusively for whites.

It was the Afrikaners of the two northern provinces, rather than liberals from the Cape, who provided the country's leadership for the next 38 years. Three Boer War generals – Botha, Hertzog and Smuts – were the only three prime ministers until a new generation of more conservative Afrikaners, under D. F. Malan, took over in 1948.

From 1910 racial discrimination began to be institutionalized. The 1913 Natives Land Act forced hundreds of thousands of Africans off farms they had either bought or were squatting on in the Transvaal and Free State. As part compensation, the African 'reserves' – today forming the basis for the self-governing and 'independent' homelands – were to be for Africans only. The legal reservation of jobs for certain races was implemented in the Mines and Works Act and strikes by contract workers forbidden. Some years later the beginnings of separate political institutions for Africans were shaped.

The institutionalization of the discriminatory franchise in the Act of Union led to the formation of what was to become the African National Congress (ANC). At first it was composed largely of African intellectuals who wanted amelioration of their people's economic plight and the extension of political rights. But the current was running against them. In 1936 the Cape Africans – the only ones allowed to vote – were taken off the common roll, put on a separate one, and given the right to elect three white MPs and four senators. In return, more land was promised to the 'reserves'. At no stage has that area of land risen beyond 13 per cent of South Africa.

The rise of African political consciousness coincided with the growth of the National Party, whose original impetus was not, however, anti-black racism but the urgent desire to uplift the white *volk* from poverty. By the 1930s a total of 300,000 Afrikaners – 17.5 per cent – were living in penury, many of them in the cities, displaced from their farms. In this period were launched campaigns for self-help for the 'poor whites' which eventually led to the growth of a large Afrikaner industrial and commercial empire. The same decade also saw the re-enactment of the Great Trek, increased national confidence which demanded equal status with

English for the Afrikaans language, and the 'theologizing' of apartheid. All these elements were blended into what the Afrikaner intellectual W. A. de Klerk calls a 'resentful nationalism', in reaction against the condescension of the more affluent English and, again in De Klerk's words, 'the newly apprehended threat of a black proletariat'.[6]

The National Party's 1948 election victory, which surprised many, including its leaders, gave the opportunity for apartheid to be put on the statute books. Movement in this direction was accelerated when Dr Hendrik Verwoerd, one of the main theologizers of apartheid, became Minister of Native Affairs and then Prime Minister. Three legislative pillars of apartheid were passed rapidly: the Population Registration Act, the Mixed Marriages Act and the Group Areas Act.

Legislation like this pushed the ANC towards a more militant stand. The result was the 1952 Defiance Campaign in protest against a number of racist laws, which was launched just as white South Africa was celebrating what it called three centuries of 'white civilization' in the country. The Defiance Campaign led in turn to the introduction of stricter 'security' laws; thousands of Africans were arrested and within a few months 52 ANC leaders had been banned under new legislation. The implementation of apartheid also led to greater unity among those at the receiving end, and the Congress Alliance was formed of the ANC, the South African Indian Congress (started after Gandhi began to put into practice the philosophy of *satyagraha* – 'soul force' and passive resistance – in the 1890s in South Africa) and the white Congress of Democrats. This sometimes uneasy unity was to lead to the drawing-up in 1955 of the Freedom Charter – today still the basis of the ANC's political demands and philosophy.

The parliamentary stage during the early and mid 1950s was dominated by the government's determination to impose political apartheid on the Coloureds. Until then, Coloured men (but not women) were still on the common voters' roll in the Cape and were registered in sufficient numbers to be able to swing the balance in half a dozen or more constituencies. Most voted for the United Party, which had lost power to the Nationalists in 1948. One of the movers behind the legislation which stripped Coloureds of their common-roll franchise was P. W. Botha, who was later, as Prime Minister, to bring in the new constitution giving them a separate parliament of their own.

A bill removing the Coloureds from the common roll was passed in the early 1950s by a simple majority in Parliament. It was then challenged in the courts on the grounds that the constitution demanded a two-thirds majority for any change in voting rights. This the National Party did not yet have. Parliament then passed a bill reconstituting itself as a

High Court with power to review legislation declared invalid by the Appeal Court. The High Court of Parliament solemnly sat and set aside the earlier court decision. This was again taken to court and the High Court of Parliament itself declared invalid. There, in 1952, the matter rested.

In 1954 the fiery J. G. Strijdom took over the premiership from the gentler and older D. F. Malan and the next stage began. First the Appeal Court was reformed to increase its membership to eleven, with a full quorum required to hear constitutional appeals. Next the Senate was enlarged so that the Nationalists would get their required two-thirds majority at a joint sitting with the House of Assembly. Both the Appeal Court and Senate were packed with government supporters. Finally, the Bill to put the Coloureds on a separate roll was introduced, passed by the new parliamentary majority, and validated by the new majority of Appeal Court judges. In compensation, Coloureds, again in the Cape only, were given the right to vote for four white MPs. The government would also nominate at least four senators who were to be 'thoroughly acquainted ... with the interests of the Coloured population'. All were Nationalists.

Shortly afterwards the government moved to end the limited franchise of the Cape Africans. Their power to elect three white MPs and four senators under the legislation of 1936 was abolished by the Promotion of Bantu Self-Government Act of 1959, which laid the legislative foundations for self-governing and 'independent' homelands.

In the late 1960s government attention turned again to the Coloureds when they showed signs of leaving the United Party for the Progressive Party, an offshoot of the UP that took a stronger stand against apartheid. The Prohibition of Political Interference Act was passed, limiting membership of parties to one race only. At about the same time Coloured representation in the House of Assembly and Senate was abolished. In its place came the Coloured Representative Council (CRC), on which nominated members tipped the balance for the pro-apartheid Federal Party against the anti-apartheid Labour Party after the first elections in September 1969. The CRC was eventually scrapped in 1980.

Amid all this legislating for apartheid, the National Party had steadily increased its parliamentary representation at successive elections. In the 1948 election it and its short-lived ally, the Afrikaner Party, which it soon absorbed, had a majority of only five seats over the United Party and others on the opposition benches. By 1966 the Nationalists had an unassailable majority: 126 seats against the UP's 39 and the Progressive Party's one (occupied by Mrs Helen Suzman, who spent from 1961 to 1974 as her party's sole MP).

As well as gaining increased representation in the Assembly, the

Nationalists ensured that many senior jobs went to like-minded *volk*. Afrikaners climbed up the rungs of the Civil Service or were imposed (notably in the Defence Force and broadcasting) over the heads of senior officials. To cope with the need to administer apartheid, as well as to provide employment for many of its supporters, the Civil Service was expanded: by 1984 there was one civil servant for every 25 people in South Africa – a total of 998,124 at an annual cost of R8.4 billions (£4.2 billion),* representing just under 40 per cent of the country's budget.[7] Despite efforts by the government, faced with a worsening economic crisis caused in part by loss of international confidence in the wake of widespread unrest, to curb the growth of the state, the Civil Service continued to grow. The state's wage bill for the second quarter of 1985 was R2,555 million – more than R10.5 billion (£5.25 billion) for the whole year. The number of public servants, excluding postal and transport workers, was more than one million, according to an estimate by the Central Statistical Service.[8] Afrikaner capitalism took off, too, while para-state organizations flourished.

This same period saw a decline in white opposition. The United Party seems never to have recovered from the psychological blow of losing the 1948 election. It compromised and changed in efforts to regain support; instead it lost votes and MPs at all but one election after 1948. Finally, in a last desperate bid for survival, it changed its name to the New Republic Party and so lost its identity and identifiability. Today it has five seats in the white chamber.

A number of the many MPs who left the United Party during its years in the wilderness came together to form the Progressive Party in 1959. Having absorbed more breakaway groups from the UP it was re-named the Progressive Federal Party, and is now, with 27 seats, the official opposition in the white chamber. The PFP got 18.17 per cent of the votes cast at the last white election in 1981. Yet when it actively canvassed a 'no' vote in the 1983 referendum on the new constitution, it could not hold much of that support and Mr Botha got the backing of two thirds of those whites who voted in the referendum – with much of the opposition coming from a completely different quarter.

The PFP found itself advocating a 'no' vote with the Conservative Party, a right-wing breakaway group from the National Party, and the even more rigid Herstigte Nasionale Party. The PFP was saying that the new constitution's exclusion of Africans from any voice in central government meant that it could not solve South Africa's problems; the

---

*A conversion rate of R2 to £1, current at the time of writing, has been used throughout the book. The rand later fell lower.

CP and the HNP, on the other hand, saw any power-sharing, however limited, with Coloureds and Indians as the thin end of the wedge and the probable downfall of 'white civilization'. Today the Conservative Party has 18 seats in the white Parliament; it has scored some notable by-election successes and near-misses, and is a constant right-wing factor among the *volk* that Mr Botha feels he has to take into account. This feeling was reinforced at the end of October 1985 when the HNP scored its first parliamentary win since its formation in 1969. With Conservative Party support, the HNP won the Sasolburg constituency in the Orange Free State, overturning the National Party's majority of 2,619 in 1981 to win by 367 votes. This result, plus strong showings by the Conservative Party in several other seats, was widely interpreted as a setback for the government's reform programme, and even Mr Botha said that he would have to 'take cognizance' of the by-elections.[9] The National Party's majority is still large, however: 127 seats against all the opposition parties' 50.

To compensate for the withdrawal of support on the right wing of Afrikanerdom, Mr Botha and his predecessor, B. J. Vorster, have turned more to the English-speaking voters. Several English-speakers have been in the Cabinet since the 1960s, and in the referendum on the constitution many English-speakers voted 'yes'. One survey showed that, of the supporters of the predominantly English-speaking PFP, seven voted 'yes' for every five who voted 'no'. The mainly English-speaking areas of Natal and the Border had the largest 'yes' majorities.

Much of this white parliamentary activity has, however, been over-shadowed by black extra-parliamentary action. The pattern of protests against apartheid, government reaction, sporadic violence and the arrest and/or banning of individuals continued throughout the 1950s, culminating in the events at Sharpeville in 1960. What protesters said began as a peaceful demonstration against pass laws ended in the police shooting dead 69 people. A state of emergency followed; the ANC and an offshoot, the Pan-Africanist Congress (PAC), were banned and thousands of people detained without trial.

At this stage the ANC and PAC went underground and resolved that the era of non-violent protest had passed. Umkhonto we Sizwe, the military wing of the ANC, and Poqo, military wing of the PAC, began the armed struggle that they are still pursuing. After some successful sabotage in the early 1960s, both appeared to be crushed by the increasing powers and efficiency of the Special Branch and the tendency of the courts to hand down heavy sentences.

After nearly a decade of sullen acquiescence, the Black Consciousness movement led by Steve Biko developed in the late 1960s and the 1970s.

W. A. de Klerk has pointed out similarities between the birth of Black Consciousness and that of Afrikaner nationalism: both originated in 'the human urge to be oneself and to live in accordance with one's essential nature, as a free intelligence with a particular idiom'.[10] Soon, however, Black Consciousness leaders attracted the attention of the Special Branch, and on 12 September 1977 Steve Biko died in detention. Five weeks later all the organizations that had sprung up through the movement were banned.

Black Consciousness had contributed to the Soweto uprising that began on 16 June 1976 in protest against the compulsory use of Afrikaans in African schools. Trouble spread almost throughout the country and hundreds of people were killed. Hundreds more fled South Africa, many of them into ANC camps for guerrilla training. For a number of reasons the ANC, the oldest of the liberation movements, emerged as the strongest force, both internally and externally.

Black Consciousness survives in several groups formed after the 1977 bannings, most notably in the Azanian Peoples' Organization (AZAPO) and an umbrella body of different organizations, the National Forum. It has, however, been overshadowed by the United Democratic Front (UDF), a similar umbrella organization, which takes as its starting point the Freedom Charter drawn up by the ANC and its Congress allies, which has a non-racial socialist state as its aim.

While black extra-parliamentary activity was in a ferment from Sharpeville onwards, the government began to implement its 'homelands' policy – that part of apartheid which, its supporters say, gives it moral legitimacy. Transkei became the first self-governing homeland in 1963, to be followed by the other nine to which Africans are meant to owe allegiance. Transkei, Ciskei, Bophuthatswana and Venda are now all 'independent', while KwaZulu, Lebowa, Gazankulu, QwaQwa, KaNgwane and KwaNdebele are self-governing.

The homelands policy is less than universally popular. Transkei, Ciskei and Venda are governed under virtual states of emergency. Some African leaders such as KwaZulu's Chief Gatsha Buthelezi have entered homeland governments under protest. Millions of Africans in the 'white' areas of South Africa have never seen the 'homelands' to which they are deemed to belong and where, in theory, they should exercise their political rights. The declared aim of the policy was that eventually there should be no more African South Africans: when all the homelands were 'independent' every African would be a citizen of one or another, merely coming to 'white' South Africa to sell labour. At the beginning of 1985, however, a possible shift in course was indicated when Mr Botha hinted that the question of citizenship was being reconsidered. Later that year, opening the Cape Congress of the National Party, he said that the government was committed to 'the principle of a geographically united South Africa, a common citizenship and universal franchise'. The President's Council would also be restructured to include Africans – the first time that he had spelled out what he meant when, at the beginning of the year, he had hinted at a consultative voice in central government for Africans.[11] Mr Botha, also for the first time, said that he would include 'non-traditional' leaders in consultations. A month later, a deputy minister said that these could include such opponents of apartheid as Bishop Desmond Tutu and the Rev. Allan Boesak.[12] These changes in policy, however, did not mean that the homelands – 'independent' and self-governing – would be abolished.

If the homelands policy has not proved universally popular, the new parliaments for Coloureds and Indians have not been widely welcomed either. In August 1984 elections for these chambers were held: fewer than 18 out of every 100 potential Coloured voters and 16 out of every 100 potential Indian voters went to the polls. In the Coloured heartland of the Cape Peninsula, the turnout of potential voters was about 5 per cent. This boycott of the polls – encouraged by a wide range of black organizations – resulted, for example, in the former leader of the Labour Party (the main Coloured political party), M. D. Arendse, taking his seat in the Coloured House of Representatives at a salary of R48,000 (£24,000) a year with 118 votes behind him in his Table Mountain constituency. Mr Arendse, however, had a short-lived parliamentary career: a year after his election he was unseated by the Supreme Court for bribing pensioners to vote for him. He was sentenced to a 12-month suspended jail term.[13]

Both the present leader of the Labour Party, the Rev. Alan Hendrikse, and the leader of the National People's Party in the Indian House of Delegates, Mr Amichand Rajbansi, are now non-departmental Cabinet ministers.

The new parliaments for Coloureds and Indians, with the existing white chamber, are meant to cater for the political needs of 27 per cent of South Africa's total population: 4.8 million whites (14.8 per cent), 2.8 million Coloureds (8.7 per cent) and 890,000 Indians (2.7 per cent). Excluded are 24.1 million Africans, about 13 million of whom live in the 'independent' and self-governing homelands.

Power, at this stage, still resides firmly in white hands, as the chapter on Parliament shows. The new constitution has been shaped so that the majority party in the white House of Assembly effectively rules. In the present circumstances this means the National Party, which in turn means the Afrikaners, estimated at 2.6 million (57 per cent of the white population or 8.7 per cent of all South Africans).

It is the Afrikaners who have become identified with apartheid – unfairly, many of them say. Some South African historians point out that much of the framework of apartheid has been in place for years: migrant labour, for example, began to be introduced on a large scale with the discovery of diamonds and gold in the late 1800s. But whatever the origins and causes of apartheid may be, it is the legislation passed by the South African Parliament, and particularly since the National Party came to power in 1948, that has focused so much attention on the country. This is what *The Apartheid Handbook* is about.

Racial Terminology

South African usage of terms to describe the people who live there is both confused and confusing. As elsewhere, it often reflects the political attitudes and position in society of the user. The apartheid system is based on the classification of the population into four main groups, at present officially called 'white', 'Coloured', 'Indian' and 'black'. However, these terms are not the only ones in everyday use. In addition, some words, whether official or unofficial usage, are unacceptable to many of the people they are supposed to identify. This note mentions some of the names historically or currently used to designate sections of South Africa's population and explains how racial terminology is used in the book.

For many everyday purposes a simple division into 'black' and 'white' is found to suffice. 'White' is used for all those classified and accepted as being of European descent. 'Black', despite its appropriation as the official term for Africans, is used by the majority of the South African population as a generic term for all those on the receiving end of apartheid, whether officially categorized as 'black', 'Coloured' or 'Indian'. Where it is unnecessary to be more specific, this usage is followed in the book, except in direct quotation from government sources.

The largest variety of terms has been applied to those of African descent. Someone holding extreme white supremacist views will often refer to Africans as 'kaffirs'. Official terminology was originally 'native', then 'Bantu' (literally 'people'), and is now 'black'. The word 'African' is officially taboo because it translates into Afrikaans as 'Afrikaner' – just the word used for the white, Afrikaans-speaking South Africans who have been largely responsible for institutionalizing apartheid. Nevertheless, except when quoting official sources, 'African' is the term employed here.

The word 'Coloured' is disliked by many of the people of mixed racial origins who are thus officially designated. There is unfortunately no other term in common usage. In South Africa there is an increasing tendency, particularly in more liberal newspapers, for the word to be used in quotes and with a lower-case 'c', but in other English-speaking countries this carries the risk of confusion with the more general sense in which the word is still sometimes used. I have therefore used the term 'Coloured' as it stands.

'Indian' and 'Asian' are used interchangeably by most South Africans to describe people whose forebears came from the Indian subcontinent. Where separate reference is needed the usage of 'Indian' is followed here.

Race Classification

South Africa is a multi-racial society, but four main groups are now officially recognized: white, African (called 'black' in government terminology), Coloured and Indian. What is South African race classification?

It is a government system categorizing every South African in a racial group defined by law. All identity documents, from birth certificate to driving licence, note the race of the bearer.

Has race classification always existed in South Africa?

The Population Registration Act, Number 30 of 1950, was one of the first major pieces of legislation brought in by the National Party government. Before that, some legislation included racial definitions, but they did not all correspond to one another and the system was not rigid: people could 'pass' from one group to another if their appearance made it possible.[1]

Why was race classification introduced by the South African government?

The government wanted a system that would end the 'passing' of people. It aimed at rigid classification based on appearance, general acceptance and repute. All people were henceforth to be classified on racial lines and entered into a register of the population.[2]

How did the 1950 Act define race?

The original Act classified people as white, Coloured, or Native (later called Bantu and still later black). Coloureds and Natives could also be subdivided according to their ethnological groups.[3]

How specific were definitions of race? Have they been refined at any time?

In Proclamation 46 of 1959, Coloureds were divided into Cape Coloured, Cape Malay, Griqua, Indian, Chinese, 'other Asiatic' and 'other Coloured'.

This was, however, declared void for reasons of vagueness by a judge of the Cape Town Supreme Court in 1967.[4]

The Population Registration Amendment Act, Number 64 of 1967, was then introduced. It said that the State President could, by proclamation, classify Coloureds and Africans into sub-groups. This was done through Proclamation R123 on 26 May 1967, repeating the earlier sub-groups declared invalid by the Supreme Court.[5]

Were the original criteria for determining race absolute?

The original Act said that appearance, general acceptance and repute were the tests. In 1962 an amending Act made it obligatory for appearance and acceptance to be considered together – until then acceptability was the main criterion used.[6]

There are many different ways of determining race. Have these definitions changed in South Africa?

The definition of a white was tightened in the 1962 amending Act and was made retrospective to 1950 in another Act in 1964. The Population Registration Amendment Act, Number 64 of 1967, again tightened the criteria used in classification, especially of whites and Coloureds. Descent was now the determining factor. Tests of 'appearance' and 'general acceptance' were set down for use in cases where people claimed to be white but could not prove that both their parents had been classified white.[7] A white person, according to the Act, is someone who:

'a. In appearance obviously is a white person and who is not generally accepted as a Coloured person; or

'b. Is generally accepted as a white person and is not in appearance obviously not a white person.'

In trying to define who is or is not a white, 'his habits, education and speech and deportment and demeanour shall be taken into account'.[8]

How do the courts apply the criteria of 'appearance' and 'general acceptance' in determining who is white?

There are no hard-and-fast rules. In 1981 a Johannesburg magistrate convicted a woman previously thought white for living in a 'white' area. The magistrate said she was Coloured because she had 'a flat nose, wavy hair, a pale skin, and high cheekbones'. The conviction was set aside by the Supreme Court judges ruling that while the woman was not obviously white, she was 'generally accepted' as such.[9]

What kinds of tests have been used in race classification?

Fingernails have been examined. Combs have been pulled through people's hair: if the comb is halted by tight curls, the person is more likely to be classified Coloured than white.[10] In July 1983 an abandoned baby, named Lize Venter by hospital staff, was found near Pretoria. To classify her by race, as the Population Registration Act demands, a strand of her hair was examined by the Pretoria police laboratory: she was then classified Coloured.[11]

Is there any scientific basis for a test using hair as a means of determining race?

Not according to a member of the International Institute of Trichology, which studies the functions, structures and diseases of the hair. He was reported to have said the test was invalid as there was no hair classification for Coloured people.[12]

Can race classifications be challenged?

To some extent. The 1967 Amendment Act removed the right of third parties to take legal action against a classification, apart from guardians of minor children. Third parties were still allowed, however, to object to the Secretary of the Interior – the Civil Service head of the department making the classification.[13]

Can people who believe they have been wrongly classified appeal to the courts?

There is a limited right. The 1969 Amendment Act lays down that a person may go to court against the decision of the departmental appeal board only if the board has altered his or her existing classification. Further, a person may go to court if the appeal board disagrees with the classification made by a lower official. But if the board confirms the lower official's classification, the person concerned cannot go to court.[14]

Can a person socially accepted as Coloured be legally classified as belonging to another group?

It can happen. The 1969 Act says that a person can be classified African if he or she appears to be African, even if that person has white or Coloured blood and is generally accepted as Coloured.[15]

Can Coloureds change their sub-group?

If a person's father is classified in one Coloured sub-group, that person must be classified in the same sub-group, according to the 1969 Act.

How many legal subdivisions are there of the racial group defined as African?

In terms of various laws, nine African 'national units' are recognized: North Sotho, South Sotho, Tswana, Zulu, Swazi, Xhosa (two units), Tsonga and Venda. Government policy assigns every African to one of these groups.

Although people cannot physically change race, can they do so in the eyes of the law?

Thousands of people have been affected in this way by the Population Registration Acts. In 1984, the Minister of Home Affairs told Parliament, 795 South Africans were re-classified. They included 518 former Coloureds who became white, two whites who became Chinese, one white who became Indian, 89 Africans who became Coloured and five Coloureds who became African.[16] In 1983, a total of 690 people changed: two thirds were Coloureds who became white; 71 Africans became Coloured; and 11 whites were classified to other groups.[17] In the year July 1981 to June 1982 a total of 997 'changed race'. Among them were one Indian who became white, four Cape Coloured to Chinese, 15 white to Chinese, three 'other Asian' to Cape Coloured, and three African to Griqua.

Do people always know what race they are assigned to?

No. In 1984, for example, a government commission studying the courts found that two pre-school children were held in detention for three years while they awaited a government decision on their race.[18] In the 1960s Sandra Laing, born to white parents in the eastern Transvaal, was asked to leave her white school at the age of 11 because she 'looked Coloured'. She was re-classified Coloured, but after a long legal battle the decision was reversed. She then lived with an African man and applied to be reclassified African so that the relationship could be legalized.[19]

There have been many reported cases of families being split by race classification. Branches of some families have been classified white while others have been classified Coloured. Dark-skinned children of Coloureds trying to pass for white are said sometimes to have been abandoned or sent to relatives of a deeper hue. Dark-skinned children of white parents, as the Sandra Laing case shows, have also caused problems.

Have people been re-classified more than once?

Yes. In late 1984, for example, a 'white' father was re-classified Coloured – the fifth time he had crossed the racial divide. His 'Indian' wife also changed and was classified Coloured. The change meant that the couple, Vic and Farina Wilkinson, could live together legally as man and wife. Mr Wilkinson was originally classified 'mixed', then 'European' (white), then Coloured, then white, and finally Coloured.[20]

Is there a 'pure' white race?

Not according to evidence given to a parliamentary select committee investigating the Immorality and Mixed Marriages Acts in 1984. Dr E. D. du Toit, senior lecturer in the University of Cape Town's department of human genetics, said there was a considerable admixture of so-called Southern African genes, mostly Khoisan (Hottentot and Bushman) as well as Negro and Asiatic. White South Africans in general had more than seven per cent mixed blood.[21]

A major row broke out in 1985 over the claim made by an academic, Dr Hans Heese, in his book *Groep Sonder Grense* ('Groups Without Boundaries') that the forebears of many leading Afrikaner families had married or had relationships with Asian slaves. At least 18 MPs in the whites-only House of Assembly have surnames indicating a racially mixed genealogy.[22] In the ensuing row about the book:

● The heart transplant surgeon Chris Barnard challenged the leader of the far-right Conservative Party, Dr Andries Treurnicht, to verify his claim to pure white ancestry by submitting to a medical test.[23]

● Sixteen people said they would sue the *Sunday Times*, which gave extensive coverage to Dr Heese's findings, for R320,000 (£160,000) unless the paper undertook not to quote again from the book. They said that they had been embarrassed and humiliated by the suggestion that they might be descended from people of colour.[24]

● A member of the extremist Herstigte Nasionale Party and of the Pretoria City Council punched a fellow-councillor in a row over mixed ancestry. Piet Rudolph said the impression was given that he was 'not worthy of representing a white electorate – that my ancestors were people who acted disgracefully towards their race and *volk* by sexually mixing with other colours'.[25]

An admission that race classification, an important pillar of apartheid, is widely resented came in a report by the Human Sciences Research Council in October 1985. It found that the system was 'probably the root cause of ill-feeling between South Africa's different groups' and that there was a 'clearly apparent link between population registration and the establishment and maintenance of white supreme authority'. The HSRC report proposed that, instead of a system where appearance and origin were the determining factor, the emphasis should be on freedom of association and acceptance.[26]

Sex across the Colour Line

The South African government has abolished two laws that prohibit inter-racial sex. What is this legislation and what does it say?

The Immorality Amendment Act, Number 23 of 1957, forbade 'unlawful carnal intercourse' or 'any immoral or indecent act' between a white person on the one hand and an African, Indian or Coloured on the other. Non-South Africans were exempt if *both* partners were foreign. The Prohibition of Mixed Marriages Act, Number 55 of 1949, which was one of the first laws introduced after the National Party won the 1948 election, made marriages between whites and members of any other racial groups illegal.

These laws were often regarded as cornerstones of apartheid. Why have they been scrapped?

In 1979 the then Prime Minister and now President, P. W. Botha, said in a BBC interview that there was no moral or religious objection to mixed marriages: the problem lay in difficulties which children of such marriages would experience. In November 1984, while stressing that he personally was not in favour of mixed marriages or 'immorality', Mr Botha said that the laws had made enemies for South Africa.[1]

'There has been [racial] mixing since Jan van Riebeeck arrived here. These laws were introduced in 1927, so what happened between 1652 and 1927?'[2]

Have other parties also called for the abolition of sexual apartheid?

The Progressive Federal Party has long called for abolition. The Labour Party which forms the majority party in the Coloured House of Representatives said in August 1984 that it would push for the laws to be repealed, which it did in 1985. The white Conservative Party was the only group in Parliament which wanted the legislation retained.

An indication of the strength of feeling among right-wingers against abolition of the Acts was given in April 1985 when 3,000 people – a large number for a South African political meeting – held a protest rally in Pretoria. The leader of the Conservative Party was presented with a petition signed by 25,000 people protesting against repeal. The rally was significant, said *The Times*, because it united the Conservative Party leader, Andries Treurnicht, with Jaap Marais, leader of the even more fanatical Herstigte Nasionale Party.[3]

What has been the churches' attitude towards the laws?

The three Dutch Reformed churches for many years supported the two Acts, with some clerics citing scriptural backing for them. When the government announced its intention to repeal the laws, the chief executive officer of the biggest Afrikaans church, the Nederduitse Gereformeerde Kerk, said it believed the Acts should be maintained, even though the last synod of the NGK had decided there were no scriptural grounds for the retention of the laws.[4] The Presbyterian and Methodist churches welcomed the move, but pointed out that it would have key implications for the Group Areas Act. The Southern African Catholic Bishops' Conference said the proposed abolition was 'only window dressing' and added: 'Such steps remain meaningless until the cornerstones of apartheid, the Population Registration Act and the Group Areas Act, are repealed.'[5]

Has the government indicated that the Population Registration and Group Areas Acts will also be abolished?

On the day the government announced its intention to scrap the Immorality and Mixed Marriages Acts the Minister of Home Affairs, F. W. de Klerk, said that there would be no changes to group areas or population registration laws. The Acts all made provision for the various problems which would be encountered by couples, and these could be sorted out by application for permits. The Population Registration Act, he said, made provision for allowing people to stay wherever they wanted, depending, for example, on acceptance by the community.[6] Problems would be dealt with 'administratively', the government said.[7]

Will mixed couples therefore still encounter apartheid problems?

Mr De Klerk said that segregated facilities would be upheld for the sake of good order and peaceful co-existence. The government had made strong points of advising marriage counsellors to tell people intending to enter into a mixed marriage about the problems that the various segregation laws would face them with.[8]

Some of the problems faced by mixed couples were shown in late 1985, only a few months after abolition of the Acts. The Herstigte Nasionale Party fought a by-election in Sasolburg largely on the issue of a white electrician and his Coloured wife who lived in the constituency. Pamphlets were circulated warning that the couple, Gerrie and Anne van den Berg, who stayed in a caravan park, 'could live in your street . . . and their children could go to your schools'. A few days after the by-election, which the HNP won, the couple moved into a Coloured township.[9]

In the Eastern Cape town of Kirkwood, death threats were made against a former Londoner, Jack Salter, and his Coloured wife. Mr Salter, whose shop was exempt from an African boycott of white-owned establishments, said that right-wing whites were responsible for the death threats.[10] Threats from a different source were made to another Englishman, Bob Seddon, who married a Coloured, Sylvia. He was reported to have been attacked by militant black youths on a beach because he was there with his wife.[11]

Was the move towards abolition a sudden one?

An Opposition MP moved a private member's bill for abolition as far back as 1962. However, it was Mr Botha's interview with the BBC in 1979 that first set the ball rolling. In 1982 he said that if the churches could agree he was prepared to amend the laws, while in 1983 he reported that he had held discussions with church leaders, who had sharply differing views of the matter.

At the end of June 1983 a parliamentary select committee was appointed to investigate the relevant Acts. In July 1984 the committee reported that the laws could not be improved: 'It is . . . the retention or repeal of the measures which is at issue.' They could not 'be justified on scriptural or other grounds'.[12]

In 1985 the Acts were put to a joint committee of the new tricameral Parliament for consideration and possible abolition. In April 1985 the committee recommended abolition and this was accepted by the government.[13] The laws were finally abolished in June 1985.

What were the penalties for contravening the Immorality Act?

Section 16, the provision dealing with inter-racial sex, said that an offender was liable for imprisonment for up to seven years with hard labour and a maximum of ten lashes when the male was under 50 years of age.[14] This was for 'unlawful carnal intercourse' or 'any immoral or indecent act'.

How did the courts define an 'immoral or indecent act'?

In some cases a kiss between people of different races led to conviction; in others charges brought on these grounds were dismissed.

How many people were convicted?

Between 1950 and the end of 1980 more than 11,500 people were convicted[15] and more than twice that number charged. In 1984 a total of 207 contraventions were investigated, 171 people were charged and 114 convicted, Parliament was told in February 1985.[16] The year before that 126 people were convicted. The number of charges laid began to decline from 1971 when the police were instructed by ministerial order 'where possible not to resort to arrest until the case has been placed before the attorney-general or senior state prosecutor for his decision'. However, when a policeman came across 'the commission of such offence, the offenders may be arrested'.[17]

What police techniques were used to catch offenders and prove guilt?

Special Force Order 025A/69 detailed the use of binoculars, tape recorders, cameras and two-way radios to trap offenders. It also spelled out how bedsheets should be felt for warmth and examined for stains.[18] Police were also reported to have examined the private parts of couples and taken people to district surgeons for examination.[19]

Did people who were charged under the Act tend to come from a particular class?

The Act caught people from every level of society: Dutch Reformed clerics, farmers, lawyers, businessmen, visiting seamen, and the secretary to a former prime minister.[20] The Afrikaans poet and writer Breyten Breytenbach, who married a Vietnamese woman in Paris, could not return legally to South Africa with her because of her race. A number of others also went into exile because of the Act, some of them overseas, while others, more recently, lived in the 'independent' homelands that had scrapped the law.[21]

How have charges under the Immorality Act affected people's lives?

Over the last 20 years at least 16 white men have committed suicide by gassing, hanging, shooting, drowning or taking insecticide after being charged. In one case a charge was withdrawn when the man concerned had already committed suicide.[22] Others charged have left the country, while social ostracism and loss of employment has also been reported.

Have the penalties under the Act always been applied identically to both partners charged?

In one case a cleric was convicted of incitement to contravene the Act and given a six months' suspended sentence. His former housemaid, who had been tried separately and earlier, was jailed for six months and served ten days before being released because of the discrepancy in sentence.[23]

If a man and a woman decided to get married, who decided which racial groups they belonged to and whether their marriage would be valid?

Initially, because race classification of the population was still incomplete, marriage officers were the arbiters. The Prohibition of Mixed Marriages Act said that if a racially mixed marriage, solemnized in good faith by a marriage officer, was later held to be invalid, any children born before the marriage was annulled would be deemed legitimate.[24] Later, when the classification system was in full operation, those wishing to marry had to produce official identity papers, which indicate the holder's racial group.

Were mixed marriages contracted outside the country recognized by South Africa?

The Mixed Marriages Amendment Act, Number 21 of 1968, said that if any male South African, or a male domiciled in the country, married outside the Republic a person he could not legally wed inside South Africa because the partner was of another race, then the marriage was void and of no effect.[25]

What could happen if a mixed couple married in another country then lived as man and wife in South Africa?

They could be prosecuted under the Immorality Act for 'unlawful carnal intercourse'.

Did earlier legislation on 'immorality' apply equally to men and women?

The first 'immorality' law in 1685 forbade marriage between whites and full-blooded 'blacks', although it was allowed between whites and people of mixed race.[26] A 1902 law banned intercourse between black men and white women, not white men and black women. The country's 1927 Immorality Act forbade all extra-marital intercourse between *all* whites and Africans, irrespective of sex. A 1950 amendment extended this to bar sex between whites and any other race – that is, Coloureds and Indians as well as Africans. The 1957 Act increased the maximum penalty to seven years' imprisonment and made it an offence for whites or blacks to solicit one another to commit any 'immoral or indecent act'.[27] The Act was scrapped by all the 'independent' homelands before the South African government decided in 1985 to abolish it and the Mixed Marriages Act.

Were there mixed marriages in South Africa while the Act was in force?

Nine were solemnized in 1983, Parliament was told in 1984. The government had not registered any of these, but documents registering the marriages had been received in apparent contravention of the Act.[28] Between 1946 and the introduction of the Act in 1949, a total of 75 people had married across the colour line, according to the historian Leo Marquard.[29] In 1939 a government-appointed commission of inquiry was told that since 1925 less than one per cent of all marriages had been racially mixed, and that the figure had currently decreased to four per 1,000.[30]

In the five months after the repeal of the Mixed Marriages Act, more than 190 mixed marriages were registered: in July, the first full month after repeal, there were 64 mixed marriages out of a total of 6,000 countrywide.[31]

Group Areas

In a democracy it is assumed that, subject to their means, people may choose the areas in which they live and work. In South Africa, however, there are group areas; what are they?

They are designated and demarcated stretches of land (usually in urban areas) which can only be legally owned and occupied by people of a particular racial group.[1]

Can the exercise of freedom of choice about where to live lead to total loss of freedom through imprisonment?

An Indian, Mr Nana Sita, served three terms of imprisonment for refusing to leave his home in Pretoria, where he had lived for 37 years, when it was zoned for whites only. There have been fewer prosecutions recently: from 1978 to 1981, 893 prosecutions were brought in Johannesburg; in 1983 there was only one.

However, in September 1985 landlords in the Johannesburg suburb of Hillbrow who had black tenants were warned that they might be prosecuted, giving rise to fears of a new clampdown on 'illegal' occupiers. A 1982 Supreme Court case prevented the authorities from evicting 'illegals' if they could not provide alternative accommodation. Little or no alternative accommodation was available, so a number of blacks – the exact total is not known – stayed on. The fear in September 1985 was that the authorities were putting pressure on landlords to do the evictions themselves, without the authorities being directly involved, merely by threatening prosecution under the Group Areas Act.[2]

What law sanctions the division of land into group areas?

The Group Areas Act. The original Act, Number 41 of 1950, like the Mixed Marriages Act and the Population Registration Act, was among the first introduced by the National Party government after its 1948 election victory. The Group Areas Act is highly complex, and has been amended numerous times since it was first passed.

How did the Act set about establishing group areas?

'Controlled' areas were to be proclaimed: eventually only people of a designated racial group would be able to live and work there. Individual buildings in a 'controlled' area could also be 'defined' and occupation limited to one race group.[3] 'Specified' areas were also to be proclaimed: in a 'specified' area only people of a particular racial group could be occupiers. Soon after the Act was passed controls were imposed throughout the country, except for African townships and reserves and Coloured mission stations and reserves. In practice, this meant that many people had to move out of their homes and businesses because they were in a group area meant for another race.

Introducing the Group Areas Act in Parliament in 1950, the then Minister of the Interior said the legislation was needed to reduce points of contact to a minimum. 'The paramountcy of the white man and of Western civilization in South Africa must be ensured in the interests of the material, cultural, and spiritual development of all races,' he said.[4]

How many people have been moved because of group areas?

The exact total is not known: government spokesmen have given figures for families only. The Minister of Constitutional Development and Planning, Chris Heunis, stated in February 1985 that a total of 126,176 families had been moved from their homes from the implementation of the Act until the end of August 1984. Of these, 2,418 (2 per cent) were white, 83,691 (66 per cent) were Coloured, and 40,067 (32 per cent) were Indian.[5]

A number of others still have to be moved: in May 1984 the figures were said to be 1,372 Coloureds (67 per cent), 684 Indians (33 per cent) and no whites.[6]

The group areas policy affected family life; did it also affect trade?

Mr Heunis told Parliament in February 1985 that 54 whites (2 per cent), 187 Coloureds (6.7 per cent) and 2,530 Indians (91.3 per cent) had been moved from business premises. Nobody else was to be moved.[7]

Are removals under the Group Areas Act in accordance with the wishes of all the people?

Coloured and Indian leaders have long and consistently called for the abolition of the Act. The Coloureds and Indians in the new tricameral

Parliament have also called for an end to group areas, as have the leaders of some white parties.

The government, however, has made it clear that the Group Areas Act will stay. In October 1985 the State President, P. W. Botha, said the Act, unlike the Immorality and Mixed Marriages Acts which had recently been abolished, was not discriminatory. 'It is not discrimination to protect black, Coloured and Indian communities in their own areas,' he said. '. . . If other population groups have rights and a rightful claim to humanitarian treatment, then I say the whites . . . are also entitled to justice and to live as citizens of the country in the manner they choose.'[8]

But Mr Botha's two black Cabinet colleagues, Alan Hendrickse (Coloured) and Amichand Rajbansi (Indian), continued to attack the Act. Mr Hendrickse was forthright at a Labour Party Congress: 'To hell with the Group Areas Act,' he said.[9] Mr Rajbansi said he and Mr Hendrickse intended to raise the issue at 'various places' and during the 1986 parliamentary session.[10]

The State President's rejection of any change to the Act was reported to have angered some members of the President's Council. Mr Botha himself had commissioned the council to examine the Act. Members of the council said that they were being told by Mr Botha what their findings should be before they had a chance to present them.[11]

Are the wishes of local authorities respected in the implementation of the group area laws?

Not necessarily. In cases where central and local government disagree, an amending Act gives central government power to act in areas normally under local control and to debit the local authority.

How do the group area laws affect Chinese people?

In June 1984 the Minister of Community Development said that Chinese would have the same status as whites under the Group Areas Act, but if a Chinese had married somebody from another racial group, 'then that Chinese will have to live in the marriage partner's group area'.[12] This was confirmed in May 1985 when the government said that the 11,000-strong Chinese community would be exempt from the Group Areas Act with immediate effect. Chinese would be allowed to own property and shops in the white areas instead of having to apply for permits as before.[13]

How are the group areas distributed among the different races?

By the end of 1984 a total of 899 group areas had been proclaimed, with an area of 895,534 hectares. Of these, 451 group areas were for whites (83.6 per cent by area), 326 for Coloureds (10.6 per cent) and 122 for Indians (5.6 per cent).[14] (Whites comprise 15 per cent of the population, Coloureds 9 per cent and Indians 3 per cent.)

How many areas are open to all races for trade?

In May 1983, 26 areas were open, against the total of 877 reserved areas. In February 1985 the government said it would open 44 selected but unidentified business districts to all races.[15] In March 1985 the prospect of blacks being allowed to manage businesses in 'white' areas was held out by the government. The law debarring this changed during the 1985 parliamentary session.[16]

Are any residential areas open, in theory or in practice?

Indians in some parts of Johannesburg and Coloureds in some parts of Cape Town live illegally in 'mixed' areas because of housing shortages. There are also some legally mixed areas in Cape Town.

In addition, a sizeable number of blacks, many of them domestic servants, live in 'white' areas. Some are accommodated legally in what are known as 'servants' quarters' attached to whites' houses or, less commonly in blocks of flats for whites. Many also live illegally in these areas. The law usually allows registered domestic servants to live in rooms provided by white owners; the servants' spouses, however, are usually forbidden to use the same accommodation.

Towards the end of 1985 some hints were given that 'grey' areas could be established giving free residential choice without abolishing the Group Areas Act. The chairman of the Human Sciences Research Council's investigation into 'inter-group relations', Dr H. C. Marais, said in late August that the Act had resulted in 'immense discrimination', but even repeal would not stop residential segregation. The HSRC investigation had recommended removing discrimination relating to access to economic resources.[17]

In October 1985 government sources said that municipalities could be given the option to recommend that suburbs be open to all races. Government strategy was to retain the Act but to put the onus on white liberal local authorities to open areas and thereby divert any white backlash away from the government. Pioneer cities were likely to be

Durban, Sandton (in greater Johannesburg) and Cape Town. This new government policy, it was said, could take effect in 1986 after the President's Council report on the Act was presented.[18]

As the law stands now, the Group Areas Act applies to the dead as well as the living. In September 1985 a victim of unrest in East London, Joseph Menold, had to be taken away from a mass funeral service to be buried in a Coloured cemetery a few hundred yards away from where 17 other – but African – unrest victims were buried.[19]

Diplomacy and politics involve negotiation and debate with people of varying colours and creeds. Are Coloured and Indian members of the new parliaments exempt from the group area laws?

No. Separate parliamentary 'villages' were built for these new M Ps. Housing for Coloured M Ps with constituencies outside Cape Town cost R2.9 million (£1.5 million). Indian M Ps' houses cost R41,000 each (£20,500). The Minister of Communications and Public Works, Dr L. A. P. A. Munnik, said in 1985 that about R26 million (£13 million) had been spent on housing, office and debating accommodation for the Coloured and Indian M Ps. The separate housing construction follows a statement in March 1983 that Coloured and Indian M Ps and ministers would have to live in separate residential areas, and not in the already existing 'white' parliamentary village.[20]

Black diplomats living in South Africa are exempt from the Group Areas Act.

National Government

South Africa has an elected government; who is the head of state?

The State President. At present this is P. W. Botha, the former Prime Minister.

How much power does the President of South Africa have?

In terms of the Republic of South Africa Constitution Act, Number 110 of 1983, the presidency was transformed from a titular and ceremonial post into an executive one. Before that Act, the State President's role was roughly similar to the British Monarch's; now he has powers akin to those of the American President – some say, even greater. His responsibilities include:

Determining sessions of Parliament;
Dissolving Parliament;
Appointing ministers;*
Proclaiming or ending martial law;
Declaring war and making peace;
Appointing and removing civil servants;
Controlling the flow of legislation to Parliament; and
Having some right of veto over legislation.

Who votes in the presidential election?

An electoral college made up of members of the three houses of Parliament: the House of Assembly for whites, the House of Representatives for Coloureds, and the House of Delegates for Indians.

Which group has the dominant voice in the electoral college?

The whites: they send 50 members to the electoral college, while the Coloureds send 25 and the Indians 13. They are elected by majority vote,

---

*In November 1985 the State President dismissed the Indian House of Delegates' minister responsible for the budget, Boetie Abramjee, for allegedly leaking information about the exploitation of oil and gas at Mossel Bay. Section 24:4 of the constitution says that matters entrusted in secret to a member of the Ministers' Council may not be revealed directly or indirectly. Mr Abramjee denied the alleged leak and complained that he was not given a chance to explain.

which means, in effect, that the President is elected by MPs of the white house, currently controlled by the National Party.

Can the State President be impeached?

The President can be impeached on grounds of 'misconduct or inability to perform efficiently the duties of his office'. In terms of the Constitution Act, he can be removed only if more than half the members of each of the three houses have petitioned the Speaker, a joint committee has been appointed by the three houses, and each house has asked for an electoral college to be formed after considering the joint committee's report. In effect, this means that any move to impeach the President could be blocked by the governing party.

Laws are passed by Parliament; how does the State President control legislation?

He decides which bills are 'general affairs' and which are 'own affairs', the latter defined as matters of concern to only one racial group. His decision cannot be questioned in any court. Once he has decided that something is the 'exclusive concern' of one house, it is debated in that house only. 'Common concern' matters go through all three houses. No amendment to an 'exclusive concern' bill can be made unless the President agrees that the amendment is also of exclusive interest to the racial group concerned.

What are 'general affairs'?

They are defined as 'matters which are not own affairs of a population group'; these are listed in Schedule I of the Constitution Act as:

Foreign affairs, defence, state security, commerce and industry, law and order, and African affairs.

Welfare policy, standards, control of welfare funds, the social work profession, and civil and military pensions.

Sport outside school.

Health issues affecting more than one racial group.

Housing finance, Group Area delimitations, rent control, and removal of squatters.

Local government matters affecting more than one racial group.

Agricultural matters affecting more than one racial group.

What are 'own affairs'?

Education of a specific race group, subject to any 'general law' on syllabuses, examinations, finance, pay and employment conditions: social welfare, health, housing, community and town development, rent control, squatter removal, local government, agriculture, water supplies, and the appointment of marriage officers, where all these apply to a specific population group only.

There are three houses of Parliament: white, Coloured and Indian. How many members are there in each house?

The white Assembly has 178 members, 166 of them elected directly by the white voters, eight elected by the MPs, and four nominated by the State President. The Coloured House of Representatives has 85 members: 80 elected directly, three indirectly elected, and two nominated. The Indian House of Delegates has 45 members: 40 elected directly, three indirectly elected, and two nominated.

While apartheid theory has it that party politics should not cross the racial divisions between each of the three houses of Parliament, the abolition in June 1985 of the Prohibition of Political Interference Act, Number 51 of 1968,* which had made multi-racial parties illegal, created a new situation. The Progressive Federal Party decided in August 1985 that, in principle, it would contest seats for the House of Representatives and the House of Delegates. It was reported, however, that the party was unlikely to do so in the near future, mainly because of the lack of support among Indians and Coloureds for their new parliamentary chambers.

How long are the houses elected for?

Normally five years, the same period as the State President's term of office.

Is the number of MPs in each house proportional to the size of the racial group which elects them?

No. There is one directly elected MP for every 26,785 whites, one Indian MP for every 21,750 Indians, and one Coloured MP for every 33,780 Coloureds.

*See chapter on unlawful organizations.

Some areas of South Africa are much more densely populated than others. Do all parliamentary constituencies contain roughly the same number of voters?

No. Since Union in 1910, constituencies have been allowed to be 'loaded' by up to 15 per cent: a rural seat can have up to 15 per cent fewer voters than the norm, an urban seat up to 15 per cent more. Thus rural voters are given more weight.

What happens if the three houses of Parliament disagree?

The issue can be referred to the President's Council. This consists of 60 members, 20 elected by majority vote in the white Assembly, 10 by the Coloured Representatives and five by the Indian Delegates, together with 25 nominated by the President. Ten of the nominated members will be opposition MPs: six whites, three Coloureds and one Indian. The Council's role is to advise the government on matters of public interest and arbitrate on disagreements between the three houses which are referred to it. In particular 'insurmountable differences' on 'general affairs' should be decided by the Council.

How can disagreements arise between the three houses of Parliament?

If one or two houses pass a bill which is rejected by the other(s), or if any of the three houses pass different versions of the same bill. In these circumstances the President may refer it to the Council, whose decision is final.

How will the Council deal with the disputed bill?

It will decide on one version of the bill, and that one will then 'be deemed to have been passed by Parliament'.

The first bill to be referred to the Council was the South African Police Special Account Bill, which allowed for secret projects by the police. The bill was rejected by the (Indian) House of Delegates although it had been accepted by the (white) House of Assembly and the (Coloured) House of Representatives. The bill was passed by 48 votes to 4 and sent to the State President for signature.

In August 1985 the President's Council again approved a bill rejected by the House of Delegates, the Local Government Affairs Amendment Bill.

Can the Council advise the President on legislation?

The President can refer a disputed bill to the Council for non-binding advice. If the President accepts the Council's recommendations, he has to change the bill and introduce it again in Parliament.

What provision exists for consultation between the white, Coloured and Indian houses of Parliament?

Joint standing committees are established to try to arrive at a consensus before legislation of 'common interest' is debated in each house.

A new constitution came into effect in 1984; what Cabinet system now operates?

There is a Cabinet, which is multi-racial, and three ministers' councils, one for each population group. At present (1986) there is one Coloured and one Indian Cabinet minister, both without portfolios; the rest are white. Members of the Cabinet, who are appointed by the President and can be dismissed by him, run the departments of state for 'general affairs'. In addition one Coloured and one Indian are now deputy ministers.

Ministers' councils consist of members appointed to run aspects of each population group's 'own affairs' and others who do not have a portfolio. The chairman of each council is appointed by the President.

What happens if one racial group withdraws from Parliament?

The constitution makes provision for the legislative function of Parliament to continue. It also permits reduction of the quorum for any house, presumably to allow it to go on operating in the event of a partial boycott. Provision is also made for the State President to take over the functions of any minister, with or without portfolio, presumably also to cope with boycotts.

Can all three houses of Parliament be dissolved at the same time?

The President can dissolve them if they all refuse to pass the main budget, or if they all pass motions of no confidence in the Cabinet.

Can one house of Parliament be dissolved on its own?

Yes, if it expresses no confidence in its own ministers' council or the Cabinet, if it rejects its own or the main budget, or if its MPs withdraw from Parliament.

The constitution makes provision for the representation of whites, Coloureds and Indians. How does it provide for African administration?

The Constitution Act says that 'the control and administration of black affairs shall vest in the State President'.

In May 1985 the government promised that Africans would have a say in the second tier of administration. Local authority representatives of all races would sit on newly created regional councils to control a wide range of services. African representation, however, will be limited, as the authorities will be represented on the councils in proportion to their contribution to the councils' revenues. Further the government-appointed administrator will have the final say as to how many members of each local council sit on the regional council. The regional councils will administer services such as water, electricity and sewerage.

The hint given by Mr Botha in January 1985 that Africans could be represented at a higher level was fleshed out on 14 November that year when the President's Council was asked to consider ways in which it could be restructured to incorporate Africans. Mr Botha told the Council that 'new circumstances call for a new approach', but he did not indicate how many Africans he thought should sit on the Council, or how they would be elected or nominated. Mr Botha's announcement met with a generally cool response among African leaders.

Later the same month the government was reported to be seeking 'new constitutional forms' to involve Africans in decision-making processes. This was said to be going further than including Africans in the President's Council, as it called for proposals to include Africans within a new constitutional system that would provide for their participation in government itself. A new range of 'embryo' constitutional options were to be drawn up. The 'independent' homelands could, it was suggested, participate in the new – but still undefined – constitutional system through some federal structure.[1]

Local Government

Do the four official racial groups have equal power in local government?

No. The second tier beneath Parliament and the central government consists of four provincial administrations. Each provincial council is elected by whites only. In urban areas municipal councils are elected and run by whites; Coloureds and Indians in the Cape lost their municipal franchise in 1972, while they had no similar vote in the Transvaal, Orange Free State or Natal.[1] New local authorities for Coloureds, Indians and Africans have been, and are being, formed around the country, but few have the same powers and responsibilities as are vested in the white municipalities.[2]

What powers do the provincial administrations have?

Subject to the approval of the government and to a number of statutes, they have limited power over education, hospital services, roads, works, nature conservation, libraries, horse racing, trade licensing, traffic control and public reports.[3] They also control municipal affairs. Just as municipal councils have to get approval from the provincial administration for bylaws to be implemented, provincial council ordinances must receive the State President's assent.[4]

Provincial council elections were frozen when the new constitution was brought in. The present councils are to be abolished in 1986 and replaced with regional councils, whose members will be drawn from local authorities of all races.*[5]

What powers do municipalities have?

Subject to provincial veto, they are responsible among other things for streets, traffic control, water, electricity, housing, planning and building control, parks and recreation services, cemeteries and crematoria, some health services, some transport, local library services, fire-fighting and sewerage.[6]

*See chapter on national government.

What provision is made at local government level for Indians and Coloureds to run their own affairs?

A three-tier system was introduced under the Promotion of Local Government Affairs Act, Number 91 of 1983. At the top is a Co-ordinating Council, made up of government, provincial, and local government members, which is to advise the government on co-ordinating, at local authority level, matters of 'general interest'.* Next are municipal development boards, whose members are decided upon by the Minister of Constitutional Development and Planning. They provide local authorities with development aid and advice. The third level is that of Coloured Management Committees and Indian Management Committees. In Natal these are called Local Affairs Committees.[7]

What powers do these committees have?

In their initial stages they can advise white municipal authorities on the provision of services. Municipal councils may later delegate some of their powers to the management committees, which can also be replaced by a Coloured or Indian council functioning independently of the white council. Some have been established as in Verulam (Indian) and Pacaltsdorp (Coloured).[8]

Have the committees accepted powers from municipal councils?

Not all cases. In Johannesburg in 1983 the Coloured Management Committee (CMC) rejected the delegated administrative powers in Coloured areas offered it by the City Council. These would have covered development and construction of parks, libraries, playgrounds, sportsfields and swimming pools; the construction of housing schemes; the erection of buildings and their use; leasing of council-owned halls, shops and stalls; allocation of bursaries and money grants; and the planning of civic amenities. The CMC refused to accept these powers because it considered them meaningless without the right to make bylaws, levy rates and raise loans, which the white City Council would not delegate.[9]

There has also been one case of an established CMC cutting its ties with the authorities. In November 1985 the CMC in Grassy Park, Cape Town, resolved to end all negotiations with the authorities, saying that to continue 'would be washing our hands in the blood of our own people'. The decision, after widespread unrest and police repression in

---

*See chapter on national government.

the Western Cape and elsewhere, was seen as a blow to the government's strategy for local government and to the Labour Party in the tricameral Parliament. Significantly, the CMC also warned people like Dr Allan Boesak and Bishop Desmond Tutu to carefully consider their intention to negotiate with the government because 'the government has no intention to negotiate with anybody but to force their policies on the people'.[10]

What powers do the committees want?

They have called repeatedly for direct representation on white muncipal councils. This has been rejected by some local authorities, although Cape Town's municipal executive committee has called for non-racial municipal franchise.[11]

Have management committee decisions been vetoed?

Yes. In 1981, for example, the CMC of Bethelsdorp, Port Elizabeth, renamed two streets after Steve Biko and Nelson Mandela. Later that year the Cape Provincial Council passed ordinances empowering the administration to change 'undesirable' street names.[12] The Biko and Mandela streets have now been changed.

What has been the level of participation in management committee elections?

This has been low in a number of areas. In September 1983 CMCs were elected in five areas of the Cape Peninsula on polls ranging from 1.81 to 11.98 per cent. In rural areas, however, the polls were higher. Before these elections there had been a call by the United Democratic Front to boycott the polls.[13]

Does the government plan further changes for the committees?

Yes. In October 1984 the Minister of Constitutional Development announced that all municipal elections, apart from those in progress, would be frozen until about 1988, when Indians and Coloureds would be given a greater share in muncipal government. The new arrangements would include:

Joint consideration of budgets before final consideration by town councils.

Special committees of town councils to liaise with Coloured and Indian committees.

Joint meetings of town council committees with Coloured and Indian committees.

Joint committees on matters of common concern.[14]

What provision is made for Africans to run their own local affairs?

Advisory boards for Africans in urban townships were established after 1921; they did not prove successful. In 1961 urban Bantu councils began to be set up; these were succeeded by community councils from 1977. African local affairs were largely controlled after 1971 by white-run Bantu Affairs Administration Boards, set up under the Bantu Administration Act, Number 45 of 1971. These at first numbered 22 but were later reduced to 14. The boards took over functions from the local authorities and got their money from rents, service and employers' fees, and profits from the sale of hard liquor in the townships (70 per cent of their income).[15] In 1983 the Black Local Authorities Act, Number 102 of 1982, began to establish a local government system intended to be based on municipalities similar to those for other racial groups. The 232 community councils in existence in the 299 townships in 'white' South Africa are to be replaced by town or village councils.[16]

What powers will town or village councils have?

They will be responsible for waste disposal, sewerage, electrification, some health programmes, sport and recreation facilities, housing administration (including illegal occupation), some welfare services, granting educational bursaries, and maintaining institutions and roads, and employment of staff.[17]

Will these new local authorities be autonomous?

The Minister of Constitutional Planning and Development will still control the making of bylaws, budgets, levies, investment and donations. The administration boards – now called development boards – will still be responsible for housing development, regarded as important, since permission for Africans to stay legally in 'white' areas depends on approved accommodation.* The boards can also take the place of local authorities where no councils have been established. They will also continue to be partly responsible (with the police) for influx control, although the Cabinet has said they should be relieved of this in time.[18] The councils will, however, take over the policing responsibilities of the development boards.[19]

*See chapter on pass laws.

How will the new councils be financed?

That income will include service charges, site rents, fines, and profits from the sale of sorghum beer, which at present is sold by the development boards. In 1983 beer production brought profits of nearly R70 million (£35 million). The government said in 1984 that the sorghum beer industry would be rationalized and, over a period of years, sold to different businesses. Privatization would be extended so that African local authorities could find alternative sources of revenue. This was opposed by a number of the new councils, as was the transfer of liquor outlets – off-licences owned by the boards – to the private sector. These outlets were a major source of revenue, bringing income of more than R562 million (£281 million) in 1982–3.

Dr Piet Koornhof, then Minister of Co-operation and Development, said in 1983 that township residents should make 'substantially increased' payments for services; water and electricity (where available) is being metered. The new councils may also get a payment from central government now being given to the development boards.[20]

Who can vote in elections for these councils?

Voters must be: aged over 18; classified as African under the Population Registration Act,* citizens of South Africa or an 'independent' homeland; qualified to live in the area,† or, if migrant workers, have lived in the area for a full 12 months.[21]

What proportion of the electorate voted in the elections for the new councils?

In the 29 elections in 1983 for new local authorities – 24 for town councils and five for village councils – the average poll was 21 per cent. In 22 instances the poll was lower than for the previous community council elections. The UDF, which together with a number of other bodies had called for a boycott of the elections, said that the polls had been even lower than the official figures indicated, because many voters were not on the roll and many wards were uncontested. The 'mayor' of Soweto, which has a population of more than a million, was elected to the council with a total of 1,115 votes.[22]

In late May 1985, as unrest continued in many parts of South Africa, with violence often directed at African councils, not a single candidate

*See chapter on race classification.
†See chapter on pass laws.

stood for election to fill 10 vacancies on the Lekoa Town Council, which is supposed to serve four Transvaal townships including Sharpeville. The election had to be cancelled.[23]

In October only one candidate stood in a new by-election and he was elected unopposed. Twelve seats were vacant at the beginning of November 1984.[24] Elsewhere in the country, councils attracted little interest. In Humansdorp, Alexandria, Kwanobuhle in Uitenhage, and Illingelible in Cradock – all in the Eastern Cape, which saw widespread unrest during 1985 – councillors resigned *en bloc*. No nominations were received for elections to the Humansdorp and Alexandria councils in August 1985, in the other two no elections were announced.[25]

What has been the response of Africans to the new local councils?

By 1985 a total of 34 councils had been introduced, of which about half had asked to establish their own police forces. Government policy is that all the local authorities should have their own police, and in October R24.6 million (£12.3 million) was allocated to help establish the forces.[26] Few of the councils were said to be operating as unrest spread to many parts of the country in 1985. By mid August at least 16 councillors had been killed by fellow Africans who regarded them as collaborators with apartheid. More than 60 councillors' homes were attacked.[27]

The councils have also been criticized for their inefficiency and corruption over housing allocations and other administrative matters.[28]

Social Segregation

There are many consequences of race classification, and one of the most visible is social segregation. What is the government policy on this?

According to a statement made in 1983 by the State President (formerly Prime Minister) P. W. Botha, discriminatory measures which are unnecessary and create ill-feeling should be removed. 'But I am not in favour of a system of compulsory integration in South Africa, and I am not in favour of endangering my own people's right to self-determination.'[1]

More recently, the Minister of Development Aid, Dr Gerrit Viljoen, said in August 1985 that any reforms would not affect 'own residential areas, own schools, own education departments and own separate political representation'.[2]

Does the President's statement of 1983 imply a modification of earlier legislation and practice?

The Reservation of Separate Amenities Act, Number 49 of 1953, legalized the provision of separate buildings, services and conveniences for different racial groups. Over the next few years provincial authorities also passed ordinances to similar effect. These were all strictly enforced over the following two decades.[3]

What public facilities were most affected by segregation?

Among others, post offices and government buildings, including police stations, were either totally segregated or had partitions erected in them so that whites could be served on one side and blacks on the other. Liquor outlets had to be segregated. Civic halls, libraries, parks, theatres, cinemas, hotels, restaurants, cafés and clubs were normally barred to blacks if situated in 'white' areas. Sports amenities and beaches were also reserved for the use of one racial group.*

---

*See chapters on sport and beaches.

Did the segregation laws impose an obligation to provide facilities of an equal standard for all races?

No. The Reservation of Separate Amenities Act said that the courts could not rule that this segregation was invalid because separate facilities were not substantially equal. Nor could the courts rule the separation invalid on the grounds that provision had not been made for all racial groups.[4]

Were exemptions from the law allowed?

Yes. The Reservation of Separate Amenities Act, and the Group Areas Act, Number 41 of 1950 (as amended), said that permits could be issued by the government to allow 'racially disqualified' people to 'occupy' premises, to visit halls, clubs and places of entertainment, to be patients in hospitals or guests in hotels.

Were many exemptions from the law granted?

The total is not known, but permits were the exception rather than the rule.

When did the segregation policy begin to change?

In January 1975 the then Prime Minister, B. J. Vorster, said that the Cabinet would seek the 'systematic and orderly elimination of unnecessary and purely irritating race discriminatory measures' not essential to separate development.[5] In 1978 the Cabinet accepted a memorandum produced after a two-year study by a Cabinet committee which stated that 'existing differentiation between white, black (African), Coloured and Indian may not be maintained where it is in disuse and no longer serves the purpose of eliminating friction and preserving a particular service for a particular group'.[6]

Did the policy affect the permit system of temporary exemptions from the segregation laws?

In December 1979 it was announced that the existing system, under which permits lasted for a year, would be relaxed and that 'open-ended' or 'blanket' permits could be issued in approved cases to legalize multiracial use of facilities.[7]

After the policy change, what facilities could be opened for multi-racial use?

Local authorities, communities or business could apply to open:

Libraries;

Private hospitals, if a doctor certified that it was in the interests of a 'disqualified' person to be admitted;

Theatres and halls used for live theatre, music recitals 'of quality', wedding receptions and concerts if alternative facilities were not available for disqualified groups and if local authorities and the Department of Community Development did not object;

Receptions for people at symposiums and congresses;

Clubs, in respect of guests;

Agricultural and industrial exhibitions and charity fêtes;

Drive-in cinemas and circuses; and

Restaurants and cafés in certain areas, in consultation with local authorities.

Hotels could be opened in terms of other legislation, including the Liquor Amendment Act, Number 58 of 1975.[8]

In practice, which facilities have been opened to all races and which remain segregated?

Libraries

Civic libraries were allowed to obtain 'blanket' exemptions in late 1979, after some larger cities – for example Johannesburg, Durban, Pietermaritzburg and East London – had begun to relax apartheid in libraries. This came after a move in 1976 by the East London City Council to open its central lending library to all. At that time the Administrator of the Cape warned the council that it, and any local authority following its example, would lose the provincial subsidy. [9] Application to end library apartheid must still come from the local authorities. Sandton, a suburb of Johannesburg, was among the latest to do so in 1983.[10] A number of other libraries are still open to whites only.

Hospitals

Public hospitals remain segregated. Several cases of hospital apartheid have aroused comment: pregnant black woman in Transvaal hospitals have had to sleep on the floor while there were empty beds in white hospitals; mothers of newly born babies had to sleep on the floor at Addington Hospital in Durban because they were Coloured and were not allowed into the less crowded white wards; and a Coloured girl had to be transferred from Pretoria to Cape Town, more than 1,000 miles away, because the Pretoria centre for autistic children was for whites only. [11]

Theatres and halls

At least 43 theatres are now open to all, after the government announced in 1978 that permanent permits would be issued for mixed audiences. Before that, in terms of Proclamation R26 of 1965, mixed audiences and mixed casts were prohibited without permit. Where mixed-audience permits were given, officials said that separate entrances, seating, toilets and refreshment facilities had to be provided. The opening of theatres came after Britain's trade union for actors, Equity, restricted their members from performing in South Africa and a cultural boycott was begun. It also followed a widespread white boycott of the Nico Malan Theatre in Cape Town, whose audiences for more than a decade were confined to whites. Permits for mixed casts to perform still have to be obtained on an individual basis: no blanket permits are issued.

Blanket permits have also been issued to open civic halls if local authorities have applied. A number have done so, while others, Pretoria for example, have not.[12] In Cape Town, however, the government has twice refused permission for two civic halls, at Sea Point and Muizenberg, to be granted 'open to all' status, although people of all races frequently use them by permit.[13]

Clubs*

A number of clubs have 'international' status, enabling them to offer visiting blacks refreshments and liquor. Clubs, Parliament was told in 1979, can decide for themselves who may be members, and also (through the 1981 Liquor Amendment Act) whether to offer black members and guests liquor.[14]

Cinemas

About 160 cinemas were due to be opened to all races, according to reports in October 1985. Most were in the central business districts of four of the country's main cities – but not the conservative Afrikaner cities of Pretoria and Bloemfontein. Most of the cinemas, in the central business districts, it was pointed out, were luxury establishments with high admission fees which would prevent underprivileged blacks from 'flooding' there.

Twenty-five cinemas (including drive-ins) were open to all before the October announcement; at the beginning of November 1985 34 cinemas

* See also chapter on sport.

and four drive-ins admitted patrons of all races: a total of at least 63.[15] A new government policy announced in 1978 allowed drive-in cinemas to apply to become open. From 1957 until then, control of audiences had been through the permit system, and a number of small-town cinemas had been given permission to admit blacks in separate seating. Under the Publications Act, however, some films can be shown only to people of a specific race or age-group.*

Restaurants and hotels

A total of 80 hotels – out of about 1,450 throughout the country – have 'international' status allowing them to admit, serve and accommodate blacks. The other 95 per cent of South African hotels are reserved for one racial group only. Before 1982 dancing had to be segregated and swimming pools were restricted to bona fide hotel guests.[16] In March 1985 it was revealed that the government had quietly dropped the restriction on mixed dancing and swimming at 'international' hotels. In answer to a question in Parliament, the government said the bars had been removed from April 1982. No official announcement had been made until the question was put in Parliament three years later.[17]

Forty-seven restaurants have 'international' status, compared with eight in 1979. A number of non-licensed hotels have been allowed to become multi-racial[18]

In January 1985 the government said that hotel and restaurant owners could decide for themselves who to admit and did not have to get prior approval from Pretoria. If owners wanted to serve blacks they could:

Apply for their premises to be granted 'international' status;

Apply for temporary 'international' status; or

Telephone Pretoria for permission to admit blacks.

Owners could admit the blacks first and get permission later.[19]

In September 1985 the government said that all discriminatory aspects of the Liquor Act, based on either race or sex, would be removed, probably during the 1986 parliamentary session. This would open public bars to men and women of all races: present legislation confines the majority of public bars to white males, although some hotels are allowed to have separate bars for Coloureds and/or Indians.

The government also said in October 1985 that shebeens – illegal African drinking places – would be legalized.[20]

*See chapter on films.

Government buildings

Apartheid partitions in post offices began to come down from 1976. In March 1985, however, it was revealed that there was racial segregation in 20 per cent of South Africa's post offices. The Minister of Communications, Dr L. A. P. A. Munnik, told the House of Representatives that structural changes to buildings had to be made before separation could be eliminated. Apartheid signs had been removed and anybody could be served at post office counters, he said.[21]

Game parks, nature reserves and pleasure resorts run by the state also began to become multi-racial from the 1970s.[22]

Parks

A number of parks were reserved for whites only under the Group Areas Act; according to the letter of the law the only blacks allowed were nursemaids with white children in their care. In many cases the law was ignored and many blacks used the parks, particularly for their meal-breaks. In the late 1970s some parks were desegregated. In April 1983 the Pretoria City Council voted to close 17 parks to blacks, while three of those remaining would be divided by fences into black and white areas. In October 1983 it was reported that the cost of this operation would be R200,000 (£100,000). In response to this the Indian Management Committee of Laudium township said it had campaigned for 20 years for parks, but had been told that Pretoria did not have the money to spend on parks for Indians.[23]

What facilities are most whites prepared to share with people of other races?

A Human Sciences Research Council survey commissioned by the Randburg Town Council found that 31 per cent of whites would refuse to accept integrated municipal services, while another 13 per cent did not know how they would react. If existing standards were maintained, most whites would not object to the dropping of apartheid in services. Most were not in favour of mixed cemeteries, municipal swimming baths, crèches, nursery schools or public lavatories. (The absence of public lavatories for blacks is said to be a health hazard in many areas.)[24]

The government says it is moving away from 'unnecessary' race discriminatory measures. Have there been cases where this has proved not to be so?

Yes. The following are recent cases:

● An application for a multi-racial gathering at a camping ground in Port Elizabeth to celebrate the East Cape Caravan Club's tenth anniversary was turned down by the Port Elizabeth City Council.[25]

● The white community of Bergville vetoed the presence of Africans, Indians and Coloureds at an open-air charity concert.[26]

● The local authority in Middelburg, Transvaal, threatened to cut its subsidy to the local country club because several Indians play golf there once a month. The club captain said: 'The Indian players just use the same course. They don't tee off with whites, so it's not mixed sport.' [27]

● Several black soccer fans in Durban were barred from watching videos of British soccer games at a local hotel because viewing was for whites only. The hotel had applied for 'international' status but had been turned down.[28]

● Johannesburg City Council's management committee recommended that 'non-residents' should be charged for admission to the city's parks. Black workers would be most affected.[29]

● An African advocate, Justice Poswo, was refused service in a coffee shop opposite Grahamstown's Supreme Court because of his race.[30]

● The restaurant at the Voortrekker Monument in Pretoria barred five black children from being served. The Adminstrator of the Transvaal promised to investigate.[31]

● Coloured and Indian MPs in the tricameral Parliament could not eat together in the parliamentary dining room. A Progressive Federal Party MP, David Dalling, said he reserved a table for himself, a newspaper editor, the Canadian Ambassador and two members of the Indian House of Delegates, but the Office of the Speaker of Parliament refused to seat the Indians.[32] Ten days later, however, the dining room was declared open to all races – but the adjacent bar and coffee shop remains for whites only.[33] Also, Coloured and Indian MPs and their spouses may only eat in the dining room if they have been invited by a white MP.[34]

● Some white franchise-holders of Wimpey restaurants put them up for sale in 1985 in protest against the group's decision to serve all races.[35]

● A hotelier in Potgietersrus, Transvaal, had to drop his plans to apply for 'international' status under pressure from the town council, all of whose members belonged to the Conservative Party.[36]

● Coloured members of the Boland provincial cricket team were turned away from a restaurant in Nystroom after playing a match against a Northern Transvaal side.[37]

Beach Apartheid

The land is segregated in South Africa, but is the sea open to all?

No. The Reservation of Separate Amenities Act, Number 49 of 1953, says that public premises 'whenever expedient' can be reserved for 'the exclusive use of persons belonging to a particular race or class'. The Cape, in 1955, and Natal, in 1967, passed ordinances giving the provincial authorities similar powers. In all cases, the term 'public premises' is defined to include beaches.[1]

How can you tell if the beaches are zoned for a particular racial group?

Usually there are signboards saying that the beach is for 'whites only', 'Coloureds only' or 'Indians only'.

Are all beaches throughout the country racially zoned under the Act, with signs to this effect?

No. Many have no signs, others are 'customarily' used by one or another racial group, and some are open to all.

If there is no signboard on a beach, can anybody swim there?

No. In Port Elizabeth, between 1 December 1981 and 6 January 1982, a total of 262 people were warned off three beaches by the police and a further 25 charged, although they said that there were no boards demarcating the beaches or that the signs were not visible.[2]

Are the borders between segregated beaches clearly indicated?

Not in all cases. In January 1984 seven people – a lawyer, a nuclear chemist, a chartered accountant, a computer manager, a teacher, a nurse and a law student – were arrested for being on a 'whites only' beach. The Cape Attorney-General's office declined to prosecute, saying that a recent government study pointed out that 'whites only' signs did not precisely define the borders of segregated beaches.[3]

What are the penalties for swimming in the 'wrong' place? Are these still imposed if the beach was not visibly segregated?

The Reservation of Separate Amenities Act lays down a maximum jail sentence of six months or a fine of £50 or both. Four of the people charged in Port Elizabeth over the Christmas holidays in 1981–2, who claimed the beaches were unsigned, were fined R20 (about £10).[4]

Are beach apartheid restrictions ever waived?

Yes. In April 1982, for example, during the South African lifesaving championships in Port Elizabeth, members of two black clubs were allowed use of all 'whites only' facilities for three days. In September 1983 apartheid signs between the Wilderness and Mossel Bay were removed for an international symposium on the Antarctic attended by more than 180 delegates from all over the world. The chairman of the symposium said requests had been made to the government to have 'any potentially offensive signs temporarily removed'.[5]

Has beach apartheid fallen into disuse as government policy moves away from 'unnecessary' racial discrimination?

Not in a number of cases. Some recent examples:

● Just before Christmas 1984 police jeeps turned away Coloureds from Sunrise Beach at Muizenberg, near Cape Town, although they had been allowed to use the beach during the rest of the year.[6]

● The Transvaal leader of the (Coloured) Labour Party, Jac Rabie, was refused admission to the Wild Waters Fun Park because it was classified as a swimming pool and it was the policy of the local Boksburg council to restrict swimming pools to whites only.[7]

● About 50 Coloureds were asked to leave a beach at Kalk Bay, near Cape Town, in January 1985, although the 'whites only' sign had been removed a year before.[8]

● The part-owner of a water-slide at Muizenberg said that police forced him to restrict entrance to whites only in January 1985.[9]

● The Cape Town City Council integrated beaches under its control in December 1984, but the rest of the area's beaches, controlled by the Divisional Council, remained segregated. The City Council also opened all but two swimming pools to everybody. One city councillor opposed to the move said: 'I'm not prepared to jump into a swimming pool with 10,000 little klonkies from Guguletu.'[10] However, the City Council also decided to erect fences on some beaches, and to treble entrance fees at the largest pools in Cape Town, producing what one city councillor said was 'cheque-book apartheid' in place of colour apartheid.[11]

● In March 1985 an African medical student at the University of Natal, Mpumezo Nxiweni, was admitted to hospital in a serious condition after being shot on a Durban beach by two white men armed with shotguns. Mr Nxiweni and friends with him on the beach claimed they were subject to racial abuse for being there.[12]

Are supervisory staff at beaches and pools from the same racial group as the users?

Usually, though there are some exceptions. In Durban, the chairman of the Bluff Ratepayers' Association organized a petition to stop a Coloured being appointed as lifeguard at the 'whites only' Brighton Beach. 'If anyone is drowning, section 37 of the bylaws forbids him to enter the water to rescue them,' the ratepayers' chairman said.[13]

However, the Durban Town Clerk said that section 39 of the same bylaws exempts municipal employees and voluntary lifeguards from the restrictions of section 37. But this still means that blacks who are not employed by the municipality and who do not belong to the South African Lifesaving Association are forbidden by law to enter the water on a white beach, even if they are the only people on the beach and a white person is drowning.[14]

In another case, a Coloured supervisor was appointed for the Brighton Beach swimming pool. Opposing the appointment, members of the Conservative Party said: 'We don't want black men walking among white women in bikinis.'[15]

Can a black nursemaid looking after white children use a 'whites only' beach?

In practice, yes, as long as she has the children in her care. If the children are not on the beach with her, she could be ruled to be there illegally. It was reported in Natal in 1984 that blacks were allowed to walk on any beach as long as they did not swim or look as if they were intending to swim.[16]

If a black nursemaid's husband stops to talk to his wife at work on a 'whites only' beach, can he be prosecuted?

Yes. The courts could rule that he was 'occupying' the beach illegally.

Are the wishes of local people the determining factor in zoning beaches?

Not necessarily. The provincial administration can direct any local authority to reserve beaches for any racial group. The Natal provincial authorities retain control over all of the seashore except for Durban and Richard's Bay. In the Cape, however, more control has been given to local authorities and away from the provincial administration.[17]

Can a local authority be prevented from allowing all races to use its beaches?

The provincial administration can override its wishes, zone beaches, and debit the local authority with the cost. In April 1982 the ratepayers' association of Hout Bay near Cape Town asked that the local beach be open to all. On the instructions of the provincial administration, part of the beach was kept for whites only. In 1983 the Natal provincial administration vetoed the Durban City Council's move to desegregate some of its beachfront.[18]

Does the law say that beaches must be 'separate but equal'?

No. Before 1953 several court cases established the principle that amenities had to be equal if separate. However, the Separate Amenities Act specifically says that zoning cannot be declared invalid by a court on the grounds that provision has not been made for all races or that separate facilities are not substantially equal.[19]

Are 'black' beaches equal to 'white' beaches in terms of quality, availability and facilities?

Not necessarily. In 1965 a National Party MP zoned beaches in the Cape: most of those for Coloureds, Indians and Africans were found to be considerable distances from their homes, lacking in amenities and sometimes dangerous. In February 1983 the Cape Provincial Council was told that in the Cape Peninsula whites had exclusive use of 188 miles of coastline, while all the other groups – who outnumbered the whites considerably – had only 5.3 miles. In Durban nearly two miles of the city's beachfront was for 'whites only', while little more than a quarter of a mile was for Indians. Durban/Pinetown has a white population of 320,000 and an Indian population of 468,000.[20] At Richard's Bay, north of Durban, there are two beaches a few hundred yards apart. Alkantsrand, for whites, is equipped with nets to keep sharks away;

Soekwater, for blacks, has no shark-nets. Richard's Bay is said to have one of the highest shark concentrations in the world.[21]

In October 1985 Durban decided to open more of its beaches to all races. The Herstigte Nasionale Party responded by calling on all 'traditionally minded' South Africans to boycott Durban hotels and the city 'to highlight belief of a separate group identity in a residential context'.[22]

Is there equal treatment for people of the 'wrong' colour using a segregated beach?

Not necessarily. In late 1984, the director of Durban beaches said that if a white complained about a black using a 'white' beach, the lifeguard would ask the offender where he came from: 'If he happened to be "Jesse Jackson from the US" he had international status and could stay. But if he was a local man from nearby KwaMashu he had to leave.'[23]

Are there moves to desegregate beaches?

In some cases. The Natal provincial administration was reported in 1983 to be getting government money to provide 'open' facilities on beaches.[24] In December 1984 the Minister of Constitutional Development and Planning, Chris Heunis, announced that R43.3 million (£21.65 million) would be spent on beach and inland resort development for 'a just dispensation in respect of recreational facilities and opportunities'.[25] Over Christmas and New Year 1983–4 and 1984–5 racial restrictions on Cape Peninsula beaches were reported to have been ignored generally during the holiday season.

Do whites want more open beaches?

A 1983 survey by the Natal Centre for Applied Social Studies found that 25 per cent of whites favoured immediate and complete beach integration, 25 per cent were willing to have limited and gradual desegregation, and the remaining 50 per cent wanted apartheid to stay. In Durban, which relies heavily on tourism, the hoteliers' association conducted a survey in which 51 per cent of holidaymakers said they would stop visiting the city if beaches were multi-racial.[26] However, despite the opening of some Durban beaches to all races, the 1984–5 Christmas/New Year season was a record one with no apparent boycott by holidaymakers.

Transport

How much apartheid is there on South African transport?

South African Airways does not enforce apartheid on either domestic or international flights, although there are no black stewards or stewardesses. The vast majority of trains were segregated until 1 September 1985, when railway apartheid was partially lifted: now there are racially unreserved coaches on suburban and inter-city trains. There are, however, still coaches marked for whites only – a facility that the Minister of Transport Affairs, Hendrik Schoeman, termed a 'national heritage' dating back to 1910.

The various Railways and Harbours Acts allow for accommodation on trains to be reserved for the exclusive use of a particular race or class.[1] A number of bus services are segregated; some others are open to all.

Have people been ordered off trains because of apartheid?

In December 1983 Colin Croft, a member of a 'rebel' West Indies cricket team touring South Africa in defiance of the international ban on cricketing contact with South Africa, was ordered out of a 'whites only' compartment on a suburban commuter train.[2] In December 1984 a woman and her five grandchildren, all classified as Coloured, were ordered to change compartments when an official changed the sign on their carriage to 'whites' from 'non-whites'. A transport spokesman said: 'Each train has a set number of coaches and if a train needs more white or non-white coaches, then we turn the boards. We try to avoid this happening, because people don't like it.'[3]

According to the Minister of Transport in 1979, local station managers could decide whether apartheid signs on stations should be removed. Toilets, bars, waiting rooms and cafeterias, however, were to remain segregated.[4] In 1983 Mr Schoeman stated that separate facilities were needed to prevent minorities being 'crowded out and trampled underfoot'. Separate platform benches, shelters, pedestrian stairs, footbridges, subways, entrances and exits existed 'where there is any danger of crowding out and thus friction', he said.[5]

In March 1985 the government was asked in Parliament to explain why the Department of Foreign Affairs claimed in overseas publications that there was no discrimination at railway stations, when a month before

Mr Schoeman had confirmed to Parliament that apartheid was still in force at Johannesburg station. The Minister had said that the 'whites' and 'non-whites' signs were for the 'convenience and effective flow' of passengers.[6]

Before the partial lifting of railway apartheid in 1985, were there exceptions to the rule?

The luxury Blue Train (from Cape Town to Johannesburg and back) and the Drakensberg Express (from Johannesburg to Durban and back) have had shared bars and dining cars for some years. In 1984 Mr Schoeman said that Coloured and Indian ministers in the new Cabinet would travel in separate compartments from whites, but later said that Coloured and Indian MPs would be allowed to use white accommodation and dining cars on trains on presentation of identity cards.[7] Most dining cars on mainline trains were supposed to be opened to all races in late 1984. In March 1985, however, a white and an Indian student travelling on the same train were forced to eat meals at separate tables in the 'open' dining car. The chief steward is reported to have said: 'We are not that multi-racial here.' The students, one travelling in a 'whites only' compartment and the other in one for blacks, were also prevented by train staff from visiting each other during the journey.[8]

How are buses segregated?

Under the Motor Carrier Transportation Amendment Act, Number 44 of 1955, local transportation boards or the National Transport Board can specify to bus operators which race group may be conveyed. If more than one group uses the buses, separate areas are reserved for each: in double-decker buses, blacks must usually sit upstairs. In most Free State and Transvaal cities, separate bus services are run for whites and blacks.

Have there been moves to integrate buses?

Under the Road Transportation Act, Number 74 of 1977, which replaced the Motor Carrier Act, bus operators can apply to the National Transport Board if they want to desegregate their buses. An integrated service began operating in Cape Town and the number of 'whites only' buses was decreased. East London also integrated its municipal bus service.[9] In Durban the National Transport Commission ruled in 1984 (for the fourth time) that the buses had to remain segregated.[10] In Johannesburg, the City Council's management committee rejected a request from the town council of Randburg, a suburb of the city, to integrate its buses within Randburg.[11]

People often take a taxi because they are in a hurry. In South Africa, can you take the first available taxi?

The Road Transportation Act of 1977 says that transportation boards should issue certificates for conveying whites, blacks or, 'in certain circumstances', mixed groups.[12] Taxi-drivers can also be segregated: in Pretoria, for example, white passengers can ask to be conveyed by a white driver.

In 1984, a three-year-old Coloured boy, on a shopping trip with a white man, was refused admission to a 'whites only' taxi to take the pair home. The boy was left at the side of the road, twelve miles from home, while the white man went back alone.[13]

How cost-effective is South African transport?

A loss of up to R400 million (£200 million) was predicted for 1985 by the Minister of Transport.[14] About R870 million (£435 million) was spent in 1982–3 to subsidize rail and bus transport, much of it for Africans commuting from townships and homelands to places of work. Employers contributed between R1 and R3 (50p and £1.50) a month to help subsidize this transport.[15]

Many Africans live far away from their work. How many of them are commuters?

A total of 773,000 commuted from homelands to work in 1982. In addition, nearly 1.4 million were migrant workers who stayed in 'white' cities during their contracts.[16] Eighty-six per cent of the 773,000 daily commuters travelled to urban area workplaces, the rest to rural areas.[17]

How do patterns and conditions of commuting for Africans in South Africa affect workers and/or employers?

A Human Sciences Research Council study of commuters between the KwaNdebele homeland and Pretoria found that:

● Most commuters, who travelled between 70 and 80 miles by bus to work in Pretoria, left home before 5 a.m. and spent two to three hours on a bus each day. More than half were away from home for more than 14 hours a day.

● A quarter spent three hours or longer on a bus each day.

● At the time of the survey 17.5 per cent of the average weekly pay of R38.50 (£19.25) was spent on transport.

● Thirty-nine per cent said they had been warned or threatened about time-keeping by their employers because of commuting problems which were beyond their control.

The study was prompted by research in London and elsewhere showing that long, uncomfortable trips had a cumulative detrimental effect in terms of illness, absenteeism and high staff turnover.[18]

Do African commuters experience particular problems?

A National Institute for Transport and Road Research study found that black commuters complained of overcrowding, lack of punctuality of buses and, even more so, trains, insufficient and infrequent transport and high costs. Nearly half also said they had experienced crime, mainly assault or robbery, as victims or witnesses.[19]

What have been the results of commuter frustrations?

A number of violent incidents have been reported regularly over the years, among them in 1983–4 a bus boycott by commuters in Mdantsane, near East London, because of an 11-per-cent fare increase, led to clashes between commuters on the one hand and Ciskei homeland police and vigilantes in which 90 people were reported to have been killed.*

Why do African commuters live far from their places of work?

The government-appointed Welgemoed Commission reported that under the Group Areas Act† 'large numbers of people were resettled, mainly from slums and as a result of slum clearance, in new areas and in many cases this resulted in employees now living further from their jobs than had been the case before'.[20] Other reasons include the relocation of older townships to homelands and the government's policy of decentralizing industry to near homeland borders.[21]

Is the large number of African commuters a result of government policy?

The government has said that it intends to reduce migrant labour by providing jobs closer to the homelands, so enabling Africans to live more

---

*See chapter on homelands.
† See chapters on group areas and removals.

with their families. This would mean more commuting. It has also said that commuting allows Africans to have regular contact with Western living while remaining in 'their own cultural context' and being able to exercise political rights in their own 'country'.[22]

Is the public transport system adequate for African commuters, or do some have to use other forms of transport?

More than 500,000 are estimated to use minibuses to and from (and within) townships every day.[23] A total of 82,000 minibuses are thought to operate in 'white' South Africa and thousands more in the homelands; about 20,000 are licensed and the rest operate illegally. Although fares are higher than public transport, commuters often prefer minibuses because of comfort, speed, safety and flexibility.[24]

What has been the reaction to the use of taxis by African commuters?

Bus operators have complained that they are carrying fewer passengers and that the service they are able to provide is suffering as a result.[25] The Welgemoed Commission said that minibuses should not be able to get permits to operate as taxis, which should carry no more than four passengers. Minibuses should provide route-bound services with approved timetables. These recommendations led to strong protests to the Minister of Transport by Witwatersrand taxi-owners.[26]

The government's proposal to phase out minibuses was rejected by the President's Council in September 1985, saying that they should be encouraged rather than be limited too much.[27]

What means of transport are there for commuting whites?

Commuter buses operate in most white towns and cities, and trains in a few. South Africa has a high proportion of car-drivers: 2.6 million cars were registered in 1982. White motor ownership is about 553 vehicles per 1,000 people – one of the highest in the world after the United States. Whites own approximately two thirds of all South African vehicles.[28]

Sport

Is there apartheid in sport in South Africa?

The government's official Yearbook for 1985 says: '... Any sportsman or sportswoman in South Africa, irrespective of population group, may play for the same club, or provincial or national team. The traditional Springbok colours, awarded to a representative national team, may be awarded to all team members.'[1]

Can all races mix freely at sporting events?

Some legal changes mean that this is now possible. The group Areas Act clause concerning sport has been scrapped. The owners of sporting facilities – private clubs and local authorities – can approve or refuse the right of people of different racial groups to 'occupy' premises in terms of the Act. The Urban Areas Consolidation Act now allows whites, Coloureds and Indians to attend sports meetings in an African township on production of a ticket. The ticket serves as a permit. A club membership card serves as a permit for a 'non-African' to take part as a player in a specific match. The Liquor Amendment Act, Number 117 of 1981, allows licensees to decide whom they will serve with refreshments.[2]

Has there been a change in government policy on sport?

Yes. Until about 1976 government policy was that all sport should, as far as possible, be segregated.

What happened in the past when foreign black players were chosen to compete against South Africa?

In 1961 the then Prime Minister, Dr Hendrik Verwoerd, banned Maoris from being included in visiting New Zealand rugby teams. In 1968 the then Prime Minister, B. J. Vorster, said that the Coloured cricketer Basil d'Oliveira, a former South African, could not play as a member of the MCC team due to tour South Africa.

What reactions were there abroad to the South African government's application of apartheid to international sport?

There were moves to boycott South African sport, either by stopping overseas teams visiting the country or by trying to prevent South African sportspeople playing abroad. As a result a number of overseas sporting bodies have refused to tour South Africa, though others have still done so. A number of South African sportspeople have been refused permission to participate in events abroad.

Have international boycotts affected the government's attitude to integrated sport?

From the 1970s government policy began to change and move away from insistence on apartheid in sport. These moves culminated in changes to the laws affecting sport.

Have the changes in policy on sports apartheid been accepted by all South African sportspeople?

No. The South African Council on Sport (SACOS) policy is that there can be 'no normal sport in an abnormal society' and that there cannot be equality in sport if facilities are not equal. The council is one of two co-ordinating organizations in SA. The other, the South African Olympic and National Games Association, accepts and welcomes the changes.[3]

How is parliamentary control of sport organized?

In terms of the new constitution, sport at school is an 'own affair' and therefore controlled individually by the white, Coloured and Indian chambers of Parliament. Other sport, including African sport, is a 'general affair' and subject to control by all three chambers.[*]

In September 1985 the government said that a single representative sports body responsible for the administration of all sports would be established. More money would be made available to the new umbrella body to be distributed to individual members.[4]

What is the government's attitude to integration in school sport?

In September 1983 Dr Gerit Viljoen, the Minister of National Education, said that the government was not moving towards total integration in

*See chapter on national government.

sport at school but was providing procedures whereby there could be increased contact between different races.[5]

In practice, how likely is it for schoolchildren of different races to play together?

School sport remains what the president of the South African Olympic and National Games Association, Rudolph Opperman, called 'a delicate issue'. The Transvaal provincial administration has issued a directive which means in effect that schools may opt for mixed or all-white leagues. SAONGA has called for a single league for children of all races to compete against each other. Over the past years there has been more mixed sport at school, although there have been incidents in which some Afrikaans schools have refused to play against private schools – the only ones that admit blacks to previously white-only institutions – which include black team members.[6]

In May 1984 a Pretoria headmaster considered holding two sports festivals to mark Republic Day – one multi-racial and one for whites. The proposal arose because the headmaster invited a neighbouring school to take part and then found that it had three Taiwanese and five Malawian pupils. The headmaster sent parents of his pupils a confidential circular asking whether they objected to their children competing in sack races, egg-throwing and tug-of-war, and having drinks and sweets, with children of another colour. If the parents did object, the headmaster said, a 'whites only' sports festival 'away from the others' could be held.[7]

There are more black people than white in South Africa. How do their sporting facilities compare?

A survey conducted by the government's Human Sciences Research Council (HSRC) found that white schools had 72 per cent of all school sports facilities. Whites owned 73 per cent of all athletic tracks, 83 per cent of swimming pools, and 82 per cent of rugby fields. They were also of better quality than facilities in black areas.[8] Parliament was told in 1983 that there were 12 sportsfields for 226,000 Africans in the Cape Peninsula and one sportsfield for more than 3,000 African high-school children.[9]

A report published by the University of Potchefstroom in 1984 found that between R7.13 and R19.71 (about £3.56 and £9.85) a head was spent on whites for sport in the various provinces, R3.61 (about £1.80) on Indians throughout the country and R0.82 (about 41p) on Africans. A 1980–81 survey showed a 49 per cent shortfall of facilities for Africans in local areas, 87 per cent at secondary schools and 83.9 per cent at primary schools. In May 1984 the government was said to be starting a R100 million (£50 million) plan to improve sports facilities, primarily for Africans, in outlying areas. Some extensions to sports facilities have taken place recently in black townships.[10]

There have been relaxations in apartheid for sport; but do sportspeople still encounter racial restrictions?

Yes. The following are some examples:

● Colin Croft, a 'rebel' West Indian cricketer touring the country, was ordered off a 'white' train carriage by a ticket collector in Cape Town in 1983. South Africa's Foreign Minister, Pik Botha, commented on the incident that he needed it 'as much as I need a hole in the head'.

● In Oudtshoorn, in the Cape, Coloured golfers are allowed to use the course but not the clubhouse.

● The Port Shepstone country club in Natal voted by 77 to two to stop blacks using the course completely, although they had previously been allowed to play at certain times during the day.

● An Indian golfer, Logie Govender, who had played for seven years on the Pietermaritzburg course, was refused membership of the club after a secret ballot.

● The Kimberley City Council banned black swimmers from training in the municipal pool.[11]

On the other hand, a West Indian cricketer of Indian descent, Alvin Kallicharran, has been allowed to live in the Orange Free State. He is one of only two Indians allowed in the province: an 1890 bylaw says that Indians may not stay for more than 72 hours without permission, although they may apply for 90-day permits. The Department of Internal Affairs said in May 1984 that the bylaw did not apply to Kallicharran: he was born in Guyana, carried a British passport and therefore was not Indian.[12]

Social Welfare

A welfare state guarantees the basic needs of all its citizens. Is South Africa by its own definition a welfare state?

Welfare services provided by the government cover a wide range, but 'against the background of the accepted policy that the country is not a welfare state', according to the official Yearbook.[1]

Welfare services may be used by all sections of society. Are South African welfare services racially integrated?

Not to any great degree. In 1959 the then Department of Native Affairs said that Africans should run their own social welfare services: 'The provision and control of such services by a body of Europeans or a joint or mixed committee of Europeans and Non-Europeans is contrary to policy and cannot be approved.' Under the Native Laws Amendment Act, Number 36 of 1957, the minister could impose conditions or debar white organizations running welfare services for Africans from leasing sites in the townships.[2]

In 1966 the Department of Social Welfare told private welfare organizations that the government was opposed to multi-racial organizations and that the executives of mixed welfare bodies should in future be white only. 'Should it be necessary for the black organization to be represented at an annual meeting, its representative would have to be a white person.'[3]

Government welfare provision is also segregated. The Department of Welfare is responsible for whites and also runs welfare services for Africans in 'white' areas, and the 10 homeland governments are responsible for welfare services for their residents.[4] Welfare is now an 'own' affair for Coloureds and Indians, with a member of each group's ministers' council responsible for it, although not sitting in the full Cabinet. Administratively, it is still handled as before by the Department of Home Affairs.

In August 1985, as South Africa's economic recession deepened, the white Ministers' Council announced that a special relief scheme would be started for whites left without income. It would concentrate on feeding schemes for white schoolchildren and cash handouts for white families. The plan was criticized by the Trade Union Council of South Africa for being confined to whites, but the Ministers' Council replied that welfare was an 'own' affair in terms of the constitution; other race groups had their own welfare departments; and no additional funds had been made available for the new scheme.[5]

How does welfare spending for the various South African racial groups compare?

In the 1984–5 budget, amounts for welfare were:

Whites	R78.9 million (£39.5 million)
Coloureds	R96 million (£48 million)
Indians	R28 million (£14 million)
Africans in white areas	R7 million (£3.5 million)[7]

In homelands, both 'independent' and self-governing, more than R622 million (£311 million) was to be spent in 1984–5. (Some homelands, however, combine departments of health and welfare, so the total for welfare services alone is lower than R622 million.)[6]

How much is spent on child welfare for different races?

Whites	R529 million (£264.5 million)
Coloureds	R303 million (£151.5 million)
Indians	R81 million (£40.5 million)
Africans in white areas	R241 million (£120.5 million)

Are grants for child foster-care paid at the same rate to all races?

The figures are R114 (£57) a month for whites, R77 (£38.50) for Coloureds and Indians and R40 (£20) for Africans.[8]

How much is spent on care for the disabled in the different racial groups?

In 1984–5 the budget allocation was:

	million (£4.3 million)
Whites	R857,000 (£278,500)
Coloureds	R118,000 (£59,000)
Indians	R845,000 (£422,500)[9]
Africans in white areas	

The Department of Co-operation and Development said in 1983 that care of the African crippled, cerebral-palsied and severely physically handicapped was the responsibility of the homelands. A R3.5 million sports complex for the physically disabled was being built in the African township of Soweto, and a workshop for the blind was also being planned there.[10]

What provision is made for care of the elderly in the different racial groups?

The 1984–5 budget allowed the following (including old age and veterans' pensions):

Whites	R363 million (£181.5 million)
Coloureds	R119 million (£59.5 million)
Indians	R25 million (£12.5 million)
Africans in white areas	R156 million (£78 million)[11]

How much are pensioners from different racial groups paid?

From October 1984 maximum old-age pension payments were:

Whites	R166 (£83) per month
Coloureds and Indians	R103 (£51.50)
Africans in white areas	R65 (£32.50) paid in the form of R130 every second month
Africans in homelands	R40–49 (£20 to £24.50) per month[12]

Has the gap between pensions paid to different races been narrowing?

In 1972 the ratio was:
   Africans 1   Indians and Coloureds 3.1   Whites 6.3
By 1979 the ratio was:
   Africans 1   Indians and Coloureds 2   Whites 3.5
The 1983–4 ratio is:
   Africans 1   Indians and Coloureds 1.6   Whites 2.6

There is, however, some dispute over pension figures. The Pietermaritzburg Agency for Christian Social Awareness said in late 1984 that in 1970 there had been a difference of only R30 between pensions paid to whites and to Africans. In 1984 the gap was R101.[13]

Another set of figures was produced to the Carnegie conference on poverty in April 1984 by the Transvaal representative of the National Council for the Aged, Mrs Zerilda Nel. She said that the white old-age pension rose 108 per cent between 1977 and 1984. In the same period African pensions rose by only 54 per cent.[14]

There is also some discrimination in means testing: to qualify for an old-age pension, an African pensioner must have a monthly income not exceeding R21. The limit for whites is R84.[15]

A slight move towards equality of pensions came in 1985, when it was announced that from October of that year all pensioners, irrespective of race, were to get an increase of R14 (£7) a month, and that a bonus of R36 (£18) would also be paid to all.[16]

Has the homeland policy affected the pension system?

In 1984 KawZulu's pension budget ran out with more than 50,000 applications waiting for approval. One reason was said to be an increase in the number of pensioners moved to the homeland from white areas in accordance with government policy.[17] In October 1985 the Natal Supreme Court ruled that the KawZulu Cabinet could not limit the number of new pensions to be paid. The Cabinet had decided in July 1983 to limit new pensions to 5 per cent over the previous year's numbers because there was a shortage of funds. At the beginning of the 1984 financial year there was a backlog of 18,000 aspirant pensioners.[18] The Ciskei, Lebowa, and Bophuthatswana homeland governments all reported difficulties in paying pensions. It has also been alleged that pension payments vary, apparently because of corruption and theft.[19]

How much money is spent on combating alcoholism and drug addiction among the different groups? How many people are treated?

In 1984–5 the budget allocation was:

Whites	R10 million (£5 million)
Coloureds	R1.8 million (£900,000)
Indians	R150,000 (£75,000)
Africans in white areas	R705,000 (£352,500)[20]

In 1981–2 a total of 7,408 whites were admitted to rehabilitation centres, mostly to be treated for alcoholism. The following year 8,262 Coloureds were treated for alcohol-related problems – a rate of 324 per 100,000 people, which is said to be very high. During 1981–2 a total of 174 Africans were treated for alcoholism and drug dependency.[21]

Health

Is there one health service for all South Africans?

The central Department of Health is responsible for community health, while provincial administrations and local authorities provide segregated health services at grassroots level. The new constitution designates the Department of Health as a planning and co-ordinating authority and most medical services, which will remain segregated, will be handed over to the country's 478 local authorities, in addition, the ten homelands are responsible for their own health services.

Do South Africans have to pay for health care?

According to the official Yearbook, all public health services are free, 'or else each patient pays according to his means'.[1] Since June 1983 in-patients at provincial hospitals have had to pay a deposit on a scale between R20 and R175 (£10 and £87.50), depending on income, before treatment. Out-patients have to pay from R2 to R13 (£1 to £6.50) before treatment.[2]

From April 1984 Transvaal hospital fees went up by between 10 and 100 per cent; those in the Cape rose by 50 per cent. As a result, attendance at clinics in Soweto, which is in the Transvaal, decreased by almost 50 per cent in June 1984.[3]

Are doctors evenly spread throughout South Africa?

According to a study presented to the Carnegie Inquiry, 5.5 per cent of doctors practise in the rural areas where 50 per cent of the population live. Half of South Africa's doctors live in Johannesburg and Cape Town.[4]

South Africa is a prosperous country with many qualified medical people. Are there equal numbers of doctors and nurses for each racial group?

There is one doctor for every 330 whites, 730 Indians, 1,200 Coloureds and 12,000 Africans.[5] In the homelands, there is one doctor for every 14,000 people in Transkei, 17,000 in Bophuthatswana, and 19,000 in Gazankulu. These figures are said to be comparable to those for the most underdeveloped countries in the world.[6] There is one nurse for every 148 whites, 745 Indians, 549 Coloureds and 707 Africans. The recommended international standard ratio for an efficient health service is one for every 500 people.[7]

How does apartheid in health care work? How does it affect medical staff and patients?

Hospitals run by the provincial administrations are segregated. Some private hospitals are, however, allowed to admit patients from different racial groups. Ambulances are usually classified for the use of one racial group. Black doctors can be stopped from treating their own patients in hospitals if this would involve the black doctor having authority over white nurses. Black specialists have been prevented from practising because they would have been in authority over white doctors, interns or medical students.[8]

Apartheid in the treatment of patients has caused some concern. Two recent cases:

● In December 1984 a black American dancer who said his arms and legs were paralysed because he was refused hospital treatment under the apartheid system sued South African authorities for $130 million. Barry Martin, aged 23, said he was involved in a car accident near Rustenberg and was left on the roadside because of his colour, while his white companion was taken by ambulance to hospital. A black passer-by, he said, took him to the local white hospital but he was refused treatment and left for several hours before being sent to the black section of another hospital 65 miles away. He said he was not treated for a further 24 hours before being transferred to the white section as an 'honorary white'.[9]

● A row developed over the death of a Coloured television announcer in April 1984. Vivian Solomons, injured in a car accident, was said to have been taken to the white Lichtenberg hospital and because of his condition transferred to Klerksdorp hospital. At the Coloured section he was thought to be Indian, and in the Indian section was thought to be white; meanwhile treatment was delayed. This was denied later by the government. The Minister of Health, Mr Nak van der Merwe, said that emergency treatment should be given to anybody immediately at any provincial hospital irrespective of race.[10]

Can South African medical students study at the universities of their choice?

Not necessarily. In 1983 Pretoria University had 230 white students but no blacks. The Natal medical school is for blacks only, as is Medunsa medical university. The universities of the Witwatersrand and Cape Town are the most integrated.

There is a shortage of hospital beds in South Africa. Does this affect the white and black populations equally?

Given a projected need for four beds for every 1,000 people, there is a shortage of 18,112 beds for whites and 81,431 for blacks in South Africa outside the homelands.[11]

Is life expectancy the same for members of all racial groups?

According to the official Yearbook, life expectancy is as follows:

Whites 72.3 years	Africans 58.9
Coloureds 56.1	Indians 63.9[12]

Life expectancy in rural areas, where most of the population is black, is lower, according to a 1985 National Medical and Dental Council study.

The United Nations Children's Fund (UNICEF) has said that South Africa has one of the highest infant mortality rates in the world in relation to national wealth; what are the figures?

Figures given to Parliament show the mortality rate per 1,000 live births in the first year after birth as:

Whites 14	Africans 80
Coloureds 58.8	Indians 18.3[13]

These figures, however, do not match those of the National Medical and Dental Council, whose study group said in January 1985 that the death rate of infants below one year was 100.2 per 1,000 live births for blacks and 20.1 for whites.[14]

In the homelands and resettlement camps, infant mortality has been estimated at between 20 and 25 per cent. At the Oxton resettlement camp in Ciskei, 61 per cent of people questioned had lost one child or more and 30 per cent had lost three or more, the Carnegie Inquiry was told in 1984.[15] Malnutrition is one of the main causes of infant mortality: it is said to be the cause of death of 55 per cent of the black children who die under the age of five.

In a television interview on SABC in March 1985, Premier Botha criticized states which allow their people to die of starvation. Is malnutrition widespread in South Africa?

According to Professor John Hansen of the University of the Witwatersrand, more than 50,000 black children died from nutritional diseases in one year (1970), 6,005 as a result of severe forms of malnutrition. In some areas of Ciskei and in Chatsworth, Durban, 60 to 70 per cent of children are malnourished. About one third of all African, Coloured and Indian children are underweight and stunted because of malnourishment. The death rate for black children from nutritional diseases is 31 times as high as for white children.[16] The Bureau for Economic Research at the University of Stellenbosch found that 2.9 million under the age of 15 show signs of malnutrition.[17]

Other research said that between 30 and 70 per cent of African school-age children were underweight and 22 to 66 per cent had stunted growth.[18]

What has been the government's response to malnutrition and infant mortality?

During the 1982–3 drought, much money was given to relief funds by the South African government, homeland governments and private organizations. In April 1983, however, the Minister of Health, Dr Nak van der Merwe, said that responsibility for the infant mortality rate had to be shared by people who 'bred uncontrollably'.[19]

What other poverty-related diseases are widespread in South Africa?

The South African National Tuberculosis Association (SANTA) says that TB increased by 22 per cent between 1977 and 1983, when a total of 62,103 cases were reported. Unemployment and the high cost of food were blamed for the increase. In Crossroads squatter camp outside Cape Town 82 children under the age of five died from TB in February 1984. Epidemics of measles and bubonic plague have been reported in recent years in black areas. Cholera broke out in 1980–81 and 1981–2, claiming 260 lives, while another outbreak between August 1982 and May 1983 killed 54 people. All these outbreaks of disease were said to be related to living conditions and the lack of clean water in rural areas.[20]

Clean water is essential to health. Are many people without access to clean water?

According to a survey carried out by a senior lecturer in hydrology at Rhodes University, Andrew Stone, reported to the Carnegie Inquiry, 90 per cent of people in the rural areas of Ciskei get their water from open sources shared by livestock. Less than half Ciskei's population have access to a reliable source of water.[21] In another Carnegie Inquiry report, 165 boreholes in the Mhala area of Gazankulu were found to be the main source of water for 152,000 people – a tap to population ratio of one to 760. A total of 48.6 per cent of people in Mhala South did not have access to clean water.[22] Ten babies in a Venda village died after drinking contaminated water.[23]

What are the main causes of death for each racial group in South Africa?

Among whites and Indians, heart attacks are the commonest cause of death. South Africa, with 11 deaths a day, is said to have the highest incidence of heart attacks in the world.[24] The official Yearbook for 1985 says that diseases of the circulatory system accounted for nearly 45 per cent of white deaths and nearly 41 per cent of Indian deaths in 1981.[25] Among Africans, infectious and parasitic diseases were the largest single killer at 21 per cent.[26] The Yearbook for 1985 says that accidents, poisonings and violence killed 18.5 per cent of Indian males in 1981 (up from 11.7 per cent in 1977), 25.8 per cent of Coloured males (15.3 per cent) and 16.3 per cent of white males (11.9 per cent).[27]

Is mental illness a particular problem in South Africa?

According to the Yearbook for 1985, a total of 652,054 out-patients were treated in 1983, more than double than those in 1977.[28] The Mental Health Society says that stress costs the country between R300 and R500 million (£150 and £250 million) a year. In 1983 increases in cases of depression and attempted suicide were reported which researchers linked to the recession and higher unemployment.[29]

Are there adequate facilities for treating mentally ill people?

There has been criticism that some mentally ill people have been held in police cells for lack of space in hospitals. Lack of facilities for Africans in the Eastern Cape has also drawn attention. An improvement has been promised.[30]

Has apartheid ever been blamed for causing mental illness?

Some members of the Royal College of Psychiatrists in London were reported as wanting the World Association of Psychiatrists to expel or censure South African psychiatrists on the grounds that apartheid caused mental hardship for blacks. Political detainees have sometimes required psychiatric treatment as a result of their handling in detention.[31] In 1983 a Soweto man, Mordecai Tatsa, who had been detained since 1979, was admitted to Johannesburg Hospital's psychiatric ward suffering from acute depression. The head of the South African Allied Workers' Union, Thozamile Gqweta, has also been treated during detention.[32]

In October 1985 the Durban Indian Child and Family Welfare Society expressed concern about the lack of protection for children detained and sentenced under the Internal Security Act.[33]

Is there any political interference with the medical profession?

Several cases have caused controversy:

● In February 1985 the South African Medical and Dental Council was forced to drop a case it had brought against Dr Aubrey Mokoape, a former political prisoner, in an attempt to have him removed from the medical register and thus made unable to practise as a doctor. Dr Mokoape had been jailed in 1976 under the Terrorism Act for organizing a banned meeting. After his release from Robben Island he was registered as a doctor, but the Medical Council later tried to have him removed because of his conviction under a political law.[34]

● In January 1985 the Pretoria Supreme Court ordered the Medical and Dental Council to hold an inquiry into the conduct of two doctors who treated the Black Consciousness leader, Steve Biko, before his death in September 1977 from head injuries sustained in detention. Evidence from the Biko inquest had been sent to the Council, but it had refused to investigate until ordered to do so by the court. Doctors who took the Council to court said that inquest evidence showed that Mr Biko had been deprived of medical attention because of neglect and the overruling of medical advice by the Special Branch.[35]

In August 1985 the two doctors were eventually found guilty of improper conduct and, in one case, disgraceful conduct by the Medical and Dental Council's disciplinary committee. Dr Benjamin Tucker, chief district surgeon of Port Elizabeth, was suspended from the medical roll for three months, that sentence being suspended for three years. Two months later the Council itself struck him off the rolls permanently. Dr Ivor Lang was reprimanded.[36]

● In the late 1960s Dr Raymond Hoffenberg of the University of Cape Town, who had played a part in the world's first heart transplant operation, was banned under the Suppression of Communism Act and prevented from continuing research.

● In late 1985 a district surgeon in Port Elizabeth, Dr Wendy Orr, successfully applied to the Supreme Court for an interim order restraining police from assaulting detainees held under the state of emergency. Describing some of the injuries she had seen, she said she believed there was an extensive, daily pattern of brutal police abuse of detainees. A week later she was reported to have been banned from visiting prisons.[37] In January 1986 Dr Orr resigned her government job after a series of telephone death threats.

● Until October 1985 detainees had no say in their choice of doctor: they would be examined and treated by a district surgeon, a government employee. The Medical Association said that month that the government, after more than two years of negotiation, had now agreed to the appointment of a panel of doctors from which detainees could select one of their own choice if they wanted an opinion other than that of a district surgeon.[38] Two organizations dealing with detainees said this did not go far enough, pointing out that detainees still could not choose a doctor but had to select from a panel. They also said that the Medical Association should insist that all doctors treating detainees should report assaults to the detainees' families or the courts.[39]

● Doctors were reported to be angry in late 1985 that the police and army were interfering with victims of unrest while they were being medically treated. Patients with gunshot wounds were reported to have been removed from doctors' surgeries. Other wounded people were said to be avoiding hospitals because police were on duty in wards.[40]

Education

There are private and state schools in South Africa. Financial considerations apart, can a child be sent to any school?

The vast majority of schools are racially segregated. Children have to go to schools run for their particular racial group. The only exceptions are some private schools – the equivalent to Britain's public schools – which now admit some Africans, Indians and Coloureds to their previously 'whites only' classrooms.

Are all schools run by the same department?

No. Whites fall under the Department of National Education, Africans under the Department of Education and Development Aid (formerly known as the Department of Bantu Education) and Coloureds and Indians have their own Departments of Education and Culture. Each homeland also has its own education department. In all, there are 18 departments and 15 ministers in South Africa controlling education: 10 in the homelands; four white provincial departments; one each at national level for whites, Coloureds and Indians; and one for Africans in 'white' South Africa.

In September 1985 the Minister of National Education, F. W. de Klerk, announced what he termed a new multi-racial Department of Education. A multi-racial Council for Education was also announced which would advise the minister on financing, salaries, service conditions, registration of teachers, syllabuses, examinations and certification of qualifications. The minister responsible for African education, Dr Gerrit Viljoen, said that the new department would draft equal education opportunities and standards for all racial groups.

The new department and council were reported to fall short of long-standing calls for a single department of education.[1]

How much does the government spend on the school systems for the different racial groups?

Per capita spending during 1983–4 (including capital expenditure) was:

White	R1,654 (£827)
Coloured	R569 (£285)
Indian	R1,088 (£544)
African in white areas and excluding self-governing homelands	R234 (£117)

In the 'independent' and self-governing homelands expenditure per pupil varied from R113 to R246 (£57 to £123).[2]

How do pupil–teacher ratios compare in the different school systems?

In 1984 the ratios were:

White	18.9 to 1
Indian	23 to 1
Coloured	26 to 1
African	40.7 to 1

The ratio in the 'independent' homelands varied from 26 to 50 pupils per teacher.[3]

By comparison, the average pupil–teacher ratio for English primary and secondary schools is calculated at just under 20 to 1.[4]

How does teachers' pay compare for the various racial groups?

Whites get most in pay, then Indians, followed by Coloureds, with Africans at the bottom. All teachers got a 12 per cent rise in January 1984, but the secretary of the African Teachers' Association said that the gap between whites and Africans was still very wide and the percentage increase would widen it.

Is education compulsory for all children of school age?

It is for whites, Indians and Coloureds up to the age of 16. Compulsory education for Africans has been introduced at those schools where the school committees have requested it. School attendance should be compulsory for six years, the government said. In 1983 a total of 113,491 pupils in the first four years of their education were at schools with compulsory education. This was 6.7 per cent of the total African school population of over 5.5 million.[5] Between 1981 and 1982 there was also a high drop-out rate of Africans supposedly at compulsory-education schools. Twenty-three per cent of those who were due to stay on until the age of 16 (seven years of education) dropped out.

Is the government committed to compulsory education for all children?

It is committed to what the then Prime Minister and now State President, P. W. Botha, termed in 1980 'the goal of equal education for all population groups'. The cost of this has been variously estimated at R5.2 billion (£2.6 billion), or about 40 per cent of total government expenditure. That estimate, by the former Minister of Finance, O. P. F. Horwood, was thought to be too high by an economist, Dr Simon Brand, who calculated that spending on education would have to rise from the present 15 per cent to 30 per cent of the total budget.

How much has spending on education risen in recent years?

In 1975–6 the state spent R644 per white pupil and R41.80 per African pupil; by 1982–3 the figures were, respectively, R1,385 and R115.19 (R192.34 using 1975–6 methods of calculation). The total education budget for all races in 1975–6 was R1,188 million (£594 million at today's conversion rate); in 1981–2 it was R2,694 million (£1,346 million). The African education department's budget rose by 1,603 per cent between 1972 and 1982, and a further 18 per cent in 1983–4 for education in 'white' areas.[6] There were 3.6 million Africans and 986,276 whites at school in 1983.

In the 1985–6 budget, R917 million (£458.5 million) was due to be spent on African education out of total education expenditure of R5,044 million (£2,522 million). This amounts to 18 per cent.[7]

Are school syllabuses the same for all?

The same core syllabuses are used and university entrance standards are the same for blacks and whites, according to the government.

What percentage of pupils in each school system complete their school education?

In 1983 only 1.6 per cent of the school-going African population was enrolled in Standard 10 (the highest school grade for all pupils irrespective of race). Coloured enrolment was 1.5 per cent, while for Indians it was 4.1 per cent and for whites 5.7 per cent.[8]

What percentage of school-leavers in each racial group pass their final-year exams?

The rate for whites is about 80 per cent, for Africans about 48 per cent, for Coloureds 71.3 per cent, and for Indians 86 per cent.[9]

Is inequality in funding the only reason for the variation in exam results?

The Department of Education for Africans attributed the poor pass rate to under-qualified teachers. In 1985 the national director of the Teacher Opportunity Programmes, a private body, said that only 2.4 per cent of black teachers were graduates. Only 15 per cent of black teachers had a matriculation certificate plus teacher's diploma, compared to 68 per cent of whites.[10]

A study at the University of the Witwatersrand in 1982 showed that African students with low matriculation results did better than their white counterparts with similar results when both groups were doing their first year of a BA degree. This led to the suspicion that African matriculation results were marked down: this was denied by the education department.[11]

Similarly, a principal of a Coloured school claimed that examinations taken by his pupils were harder than those for whites.

What percentage of candidates from each racial group pass the university entrance exam?

For Africans the figure in 1984 was 12.25 per cent, for Coloureds 14.9 per cent and for Indians 40 per cent. The most recent (1983) figure available for whites is 40.4 per cent.[12] A retired educationalist in the old Department of Bantu Education, Dr Ken Hartshorne, said during 1983 that the figure for African university entrance passes had begun to drop in 1976, the year of the Soweto uprising. He added that African results would improve only when there was a single department of education for all races.

Are there moves towards a single department of education?

A government-appointed commission of inquiry into education recommended this, but it was rejected.

What reasons have been given in the past for segregating education?

'Bantu education' was introduced in 1953 under the then Minister of Native Affairs and later Prime Minister, Dr Hendrik Verwoerd, who said: 'Native education should be controlled in such a way that it should be in accord with the policy of the state . . . If the native in South Africa today in any kind of school in existence is being taught to expect that he will live his adult life under a policy of equal rights, he is making a big mistake . . . There is no place for him in the European community above the level of certain forms of labour . . .'

Has policy on segregated education changed during the last few years?

Yes, according to recent government statements. Critics argue that more needs to be done to move to more integrated education.

How big a problem is illiteracy in South Africa? How do literacy levels among the different racial groups compare?

According to a study by the government-sponsored Human Sciences Research Council released in 1983, some six million adults in 'white' South Africa and the homelands had not received enough education to be regarded as literate. Among Africans the literacy rate was 50 to 60 per cent and among whites 98 per cent. Half of African and Coloured pupils leave school with four years or less of education, which means they are functionally illiterate.[13]

What reasons have been suggested for the high African illiteracy rate?

Dr Marius Barnard, brother of heart surgeon Chris Barnard and the official opposition's spokesman on health, suggested that malnutrition was a prime reason. A Stellenbosch University researcher has made the same claim. Other causes that have been suggested include insufficient and under-qualified teachers (77 per cent of African teachers are not properly qualified), overcrowding, poor facilities and lack of books and stationery. A survey by the Institute of Race Relations in 1984 showed the lack of facilities: 36 per cent of pupils in the two final years of schooling did not have electricity at home, 40 per cent did not have teachers for all subjects, 5 per cent had 70 to 80 pupils in their class, 51.8 per cent did not have access to a library and 72.2 per cent lived in a four-roomed house. Such conditions have resulted in teaching by 'double sessions' (the same teacher taking two classes a day in the first two years of schooling: 187,354 African pupils had their schooling arranged this way in 1982), or by the 'platoon system' (two teachers for two classes, but in the same room: 41,720 pupils were taught under these conditions in 1982).[14]

Political disruption of schools has also played a role. About 200,000 pupils – just over 10 per cent of the 1.8 million in urban areas – were boycotting classes at the end of 1985, and about half of the 24,000 eligible to write their final examinations did not take them. At the end of December 1985 a conference in Johannesburg on the crisis in black education recommended that pupils return to school. But if a series of demands – including freely elected students' representative councils, the ban on the Congress of South African Students (COSAS) to be lifted, student leaders to be freed from detention, and the scrapping of 'ethnic' education – were not met by March 1986, futher strike action should be taken, the conference said.[15]

Higher Education

University entrance exams are the same for all. Can those who pass them apply to any university?

The overwhelming majority at any one university are of one racial group, but in the past few years more black students have been admitted to 'white' universities and vice versa. In 1984 the Afrikaans-language University of Pretoria had only one African student, two Coloureds and three Indians; there were nearly 17,400 whites. At the African University of QwaQwa there were three whites and 458 Africans.[1]

There have been moves to make two Afrikaans universities more 'open' which have aroused controversy. In October 1985 it was announced that Pretoria University would be open to all races 'taking the university's traditional Afrikaans character into consideration'.[2] Later the same month a supposed 'mass' meeting of students, attended by less than 250 people, voted against opening the campus. The meeting, called by the right-wing Afrikaner Studentefront, said the students did not want to 'attend classes or play rugby' with people of other races. Those attending voted by 155 to 77 against opening the university; but after it was pointed out that the 'mass' meeting was no bigger than the first-year Afrikaans language class, it was decided that the issue would be put to a secret ballot to the 20,000-strong student body.[3]

At Stellenbosch, students and academics supported a call by the rector to ease the entrance of blacks to the campus. At present black post-graduates are admitted on merit, but undergraduates only if their course was not offered at their 'own' university.[4]

If passing entrance exams is not the only determining factor in university entrance, who decides whether blacks, for example, may attend 'white' universities?

Until 1983 the decision was made by the Minister of National Education, who issued permits if applicants were successful. Now the decision is up to the university authorities.

What powers does the government have in relation to university admissions?

The University Amendment Act, Number 83 of 1983, empowers the education minister to set quotas for the number of students allowed to attend universities established for other racial groups. After strong protests by the English-language universities, the minister said the Act would remain on the statute book but the quota clause would not be implemented unless there was a substantial change in ratios. The old system of permits would still apply to blacks wanting to study medicine, dentistry, pharmacy, nursing, paramedical courses, optometry, surveying, agriculture and veterinary science at 'white' universities.[5]

How many black students were refused university entrance permits under the old system?

In 1983 a total of 954 Africans were granted permission and 1,651 refused (a success rate of 36.6 per cent). For Coloureds the figures were 1,255 and 116 (91.5 per cent success) and for Indians 1,323 and 356 (78.8 per cent successful).[6] Between 1980 and 1983 the success rate for Africans varied from 36.6 to 48 per cent, for Coloureds from 89.2 to 92.2, and for Indians from 78.8 to 90.7.[7] Over the years the numbers of applicants has increased.

What percentage of students at 'white' universities are black?

In 1984, at the four English-speaking universities of Cape Town, Witwatersrand, Natal and Rhodes, 15.7 per cent were black. The five Afrikaans universities had 0.6 per cent black enrolment.

How many whites attend 'black' universities?

A total of about 600 out of more than 33,000 in 1984.

Most university teaching staff are white. What percentage of academics belong to other racial groups?

Excluding the 'independent' homeland universities of Bophuthatswana, Transkei and Venda, in 1984 Coloureds made up 1.2 per cent, Indians 2.8 per cent and Africans 4 per cent.[8]

Are black academics in the majority at 'black' universities?

No. They are still outnumbered by whites.

Have South Africa's universities always been segregated? What changes in admissions policy have there been over the years?

The Afrikaans universities did not admit blacks as undergraduates. Cape Town and Witwatersrand were 'open', and some blacks went to Natal in segregated classes. Fort Hare, attached to the white Rhodes University, was the only 'black' university in existence until 1959. In that year UCT and Witwatersrand were made to close their doors to blacks, Fort Hare was detached from Rhodes and made an ethnic Xhosa university college, and two new university colleges for Africans were founded. A university college was established for Coloureds in 1960 and one for Indians the following year. Other universities have been set up since, all intended to cater for a particular racial group. Since 1980, however, the government has become less rigid in demanding apartheid for students.

Are there religious or political restrictions on academic freedom in South African universities?

Universities are subject to the law of the land: lecturers and students have been banned under the Suppression of Communism Act and the later Internal Security Act, notably in 1974 when action was taken against the leadership of the non-racial but white-led National Union of South African Students and that of the South African Students' Organization, part of the Black Consciousness movement. The 'conscience clause' forbidding discrimination on grounds of religion has been confined to white universities, except for Potchefstroom where it never applied. Strict rules governing students were enforced at the new 'black' universities. At Fort Hare, for example, when the government assumed control from Rhodes University in 1959, the black Principal and eight other staff were not re-appointed on political grounds.

Academic books have also been censored and in several social science areas there is limited access to some 'political' books, particularly those dealing with Marxism. Visas have also been refused to lecturers from overseas.

At Potchefstroom in late 1985, eight students were fined and given suspended expulsion sentences after they tortured a member of a newly formed branch of the liberal National Union of South African Students. Among other things, he was given electric-shock treatment, which included having an electric generator attached to his genitals.[9]

Employment

Can any South African work anywhere in the country?

There are a number of restrictions. Africans, for example, have to be legally qualified in a 'white' area before they can take employment.* Indians may not work or live in the Orange Free State without permission. Africans are also prohibited from taking certain jobs in the mining industry. The Group Areas Act, among other laws, also lays down where commercial activities can take place.

Have there been fewer or more openings for blacks in employment in recent years?

More. The Industrial Conciliation Act, Number 28 of 1956, as amended, made it possible for the government to restrict certain work to particular racial groups: this was known as job reservation. In the two decades after the passing of the Act, 28 job reservations were made. They covered the building, clothing, footwear, furniture and motor assembly industries, transport, the wholesale meat trade, road construction, some lift operators, and barmen in white public bars. Other rulings restricted Africans in mine work, and in Cape Town only whites could be ambulance drivers, firemen, and traffic policemen above the rank of constable.[1]

These job reservations have now been withdrawn. The last to go was that covering the mines, lifted in June 1983. However, the Mines and Works Act still prevents blacks from doing skilled work by not allowing them to qualify for blasting certificates.[2] In May 1985, however, the government said it would scrap this provision in 1986 even if agreement could not be reached with white miners, many of whom have strongly resisted opening all jobs on the mines to all races.[3]

In November 1985 the Chamber of Mines, which controls the industry, said that security of employment would be guaranteed to whites when the last job bars on Africans were lifted. Nobody would be dismissed 'to create a vacancy to be filled with someone of another race' – reflecting fears among some white mine-workers that they would be fired and replaced by cheaper black labour. The Chamber also promised equal pay for all races: in August the black National Union of Mineworkers said its members averaged R300 (£150) a month, compared with R1,200 (£600)

*See chapter on the pass laws.

for whites. The NUM also said that it had doubts about how many Africans would be given jobs previously reserved for whites.[4]

What other employment restrictions have been lifted?

In late 1984 the government announced its intention to drop the Coloured labour preference policy – which barred Africans from a wide range of jobs in the Western Cape if Coloureds were available. However, the policy was still being applied in 1985 through what the *Financial Mail* termed 'bureaucratic lethargy rather than weak political will'. Officials in Cape Town were awaiting an official directive from Pretoria and until it arrived the policy would be implemented.[5] A notice in 1970 that Africans could not be employed as shop assistants, hotel reception clerks, telephonists, typists, clerks or cashiers in shops, offices, factories and hotels was never applied. Another statement that Africans should not be given many kinds of managerial posts was also dropped.[6] African traders were also formerly restricted, as were professional men, in terms of the Natives (Urban Areas) Consolidation Act, Number 25 of 1945. These rules were abandoned under the government's new labour policy, following the 1979 report of the Wiehahn Commission.* In September 1985 a section of the Physical Planning Act, Number 88 of 1967, which restricted the employment of Africans on the Witwatersrand – the country's main industrial area – by laying down a ratio of black to white workers, was scrapped.[7]

Have blacks moved into jobs previously reserved for whites?

As South Africa experienced a graver shortage of skilled labour, more blacks moved into positions customarily, or by law, held by whites. The Human Sciences Research Council said in a study quoted in 1984 that in 1965 only 9 per cent of clerical workers had been black, but by 1981 this had increased to 18 per cent. Over the same period black foremen and supervisors had risen from 13 to 26 per cent of the total. The percentage of whites who held clerical, sales, artisan and supervisory jobs decreased from 82 to 66 per cent in the years 1965 to 1981.[8]

* See chapter on trade unions.

When members of different racial groups do the same work, how does their pay compare?

According to figures for 1983 the percentage differences (with whites rated at 100 per cent) are:

	Unskilled	Semi-skilled	Skilled
Whites	100	100	100
Indians	73	85	84
Coloureds	65	77	70
Africans	56	65	60

The gap between unskilled whites and blacks, particularly Indians, widened over the previous year, while there was a significant narrowing of differentials in semi-skilled and skilled jobs.[9]

These percentages do not tell the whole story, however, because most whites are in higher-paid jobs. The government's Central Statistical Service said in July 1984 that average earnings in March that year were:

Whites R1,300 (£650)
Coloureds R440 (£220)
Indians R630 (£315)
Africans R330 (£165)

These figures, which exclude payment in kind, cover most sectors of the economy but exclude farmworkers and domestic servants.[10] Calculated on this basis, average African earnings come out at 25.4 per cent of those of whites. Coloureds earn 33.8 per cent of white earnings, and Indians 48.5 per cent.

The biggest wage gap is in mining and quarrying, where average African earnings are 19 per cent of white earnings. The smallest gap is in banking institutions, building societies and insurance companies, where Africans earn 42.1 per cent of the average white salary.[11]

There are regional factors in unemployment patterns. Are many people unemployed in South Africa?

Precise figures are not available: some academics have estimated the total number of African unemployed at more than three million people.[12] Unemployment in the homelands taken together is said to be 27.5 per cent of the economically active population, and in many areas 50 per cent of people are out of work.[13]

White unemployment rose by more than 33 per cent between 1984 and April 1985, with an estimated 100,000 out of work. Young men who have completed their military service have been hit particularly hard and the Defence Force Orientation Services in Natal put the figure in mid 1985 at 30 per cent.

Registered Coloured and Indian unemployment nearly doubled from 17,000 to 31,500, but since many people do not register the true figure is considerably higher.

Is everyone eligible for unemployment benefit?

Those excluded from the Unemployment Insurance Act's workings are domestic servants, agricultural workers, public servants, African mine-workers, contract workers, casual workers and some seasonal workers. Those earning below a certain sum are also excluded, as are those earning above a maximum.[14] Unemployed people who have never contributed to the fund are not eligible for benefits.

How much is paid out in unemployment benefits?

In 1980 a total of R38.2 million (£19.1 million) was paid; by 1983 it had risen to R104.2 (£52.1 million) and in the first eight months of 1985 to R130 million (£65 million). In mid 1985 the Unemployment Insurance Fund had sold investments worth R300 million (£150 million) because pay-outs were running at R2 million to R3 million (£1 million to £1.5 million) more than the fund was receiving.

Benefits are also paid for illness and maternity, and to dependants of deceased contributors.[15]

Some homelands are 'independent'. How is unemployment benefit organized for people designated as their citizens?

All four 'independent' homelands* have started benefit schemes. Contract workers from the homelands pay into the South African fund while they are working in 'white' South Africa. Their contributions are then transferred back to their homelands and they have to apply for benefits there if they lose their jobs.[16]

Is there a legal minimum wage in South Africa?

The National Manpower Commission reported in June 1983 that there was room for a 'partial system of minimum wage determinations', but no

*See chapter on the homelands.

justification could be found for a general or regional system.[17] In industrial growth-points on the borders of the homelands, statutory wage determinations do not apply and pay is therefore lower.

Employment in some homelands caused concern in 1985. Among the cases were:

● Some factory labourers in QwaQwa were being paid $7* a week – less than 20 per cent of the minimum wage laid down for such workers by industrial agreements in the rest of South Africa. Employers themselves were paying only a fraction of this: the South African Government paid most with a 95 per cent wage subsidy. The Decentralization Board, set up to help attract industries to the homelands and border areas, will pay, on agreement, 95 per cent of wages of those earning up to $55 a month. By paying many much less than $55 a month, employers could keep their entire wage bill – including salaries for highly paid white managers – within the limit for which they could claim the 95 per cent subsidy. In this way some industrialists were paying as little as $1,400 a month for a labour force of 500.[18]

● Payrolls were also reported to be padded in Ciskei to claim the 95 per cent wage subsidy: two firms that shared a factory listed 520 cleaners, 326 security employees and 126 gardeners. There were no gardens at the factory. The employers said that the workers were 'fulfilling necessary roles in our company structure'.[19]

● The American company Tidwell Housing in KwaZulu was reported in late 1985 to have been paying its black workers R23 (£11.50) a week compared to the average R78 (£39) being paid in a nearby white town.[20]

● Also in KwaZulu, African magistrates and prosecutors said in August 1985 that they were being paid less than half of their white counterparts despite similar qualifications.[21]

Where there is no minimum wage, are workers sometimes paid below subsistence level?

In December 1983 a farmer from Colenso, Natal, admitted in court that he paid one of his workers a monthly cash wage of R2 (£1). The worker had been found guilty of stock theft and pleaded in mitigation that he was compelled to steal cattle to support his wife and two small children.[22]

---

*A conversion rate of approximately R1 to $2 applied at this time.

Where wage rates are set by statutory bodies, are workers always paid a living wage?

In October 1983 two Industrial Council agreements in Cape Town fixed wages that were well below the minimum poverty line. Watchmen, for example, were to be paid R36.30 (£18.15) for up to 72 hours' work a week. The lowest minimum in the textile industry was to be R41.25 (£20.63) a week. The Minimum Living Level for Cape Town, providing only for bare necessities, was calculated by the Bureau of Market Research at R52 a week.[23] Minimum wage levels for labourers, who comprise about 20 per cent of the working population, were below the Supplemented Living Level (see next question) in all but one of the 84 wage agreements set by Industrial Councils throughout the country.[24]

In 1985 the South African Labour and Development Research Unit (Saldru) said that real wages for labourers and artisans were dropping and in 10 years artisan wages set by industrial councils had fallen by 16 per cent. From July to September 1985 the real value of minimum wages fell in 21 of 23 industrial council agreements. One, for the building industry in Bloemfontein, actually reduced the minimum wage at a time when inflation was calculated to be running at about 16 per cent.[25]

Saldru also said that watchmen in one area were being paid 20 per cent less in real terms than in 1977. The legal minimum wage for watchmen was R52.50 (£26.25) for a 72-hour week, although the Basic Conditions of Employment Act, Number 3 of 1983, prescribed a maximum 60-hour week for nightwatchmen. Despite this, some industrial council agreements allowed even an 84-hour week, and over half of these agreements and wage determinations prescribed a maximum 72-hour week. In one case a watchman who worked two months with no days off was fired when he complained.[26]

The Supplemented Living Level is sometimes used to define standards of living in South Africa. What is it?

It is a measure of the cost of living in specific areas and does not include any luxuries. According to papers presented to the Carnegie Conference on Poverty in April 1984, 'any income less than the SLL must be termed a condition of poverty'.[27]

Can links be found between economic stress and unrest in South Africa?

A study by the University of Port Elizabeth reported in October 1984 that Africans in townships on the Witwatersrand – areas most affected by riots that year – had the highest cost of living and saw the steepest price increases. A family of six had to bring in R330.25 (£165.13) a month to meet the basic costs of food, housing, and transport.[28]

Where is most poverty to be found in South Africa?

According to a paper presented to the Carnegie Inquiry, 93.7 per cent of South Africa's poverty was in the homelands or among Africans working on white farms.[29] In Transkei, the most highly developed homeland, 66 per cent of the people live below subsistence level.[30] In Ciskei, the average income in three resettlement camps was R55 (£27.50) a month per family.[31] A total of 1.43 million people living in the homelands have no income and nearly nine million people there live below the breadline.[32]

Is there poverty in the cities as well as in rural areas?

Between 20 and 40 per cent of the population of Soweto (estimated at more than one million) live below the poverty datum line.[33]

In view of the poverty and unemployment, has the government taken steps to alleviate conditions?

In September and October 1985 it announced a special scheme to train about 100,000 unemployed, mainly Africans. A few weeks later a R600-million (£300 million) emergency plan to combat unemployment was unveiled. A flat rate of R4 (£2) a day would be paid to urban workers and R3 (£1.50) to rural workers, regardless of race. They would be involved in soil erosion works, weed and bush eradication, cleaning canals, repairing and maintaining dams and roads, and developing community recreation areas.[34]

The growing threat of international sanctions against South Africa, plus the resulting unemployment because of disinvestment and boycotts, led the government in November 1985 to prepare contingency plans to repatriate foreign African workers. 'Since charity begins at home, the government has no option but to give preference to the needs of its own citizens as regards job opportunities,' the Minister of Manpower, P. T. du Plessis, said. About 1.5 million foreign Africans are said to work in South Africa, of whom about 350,000 were lawfully employed. Most are contract workers on the mines. Mining leaders strongly opposed repatriation, saying it would disrupt production and would have serious implications for the rand.[35]

Trade Unions

Can workers belong to the trade unions of their choice in South Africa?

In theory yes, but a number of unions are racially exclusive: 54 for whites, 38 Indian and Coloured, and 19 African. Another 83 cater for several races.[1] In addition, four 'independent' homeland governments have restrictions on union membership: Ciskei has banned the South African Allied Workers' Union (SAAWU); Bophuthatswana does not allow unions that operate in South Africa to organize in the territory; and both Venda and Transkei view trade unionism as 'Western decadence' or incipient 'subversion'.[2]

What laws restrict trade union activities in South Africa?

Apart from the limitations imposed by the homeland governments, several other laws have been used to restrict unions. One labour lawyer has cited 17 Acts which contain restrictions on unions' freedom. Some, like the Black Administration Act and the Development Trust and Land Act, which apply to Africans only, have been used to prevent unions holding mass meetings of their members. The Trespass Act has been used by police and employers to remove strikers from employers' property and the fine for contravening this law has been increased to R2,000 (£1,000). A number of labour laws also limit the right to strike, and the Armaments Act prohibits employees of the state-run Armaments Corporation from belonging to multi-racial unions. The Intimidation Act has also been used to restrict unions' organization of strikes.[3]

How many South Africans belong to trade unions?

Nearly 1.5 million, roughly 15 per cent of the economically active population. In Britain 50 per cent of the economically active population are union members; the figure is 24 per cent in the USA, 38 per cent in West Germany and 83 per cent in Sweden.[4]

Is the number of unionized workers in South Africa growing or declining?

It is growing: in 1972 there were 637,480 union members, compared with 1.5 million at present. There were no registered – that is, officially recognized – African unions until the law on this was changed in 1979.[5]

Have any groups of South African workers been legally excluded from union membership?

The Native Labour (Settlement of Disputes) Act, Number 48 of 1953, as amended, redefined the term 'employee' in the Industrial Conciliation Act so as to exclude all Africans from being thus described. This meant that Africans could not remain members of registered racially mixed unions and that unions for Africans only, of which there were over 30 at the time, could not be registered.[6]

How did the law affect racially mixed trade unions after 1953?

The Industrial Conciliation Act, Number 28 of 1956, as amended, said that no new racially mixed unions could be registered. The Act also attempted to get existing mixed unions to split into racially exclusive organizations or to set up separate branches for different racial groups.[7] Nevertheless, mixed unions continued to exist: by 1974 there were 85 unions with white members only, 48 with Coloured and/or Indian members, and 41 with white, Coloured and Indian members. After 1979 mixed unions were given more freedom.

Under what law were Africans allowed to belong to unions?

The Industrial Conciliation Amendment Act, Number 94 of 1979, said that Africans with Section 10 rights* living permanently in South Africa and in employment could belong to unions. The same year migrant and commuter workers from the homelands were also allowed to join unions. In 1981 all 'foreign' workers (i.e., those from the 'independent' home-lands and neighbouring states) in the country permanently were made eligible for membership.[8] The Act provided for African unions to be registered; however, a number have not applied for registration.

*See chapter on pass laws.

What does registration of a union mean?

Registration means that unions have to submit their constitutions, membership records and financial books to government inspection. They also agree not to affiliate to any political party. In return they get the right to take part in the official bargaining system: they can be represented on the industrial councils which make agreements for different economic sectors, use official conciliation boards to get employers to the negotiating table, and strike legally.[9]

Why did some South African unions object to registration?

They said, among other things, that registration would mean participation in government-created labour schemes, which they would not do unless all discriminatory laws were scrapped. They felt that the centralized industrial council system tended to produce bureaucratic unions which became cut off from the rank and file. The disadvantages of control by the Department of Manpower were thought to outweigh the benefits of official bargaining rights.[10]

Has the law on registration stayed the same? Is there still opposition to registration?

Unregistered unions must now also submit records to the Department of Manpower and are barred from affiliating to a political party. Unregistered unions can also use official conciliation boards and the industrial court and strike legally. Registration or non-registration is now not really a matter of dispute in the trade union movement.

There is now an industrial court in South Africa. When was it established and what are its functions?

It was established after the Wiehahn Commission Report, which in 1979 recommended many labour-law changes. It exists to interpret labour law, industrial agreements and wage determinations, to hear cases of irregular and undesirable labour practices, to settle disputes, and to develop labour case law.[11]

What kinds of judgements has the industrial court made?

Among other judgements the court has:

- Ruled that it is an unfair labour practice to call a worker a 'kaffir' or a 'boy';
- Said that in some circumstances employers must recognize representative unions even if they are not registered, and that they should bargain 'in good faith' with unions;
- Ordered an employer not to favour one union over another;
- Told employers not to dismiss workers without adhering to equitable procedures and ordered the reinstatement of sacked staff.[12]

Increasing use is being made of the court; it dealt with more than 400 cases in 1984, double the number of 1983, which in turn saw a fourfold increase over 1982.[13]

Is there general satisfaction with the way the court is working?

Some employers believe that the definition of an unfair labour practice is too wide and that the court's power to set precedents, which must be obeyed, is too great. Mike Rosholt, the chairman of the large Barlow Rand Group, which is linked with Anglo American, industrial councils, and at least one trade unionist, have called for a tighter definition of an unfair labour practice. The government said this would be done, and the power of the court curbed.[14] This appears to be happening, although without legislation. In 1984 African unions particularly complained that more restrictions were being placed on the court's powers, especially over the hearing of unfair labour practices. The Council of Unions of South Africa (CUSA) said that the replacement of Fanie Botha as Minister of Manpower by P. T. du Plessis had meant 'a new era of conservatism . . . in labour relations'.[15]

Are there union co-ordinating bodies like Britain's TUC and America's AFL–CIO?

There are four main bodies:

The Trade Union Council of South Africa (TUCSA) with 43 unions representing about 350,000 workers. It included African unions from 1962 to 1969 and in 1973 voted that existing affiliated unions should form parallel unions for Africans. Few African unions are affiliated and several other unions have left.[16]

The South African Confederation of Labour (SACLA), whose 11 unions with more than 100,000 members are all white. It consistently opposed most of the recommendations of the Wiehahn Commission.[17]

The Congress of South African Trade Unions (COSATU) is a federation of 34 unions representing 500,000 black workers. It was formed at the beginning of December 1985 after years of negotiations, but two important groups, CUSA and AZACTU (see below), have not joined. The biggest previous grouping, the Federation of South African Unions (FOSATU), with about 110,000 members, the National Union of Mineworkers (150,000) and many others came together in COSATU and immediately threatened to launch a campaign of defiance if the government did not abolish the pass laws within six months. It appeared as if the new Congress would play a militant political role rather than limit itself to industrial relations. COSATU's first president, Elijah Barayi, predicted that it would take over from P. W. Botha's government and dismissed the argument that blacks would suffer first if economic sanctions were imposed against South Africa. 'Blacks have starved since 1652,' he said. 'COSATU is therefore in favour of sanctions.'

The Azanian Confederation of Trade Unions (AZACTU), like CUSA, leans towards Black Consciousness. With CUSA it was ejected from the talks leading to the new 'super-federation' of COSATU because they refused to accept the non-racial philosophical cornerstone of the other unions involved, being hostile to whites at leadership level. AZACTU claims that its seven affiliated unions have organized a total of 75,000 members. It is hoping for a 'closer working relationship' with CUSA.[18]

The Council of Unions of South Africa (CUSA) has 150,000 members. It grew out of a Consultative Committee of unions set up in Durban after a widespread series of strikes in 1972 that provided the impetus for the government to re-examine its labour legislation. It has tended to adopt Black Consciousness, and it refused to join FOSATU, alleging that the latter was dominated by non-Africans. Recently a small number of whites have joined CUSA unions. Like FOSATU, CUSA has spoken out against government legislation and the detention of trade unionists. Most of its unions are registered.[19]

Are there unions which are not affiliated to any co-ordinating body?

A number are not affiliated: the South African Boilermakers' Society, the Motor Industry Combined Workers' Union and the Amalgamated Engineering Union are among the largest.

What has been the attitude of established unions towards the new black unions?

TUCSA which in the 1960s called for Africans to be given union rights, in 1983 urged the government to make it an offence for unregistered unions to operate and for employers to recognize them. SACLA opposes extending union rights to Africans.[20] Three unions withdrew from TUCSA after the call to bar unregistered unions.

Has the government taken particular action against the new black unions?

In late 1984 a number of trade unionists were detained without trial after unrest on the Witwatersrand. Employers' organizations, in the first combined statement they have made on the issue, called on the government to charge or release the detainees. The president of the pro-Black Consciousness SAAWU, Thozamile Gqweta, has been detained at least eight times by the security police of South Africa and Ciskei: he has not been found guilty of any offence. In February 1985 he was detained on treason charges.[21] Dozens of others have been detained. At least two, Neil Aggett, a white who was Transvaal secretary of the African Food and Canning Workers' Union, and Andries Raditsela, another Transvaal union leader, died as a result of their treatment in detention. Others have been banned.

What has the South African government said about the political leanings of the unions?

The Minister of Law and Order, Louis le Grange, has said that labour has been 'targeted' by groups supporting the banned African National Congress. The Ciskei government has said that SAAWU and the ANC are synonymous.[22]

How many strikes and stoppages have there been in South Africa in recent years?

In 1982 there were 394 strikes and stoppages involving 141,571 workers, 86 per cent of them Africans. In 1983 there were 336 strikes involving 64,469 workers.[23] In 1984 there were 469 strikes with a loss of 378,000 worker-hours involving 181,942 workers. In the first nine months of 1985 the lost time was up by 30 per cent.[24]

How do these figures compare with those of other countries?

Working from the 1982 figures, the National Manpower Commission found that South Africa lost 40.7 days' work per 1,000 workers. This was lower than Britain (204.7) and the USA (254.9) and roughly comparable with Sweden (52.4). South Africa's figure is higher (66.7) if employees in agriculture, domestic service and central government are excluded from the calculation: these do not have statutory trade union rights or the right to stage legal strikes.[25]

What legislation is used against striking workers?

Some have been charged under the Intimidation Act, while others have been in court under the Trespass Act. In Transkei 90 workers were charged in 1983 under that homeland's Labour Relations Act for refusing or failing to work.[26] Although more than 90 per cent of strikes in South Africa are technically illegal – usually because the cumbersome and lengthy statutory procedure for calling a legal strike has not been used – it is rare for laws dealing directly with unions to be invoked.

A number of South African workers are often sceptical about 'official' mediating bodies. How many workers are covered by industrial agreements?

More than 1.1 million workers were covered by 104 industrial councils in 1983. The councils, composed of equal numbers of trade union representatives and employers, have jurisdiction over particular industries or areas and conclude agreements and settle disputes. Mediators can be called in to help industrial councils reach agreements. Because Africans were excluded for many years from the unions operating in the industrial councils, many councils are still dominated by TUCSA affiliates which have used their veto power to resist applications for membership by African unions. Less than half the workers who are governed by these industrial council agreements belong to unions which sit on the councils. The agreements are made binding on a particular industry and any breach is a criminal offence.

Conciliation boards can also be set up if there is no industrial council to deal with disputes. In 1983 101 boards were appointed. This is said to indicate increasing use of the official dispute-settling machinery.[27] Some of the new black unions see membership of industrial councils as a supplement to factory-floor bargaining, rather than a replacement for it.

Are there closed-shop agreements in South Africa?

Yes. They have been criticized by new black unions on the grounds that established unions have been using them to maintain their own positions. They have also been criticized as a way of keeping blacks, particularly Africans, out of skilled jobs. The law allows industrial councils to grant exemptions from closed-shop agreements.[28]

Can individual unions make agreements outside the official collective bargaining system?

Several hundred local agreements are in force at individual factories and commercial institutions. Many of the efforts of the new black unions have been at this level.[29]

The Homelands

Certain parts of South Africa have been designated as 'homelands' for Africans. How does the government define the homelands policy?

According to the Official Yearbook of South Africa, it 'provides for the full political development [of Africans] including the option of sovereign independence based in their traditional territories'.[1] Every African is classified into a 'national unit'; his or her political rights are to be exercised in an area demarcated for that unit.

How many homelands are there?

Ten (based on 'ethnic' groups): Transkei (for the Xhosa-speaking people), Ciskei (also Xhosa), KwaZulu (Zulu), Lebowa (North Sotho), Venda (Vhacenda), Gazankulu (Machangana-Tsonga), Bophuthatswana (Tswana), QwaQwa (South Sotho), KaNgwane (Swazi), and KwaNdebele (Southern Ndebele).

However, the homelands are not necessary geographical entities; one homeland may consist of several distinct parts, separated by areas allocated to 'white' South Africa and controlled by Pretoria. Originally there were 98 sections of homeland,[2] but consolidation of land areas, which is still continuing, has greatly reduced this number. At present Bophuthatswana consists of six distinct areas, Lebowa six and KwaZulu ten.

South Africa has declared some homelands independent states: which are these?

Transkei (in 1976), Bophuthatswana (1977), Venda (1979) and Ciskei (1981). The others are at varying stages of self-government. Several, notably KwaZulu, have said that they will not ask for 'independence' from Pretoria.

Are the 'independent' homelands internationally recognized as independent states?

They have recognition only from South Africa and each other. Most of the countries of the world maintain that South Africa is, and should be, one state and that the homelands are too dependent on Pretoria to be recognized as sovereign states.

Apartheid is now a policy of separate development of races in one country. Did Africans want the homelands policy introduced? Did whites?

Africans were not consulted when the Promotion of Bantu Self-Government Act, Number 46 of 1959, was introduced in Parliament. The Act removed from Africans throughout the country their right to elect four whites to the Senate through a system of electoral colleges,[3] and was passed against strong protests from these representatives, as well as from most African and non-racial organizations. Whites were not consulted either, apart from the caucus of the ruling National Party. One MP, Japie Basson, protested against the abolition of African representatives before the introduction of 'self-government' and was forced out of the party. The architect of the policy, the Prime Minister, Dr Hendrik Verwoerd, said in 1961 that it was 'a form of fragmentation which we would rather not have had if it was within our control to avoid it'. In part, the policy was designed to defuse international criticism of apartheid, or *baasskap* (white domination), as it was also called.

How much land do the homelands occupy, and how many people live in them?

Together the homelands cover about 13 per cent of South Africa's total area of 122 million hectares. According to calculations made by the South African Institute for Race Relations, 13 million people – 40 per cent of the total South African population – live in the homelands.[4] This is estimated to include about 55 per cent of Africans.

Approximately 11 million Africans live outside the homelands. What is their official status?

Until late 1985 official policy was that they were citizens of one or another homeland and were meant to exercise political rights there, not in 'white' South Africa. In September a shift was announced when the State President, P. W. Botha, pledged to restore the citizenship of the 5 million Africans regarded as nationals of the 'independent' homelands who live permanently in 'white' South Africa. The government, he said, would also negotiate with the 'independent' homeland governments over the citizenship of the 5 million Africans living in those territories. 'We propose that this be done on the basis of dual citizenship, which implies that these persons may have the option of accepting South African citizenship as a second citizenship in addition to their current citizenship.'

Mr Botha also said that the 'legitimate aspirations' of all Africans in the country would be 'accommodated by structures within South Africa'. In November 1985 he asked the President's Council to consider how it could be restructured to incorporate Africans – the first move to include Africans at central government level.*

It was made clear, however, that restoration of citizenship did not mean the end of the homelands system: 'Whatever the constitutional future ... the existence of the self-governing states will be part of the solution,' the Minister of Constitutional Development and Planning, Chris Heunis, said in September 1985. It also did not mean, he said, that citizens of 'independent' homelands would get political rights in 'white' South Africa.[5]

Are the homelands close to where Africans live and work?

Not necessarily. Most Africans in Cape Town, for example, are Xhosa-speaking: their nearest homeland is Ciskei, more than 500 miles away. Similarly, many Africans in Soweto, near Johannesburg, are Zulu: their homeland of KwaZulu is several hundred miles away. On the other hand, parts of Bophuthatswana and Lebowa are closer to the main industrial area of the Witwatersrand, centred around Johannesburg, where many Africans are employed.

Are any of the homelands economically self-sufficient?

All rely on South Africa to balance their budgets and none alone can feed their own people.

To what extent does South Africa support the homelands financially?

Parliament was told in July 1984[6] that South Africa spent R2.2 billion (about £1.1 billion) on the homelands in 1983 – almost 9 per cent of its total budget. According to figures supplied by the Department of Foreign Affairs, annual payments by South Africa to homeland governments for 1983–4 were:

*See chapter on national government.

Venda R119.2 million

Transkei R481.2 million

Lebowa R395.3 million

KwaNdebele R68.1 million

KwaZulu R466.8 million

Bophuthatswana R312.4 million

Ciskei R247.7 million

Gazankulu R188.8 million

KaNgwane R31.7 million

QwaQwa R97.5 million

What percentages of the homeland budgets are contributed by South Africa?

For the 'independent' homelands in 1984–5 the figures were: Transkei 77 per cent, Bophuthatswana 42.9, Venda 71.7 and Ciskei 75.

In what form is financial aid granted to the homelands?

Some is in the form of direct grants, the rest through bilateral agreements on tax, customs duties and the Rand monetary area. In addition, aid projects and secondment of officials to the homelands account for many millions of rand more.

What has been done to create more jobs in the homelands?

A variety of schemes for industrialization, inside the homelands or near the borders, have been planned through tax incentives, transport rebates, wage rebates, etc. Commercial opportunities have been increased in the homelands, agricultural improvement schemes implemented and their civil services expanded.

How high is the unemployment rate in the homelands?

No really accurate figures exist, but one estimate is that in Ciskei, for example, it is 35 per cent.[7] The Director of the Development Bank of Southern Africa, John Maree, said in 1983 that more than 70 cent of workers from the homelands entering the labour market depend on 'white' South Africa for jobs.[8] The Official Yearbook quotes a study by the Bureau for Economic Research: Co-operation and Development (BENSO) which found that between 1972 and 1975 jobs were found for only 28.4 per cent of the 100,000 young men and women who entered the labour market in the homelands every year.[9] The chairman of the Corporation for Economic Development, Dr. J. Adendorff, said in 1983 that R1,200 million a year needed to be spent in the homelands merely to prevent unemployment worsening.[10] Overall, unemployment in the homelands is said to be 27.5 per cent of the economically active population.

Has South Africa's aid policy towards the homelands succeeded in raising living standards?

Not by very much, Parliament was told in 1984.[11] The Gross Domestic Product per capita, at 1970 prices, of the self-governing homelands increased from R40 in 1970 to R46 in 1980 – an average annual income rise of 1.3 per cent. In the same period, South Africa's annual increase in GDP was 3.6 per cent in real terms.

Although the proportion of people living below the poverty datum line dropped from 99 per cent in 1960 to 81 per cent in 1980, the homeland population more than doubled, from 5 million to 11 million, in the same period. 'In other words,' Parliament was told, '99 per cent of five million is 4.1 million, but 81 per cent of 11 million is 8.9 million.'[12]

Has the number of destitute people in the homelands increased despite South African aid?

According to figures given to Parliament, the number of destitute people, defined as those with no jobs, no pension payments, no land and no cattle, rose from 250,000 in 1960 (5 per cent of the African homeland population) to 1.43 million (13 per cent) in 1980.[13]

If more people are destitute despite increased aid to the homelands, where is the money going?

To a large extent, on increased governmental and administrative spending. In Transkei, for example, the total cost of the public service is R226.58 million – 36 per cent of the total budget in 1983–4. There are 44,127 Transkei civil servants – one for every 59 people.[14]

Outside the civil service, what access is there to earned income in the homelands?

Most income is earned by migrant workers who travel to 'white' South Africa in search of employment: this source supplied 72 per cent of the total gross national income of the homelands in 1980. Those actually living and working in the homelands earn little. In Transkei, for example, 85 per cent of rural households earn less than the minimum subsistence level. In 1979 the poorest 20 per cent of rural households earned R242 a year – 15 per cent of the minimum subsistence level.

How does the pay of the homelands' elected leaders compare with the incomes of ordinary inhabitants?

Figures published in February 1983[15] said that the Chief Minister of Venda, for example, earns R48,700 a year plus a tax-free allowance; his chauffeur earns R1,896 a year. The average annual per capita income there is less than R450. In Ciskei, the average annual income is R212; the President earns R42,808.

Inhabitants of the homelands live within the area recognized by the rest of the world as South Africa, but the homelands themselves have no international status. Is it possible to be a citizen both of South Africa and of a homeland?

More than eight million Africans were made citizens of the homelands between 1976 and 1981, according to Sheena Duncan, National President of the Black Sash, a women's organization concerned with civil rights. Citizenship of an 'independent' homeland has meant loss of South African citizenship.[16] These 'ex-South Africans', as they are described by Professor John Dugard of the University of the Witwatersrand's Centre for Applied Legal Studies, do not qualify for South African passports and may be deported to their 'independent' homeland. They may also be refused admission to South Africa. According to Professor Dugard, 'Denationalized black South Africans living in the poverty-ridden homelands are refused admission to the industrial centres of South Africa; and those denationalized South Africans without special permission to remain in South Africa are deported to their national states. Resettlement camps and rural poverty are therefore the products of the policy of denationalization.'[17]

How does an African become a citizen of a homeland?

Africans become citizens of the homelands under agreements between Pretoria and the homelands, in terms of the Bantu Homelands Citizenship Act, Number 26 of 1970, or by Acts passed by homeland parliaments.

An amending Act of 1974 said that an African would become a homeland citizen if born in the area, if living there, if speaking any language or dialect used there, related to any member of the population of the homeland, identified with any part of the population there, or associated with any part of the population 'by virtue of their cultural or racial background'.[18] A memorandum released with the bill said that 'all indigenous Bantu groups thus fall within the scope of this clause'.

Did the homeland policy mean that eventually all Africans in South Africa should have only homeland citizenship?

The then Minister of Bantu Administration and Development, Connie Mulder, said in 1978: 'If our policy is taken to its logical conclusion as far as the black people are concerned, there will not be one black man with South African citizenship ... Every black man in South Africa will eventually be accommodated in some independent new state in this honourable way and there will no longer be a moral obligation on this parliament to accommodate these people politically.'[19]

This policy is resented by many, particularly Africans deprived of their citizenship, and Professor Dugard has questioned whether denationalization is against international law.[20]

Is government policy on citizenship changing?

Opening the new tricameral Parliament in January 1985, President Botha said that the government was reconsidering the citizenship issue. 'Clarity must be reached soon ... The government confirms that it is its intention to do so.' A special Cabinet committee is investigating citizenship. There has been speculation that some form of dual citizenship is under consideration.[21]

In April 1985 Mr Botha hinted that citizens of the 'independent' homelands might be allowed to retain their South African nationality. He invited opposition parties to serve on the special committee investigating how best to accommodate politically blacks living outside the homelands. Only the Conservative Party in the white House of Assembly refused to join the committee.[22]

In September 1985, as detailed on pp. 111–12, Mr Botha promised to restore citizenship to those nationals of the 'independent' homelands living in 'white' South Africa and to negotiate some kind of dual citizenship for those living in the 'independent' homelands. Mr Botha's statement was generally welcomed by homeland leaders and white politicians, apart from those on Mr Botha's right-wing.[23]

Are passports issued to citizens of the homelands internationally recognized?

Not outside South Africa and other homelands. The South African government issues travel documents to get around this difficulty.

Do people travelling between 'white' South Africa and the 'independent' homelands need passports?

Some documentation, usually a passport, is needed at border posts. The posts, however, do not guard every entry and exit: there are many roads which are not checked. Foreigners, that is, non-South Africans, need visas to visit the 'independent' homelands.

Do the homelands have apartheid laws?

A number of such laws have been abolished by the 'independent' homelands, where, for example, hotels and bars are multi-racial, housing is not segregated by law and the Immorality and Mixed Marriages Acts do not apply. In these homelands there are, however, some schools which still cater for whites only and are administered from Pretoria.

The 'non-independent' homelands are subject to every law applicable in 'white' South Africa.

Do the 'independent' homelands have trade and investments links with countries outside South Africa?

Israel and Taiwan, two of South Africa's closest allies, have some trading ties with all four 'independent' Bantustans. Among others, Israeli companies have been involved in agricultural projects in Bophuthatswana and Ciskei, and by March 1983 a total of 29 Taiwanese firms had applied for decentralization concessions to set up factories in or near the homelands.[24]

Have there been contacts at governmental level between the homelands and nations outside South Africa?

The homelands have no official diplomatic links except with South Africa and each other. There have been other connections, however. Presidents Sebe (Ciskei) and Mangope (Bophuthatswana) have visited Israel, the former on several occasions, while Venda's Chief Mphephu and Lebowa's Dr Phatudi have been to Taiwan. In September 1984 there was reported to be official concern and embarrassment about links between Israel and the homelands at a time when Jerusalem was trying to repair ties with black African states. Israeli firms have been reported to be training Ciskeians to become pilots. The cost of the courses to train 20 Ciskeian pilots was reported to be R4 million (£2 million) while the cost in South Africa would have been about R40,000 (£20,000). Some of the pilots were said to have only the education of 13-year-olds. Israeli planes for a fledgling Ciskei air force are reported to have been sold to the homeland, together with a private jet for President Sebe. It is believed to have cost R900,000 (£450,000), although the same aircraft was advertised in Israel for R150,000 (£75,000). The Israeli government has denied that there are any government-to-government links with any homeland. The former head of Ciskei security, Lieutenant-General Charles Sebe, travelled to Israel in early 1983 and spoke at a seminar of security experts.

In late 1985 the telephones of all senior Ciskeian civil servants were reported to be tapped with special equipment provided, on President Sebe's orders, by an Israeli security firm. Israelis were also said to be guarding the gaming tables at Sun City casino in Bophuthatswana.

Ciskei is developing an air force. Do all 'independent' homelands have defence forces?

Yes. In 1984–5 Bophuthatswana's defence budget was R21 million, Transkei's R16 million, Venda's R8.7 million, and Ciskei's commitment for 'state security' R10.3 million. In late 1984 Ciskei was also reported to have sent 30 of its troops to help South African forces in Namibia.

What is the relationship of the homeland defence forces to the South African Defence Force?

In September 1983 Professor Ken Grundy, a US political scientist, said in a paper published by the South African Institute of International Affairs that the homeland forces were 'part of Pretoria's regional defence system against insurgents of the ANC'.[25] All four homeland forces have clashed with African National Congress guerrillas. Professor Grundy said: 'It would appear that the SA Government would ideally like to transform the homelands, as each gains independence, into an inner ring of buffer states to replace what had been a defence in depth prior to the fall of the Portuguese holdings in Africa and the Zimbabwean resolution.' Pretoria has signed non-aggression pacts with each of the 'independent' homelands.

Are the 'independent' homelands' security laws and services similar to those of South Africa?

There are many similarities, examples of which are given below.

Transkei

A state of emergency has existed since 1960 except for eight months in 1976–7. Under first Proclamation R400 and then the Transkei Public Security Act of 1977, police may detain anybody; enter buildings with warrants; seize vehicles, firearms, and publications; close roads and public places; prohibit meetings; prevent any person entering an area or leaving an area. The Act also incorporates provisions of South Africa's security laws and makes it an offence to advocate that Transkei, or parts of it, should form part of another country – an attempt to stop criticism of Transkei taking independence.[26]

Opposition politicians have been detained without trial.[27] A powerful Paramount Chief, Sabata Delindyebo, was found guilty of injuring the reputation of the State President and forced into exile. Organizations have been banned, journalists detained and deported, University of Transkei academics deported – the most recent being two professors in August 1984[28] – and students held. In addition, a number of people have been charged with supporting the banned African National Congress and Pan-Africanist Congress.

Three policemen were found guilty of culpable homicide and assault of a detained murder suspect, and a Durban advocate was paid damages for detention without trial.

In 1985, as unrest spread to many parts of the country, Transkei was also involved. A curfew had to be imposed in the capital, Umtata, and a number of people detained after a fuel depot was destroyed by a bomb.[29] In September 1985 a former student leader, Batandwa Ndondo, was abducted by people identified as Transkei security police. Trying to escape apparent assault by the police in a van, he was gunned down in the village of Cala. Several witnesses to the shooting were later detained, as were pall-bearers at Mr Ndondo's funeral – joining at least 880 people who had been detained in September 1985. Transkei's President K. D. Matanzima blamed Mr Ndondo for the bomb that destroyed the Umtata fuel depot in June 1985. This was interpreted by one South African white MP as 'suspiciously like a tacit admission by President Matanzima that the killing was officially sanctioned'. The Transkei police were reported to have opened a murder investigation into Mr Ndondo's death.[30]

Bophuthatswana

This is the only 'country' in Southern Africa to have a Bill of Rights. In June 1983 the general secretary of the opposition National Seoposengwe Party, Victor Sifora, was detained without trial – although the Bill of

Rights does not allow for this. Three other members of the party were also detained.[31] Several chiefs have been deposed, allegedly because they support the opposition.[32]

Venda

At least two people have died while being held in detention without trial, the latest, Samuel Tshikhudo, in January 1984.[33] In mid 1983 the family of the first person to die in detention, Tshifiwa Muofhe, were given an out-of-court payment of R150,000. Two policemen were found not guilty of causing the death.

In February 1984 two men were re-arrested under security laws within minutes of being released from detention, after the Venda police chief had given an undertaking in the Supreme Court to free them.[34] In 1983 detainees filed claims totalling more than R300,000 for torture while in detention.[35]

The ruling Venda National Party has twice been defeated in elections by the opposition Venda Independence Party. The first time this happened the nominated chiefs, who are in the majority in the assembly, were reported to have been induced by bribery to support President Mpephu.[36] On the second occasion, he detained the entire opposition until they co-operated.[37] In 1982 a Venda Cabinet minister was executed for ritual murder; in 1983 one of his sons was sentenced to death for the same crime.[38]

Ciskei

Under President Sebe, confirmed in office for life in August 1983,[39] Ciskei has attracted the most attention over the use of its security laws. The National Security Act of 1982 replaced Proclamation R252 of 1977, which had provisions similar to Transkei's state of emergency Proclamation R400. Among other things, it provides for detention without trial, banning of individuals and organizations – the most notable of those affected being the black South African Allied Workers' Union – and the prohibition of strikes and encouragement to strike.[40]

In 1983 up to 90 people were reported to have died in a long-running dispute between the Ciskei government and commuters in the major township of Mdantsane. A boycott of buses was organized in protest against fare increases: the Ciskei police and army detained at least 800 people, beat commuters back into buses, tortured dozens in a soccer stadium and shot Mdantsane residents trying to board trains. The Ciskei government is facing claims totalling R1 million (£500,000) for damages as a result.

The bus boycott came as an alleged coup was being mounted by

Lieutenant-General Charles Sebe, President Sebe's brother. General Sebe, described as 'the most powerful cop in Southern Africa',[41] was detained and eventually sentenced to 12 years' imprisonment. At least six other members of the Sebe family were also detained. President Sebe was reported to have fled during the bus unrest to nearby East London, in 'white' South Africa.[42]

Hundreds of trade unionists have been detained without trial: the leader of SAAWU, Thozamila Gqweta, at least eight times by the Ciskei and South African security forces. He has not been found guilty of any offence. Mdantsane, the dormitory township for industrial East London, is in Ciskei: workers find that they may belong to a trade union like SAAWU by day at their workplace, but not at night when they return home.

In early 1985, amid signs of deteriorating relations between South Africa and Ciskei, Pretoria withdrew all of its Defence Force members seconded to Ciskei. A few days before, President Sebe had suspended three senior officers, detained at least two leading educationalists, and reshuffled his Cabinet for the twelfth time since Ciskei was declared independent in December 1981.[43]

South African unrest in 1985 did not leave Ciskei unscathed. A number of people were killed; three schoolchildren drowned in a river while trying to escape from Ciskei police; and thousands of people were detained, including in September 1985 one crowd of 2,900 people who were alleged to be holding an illegal gathering.[44]

The Pass Laws

Can South Africans move freely around the country?

Various Acts bar certain people from defined areas. Until mid 1985 non-Africans, for example, could legally enter African townships only if issued with a permit to do so. This was changed, but the police are able to bar people considered 'undesirable' from entering a particular township for up to three months. Anybody failing to comply can be summarily ejected and charged. There is a maximum penalty of a R500 (£250) fine or a prison sentence of up to six months or both.[1] In August 1985 Dr Allan Boesak and 18 others were arrested after they ignored an order not to enter Guguletu township, Cape Town, to attend the funeral of an unrest victim.[2]

Indians are at present not allowed to live and work in the Orange Free State without permission. In September 1985, however, the Free State congress of the National Party voted overwhelmingly in favour of repealing the old Free State Republic statute that barred 'coolies, Chinese and other Asians' from the province.[3]

Africans can live and work in 'white' South Africa only if they have documents entitling them to be there: the Acts enforcing this are known as 'influx control' or the 'pass laws'.

What is a 'pass'?

It was defined by the government-appointed Fagan Commission in 1948 as a document

'(a) which is not carried by all races, but only by people of a particular race; and which either

(b) is connected with restriction of the freedom of movement of the person concerned; or

(c) must at all times be carried by the person concerned on his body, since the law lays the obligation on him of producing it on demand to the police and certain other officials and the mere failure to produce it is by itself a punishable offence.'[4]

The first pass laws were introduced in 1760 when all slaves in the Cape had to carry them. All male Africans have had to carry their 'reference books', as passes are also called, since 1 February 1958, and African women from 1 February 1963.

Despite its name, a pass does not give its holder total freedom of movement. What is the official purpose of a pass?

It provides proof that an African's presence in a specific area is legal or otherwise. Under the Native Laws Amendment Act, Number 54 of 1972, any African born in the country may not visit an urban area for more than 72 hours without obtaining a special permit. A pass, therefore, carries information showing whether its holder is a legal resident of a prescribed area.[5]

Why were the pass laws introduced?

The aim was to facilitate the control of population movement. By this means, African labour could be directed where it was needed, whether in the mines and industry or on white farms. In particular it was hoped to check the drift to the 'white' cities of Africans seeking work, or better-paid work, they could not obtain in the country. This policy, which is expressed in numerous laws and regulations, became known as 'influx control'.

Do people from other racial groups have to carry identity documents similar to those for Africans?

Whites, Coloureds and Indians are issued with identity documents which 'must be produced within seven days when demanded by any peace officer'.[6]

In March 1985 the State President said that 'all South Africans' were forced to carry identity cards, including himself. To establish the accuracy of this statement, which seemed to imply that black and white were treated equally over identity documents, Parliament was asked about arrests over the past 10 years for not carrying official identity documents. The figures were:

Africans	637,584
Coloureds	2
Indians	None
Whites	None[7]

Do Africans have to carry their passes on them at all times?

The Natives (Abolition of Passes and Co-ordination of Documents) Act, Number 67 of 1952, said that any authorized officer could at any time order any African to produce to him a reference book. Failure to comply is an offence.[8]

In 1984 an African marathon runner was told that in terms of the law he should really carry his pass on him while running. Officials then relented: it would be all right, he was told, if he pinned a photostat of the first page of his pass book to his vest while in a race.

Are Africans without their passes given a chance to produce them?

The second Bantu Laws Amendment Act, Number 102 of 1978, allowed Africans who did not have their reference books on them to fetch them if the pass was not more than five kilometres away from where the demand was made. Ministers have said that police have been instructed to allow Africans a 'reasonable' opportunity of fetching their passes: this has not been defined in law. It has been reported that in practice these provisos are not often observed. The same Amendment Act also provided that Africans could carry citizenship documents issued by a homeland government instead of a pass.[9] In terms of this and other legislation, Africans belonging to 'independent' homelands are no longer South African citizens.

How many people are arrested under the pass laws each year?

In the past nine years for which figures are available, more than 1.9 million people have been arrested. The individual figures are:[10]

1975–6	381,858	1981	162,024
1976–7	297,374	1982	206,022
1977–8	279,957	1983	262,904
1978–9	162,054	1984	163,862
1980	158,335		

Parliament was told that the 1982 arrest figures meant that the rate was one person every two and a half minutes.

Between 1916 and 1981 a total of 17.12 million Africans had been arrested under the pass laws, the President's Council said in September 1985.

How many people are convicted under the pass laws each year?

The exact total is not known: from 1980 the report of the Commissioner of Police no longer gave the figures. However, figures for the nine main urban areas show that in 1983 a total of 142,067 people were convicted, most in the Transvaal industrial area. The comparable figure for 1981 was 75,176.[11]

What sentences are given for pass law offences?

According to a study done in the Johannesburg Commissioner's Courts, the usual sentence is a fine of between R30 (or 30 days) and R90 (or 90 days). The heaviest fine was R250 and the longest jail term 250 days.[12]

What happens to pass law cases in the courts?

In the cases surveyed at the Johannesburg Commissioner's Courts, hearings took from 30 seconds to seven minutes. Only five of 369 people charged had legal representation. Fewer than one in 10 were discharged or acquitted. About 60 per cent were convicted on their first appearance in court; many other cases were postponed for between one and 19 days and bail, when requested, was often fixed at between R70 and R100. No investigating officers were called to prove that the accused were illegally in an urban area. In 48 of the 369 cases the accused had passes that, it was said, they were given no opportunity to fetch at the time of arrest.[13]

Less than one per cent of the Africans who appeared in all the country's commissioners' courts – most of them on pass law charges – were defended by lawyers, according to government figures issued in 1984.[14] The state received R1.15 million (£557,920) in fines paid by Africans convicted under influx control regulations in the major urban areas in 1983.[15]

In October 1985 it was reported that Africans arrested under the pass laws would soon no longer be tried in the commissioners' courts but in ordinary courts. Special courts for Africans were termed 'obsolete'.[16]

The pass laws are intended to control population movement. Are other laws used for this as well?

In 1983 a total of 104,607 Africans were arrested under the Trespass Act.[17] The fines for transgressing this Act were raised in 1983 from R50 to R2,000. In March 1983 blacks living on plots in southern Johannesburg were raided and many charged under the Trespass Act. The Black Sash civil rights organization was reported to have said that the law could be used against blacks squatting on public land or living illegally in servants' quarters.[18]

In July 1983 six people were convicted under a 1968 government regulation making it an offence for a 'registered occupier' – anybody with a permit to stay in a township – to occupy a site, dwelling or accommodation other than that specified in the permit. Five of the six, who told the court that they had been visiting friends or relatives, were fined R10 (or 10 days' jail).[19]

Legislation against squatting has also been used. In June 1983 six people who had been squatting at the KTC camp near Cape Town were fined R50 (or 50 days' jail), suspended for two years on condition they left the area. Evidence was given that officials raided the camp, destroyed the squatters' shacks and confiscated their personal belongings. The accused said that they came to the Cape from Transkei because they were starving.[20]

Action is being taken against 'foreign' Africans – from the 'independent' homelands or neighbouring states – under the immigration laws. The 1937 Aliens Act and the Regulation of Admission of Persons to the Republic Act, Number 59 of 1972 (now amended by the Aliens and Immigration Amendment Act of 1984), were used to send back to Transkei or Ciskei 2,000 squatters from Nyanga outside Cape Town in August 1981.[21]

In June 1984 an investigation was ordered after press reports that several Africans had been detained without trial on suspicion of being Zimbabweans. Some, with valid identity documents, had been held for up to 13 months to make them confess to being aliens so that they could be deported to Zimbabwe.[22] An official responsible said he had been instructed that none of the people being held were to be allowed bail. When a person did appear in court and was found not guilty, he had him re-arrested immediately, as he was allowed to do under the terms of the Admission of Persons to the Republic Act, and held him until he confessed.[23]

How do Africans qualify to live legally in urban areas in 'white' South Africa?

The law is immensely complicated and administration of it said to be often arbitrary. For Africans to be 'legals' they must have what is called 'Section 10' rights. This is Section 10(1) of the Urban Areas Consolidation Act of 1945 as amended – most recently in June 1985 – which says that an African may not be in a prescribed area unless he or she:

'(a) had been born there and resided there continuously since birth; or

'(b) worked continuously for 10 years in any prescribed area for any employer; or lived continuously in any such area for a period not less than 10 years; or

'(c) was the wife, unmarried daughter, or son under 18 years of age of an African falling into classes (a) or (b), and ordinarily resided with him, and initially entered the area lawfully; or

'(d) had been granted a permit to remain by a labour bureau.' [24]

The onus of proving legality is on Africans, not the state.

The June 1985 amendments to Section 10 were said to be a considerable relaxation of the law. Previously Africans had to work continuously for 10 years for one employer in one area: a change of job, a dismissal or a relocation meant the loss of qualifying rights. The amendment allowed Africans to change employment without loss. Further, until June 1985 an African could qualify only if he or she 'had been there [in a prescribed area] continuously and lawfully for 15 years and had thereafter continued to reside there, and was not employed outside the area, and while in the area had not been sentenced to a fine exceeding R100 or to imprisonment for a period exceeding six months'. In terms of the June 1985 amendment the qualifying period of continuous and lawful residence was reduced from 15 years to 10. [25]

The law said that Africans could qualify to live in an urban area by working there continuously for ten years or more. Could this right always be exercised in practice?

A 1968 government regulation stated that migrant workers in urban areas in 'white' South Africa had to return home every year to renew their contracts. Officials said that because migrants had to leave their employers for this purpose each year they could never work for one employer 'continuously' for more than a year, and so could not claim their right under Section 10(1)(b). [26] A change resulted from the 'Rikhoto judgement' in the Appeal Court in May 1983. This decision, which affected thousands of migrant workers, was that enforced absences did not mean a break in service. This was seen as a landmark case. It followed two other judgements, regarded as equally important. The Komani case of 1980 said that the wife of a man legally resident in Cape Town in terms of Section 10(1)(c) could remain with him. The Booi judgement of May 1982 gave a ruling along similar lines to the later Rikhoto judgement. [27]

However, Parliament amended the pass laws under the Laws of Co-operation and Development Amendment Act in August 1983 to say that only dependants of a man who is a legal tenant or owner of a housing unit could qualify to be in the area. Only people who are members of a 'legal' family and in 'legal' lodgings can get on to township housing waiting lists.

In September 1985 another decision that has implications for contract workers was delivered by the Appeal Court. The 'Mthiya judgement' said that a contract worker who took long leave – ranging in this case from four to eight months – during the period that he was qualifying for Section 10 rights should be given those rights on the basis that he would be re-employed before he took the leave. Before the judgement, thousands of contract workers were said to have been refused Section 10 rights because development boards had interpreted periods of long leave as interrupted service.[28]

How many people stood to gain urban residence rights through the Rikhoto judgement?

It was estimated that about 143,000 out of the 800,000 migrant workers would benefit. The government stated in February 1985 that about 50,000 people had won residence rights as a result of this case.[29] After the judgement, officials of several (African) development boards, which deal with pass laws and residence rights, were said to be turning away applicants or slowing the administrative process.[30] Because of the shortage of black housing and because its allocation is controlled by officials, it was thought that there would not be a large influx of dependants of men who qualified for residence in terms of the Rikhoto judgement. Housing also has to be 'approved' by government officials before dependants are allowed in legally.[31]

What can happen to Africans who are not employed?

Section 29 of the Urban Areas Consolidation Act says that 'idle and undesirable' Africans may be sent to a prison farm for up to two years and stripped of their city rights. One criterion for deciding whether a person is 'idle and undesirable' is that he must be unemployed and have spent less than 122 days of the past year in lawful employment. This was challenged by the Natal Supreme Court in June 1983, when it ruled that courts had to take into account the ordinary dictionary definition of 'idle'. This ruling applies to Natal only.[32]

In the period between 30 June 1983 and 31 January 1984 inquiries had been made against 5,359 people in terms of the Act and 313 had been declared 'idle'.[33]

Can whites employing 'illegal' Africans be prosecuted?

Yes. There is a maximum fine of R2,000.

Do Africans lose their Section 10 rights if they move to the homelands?

There was some confusion about this. The Minister of Co-operation and Development, Dr Gerrit Viljoen, said that people would 'not lose such privileges if they move to a trust area of a national state'. But it was pointed out that this pledge did not include the children of such people.[34]

Are there moves to liberalize or scrap the pass laws?

In September 1985 the President's Council recommended abolition of the pass laws and their replacement by a colour-blind 'strategy for orderly urbanization'. All South Africans irrespective of race, it said, should carry uniform identity documents, but failure to do so should not be an offence. Pass law abolition should also be extended to citizens of the 'independent' homelands who had been subject to the rigorous controls of the Aliens Act. The Council also recommended that Africans anywhere in the country should have the right to have their wives and families live with them – subject to the Squatters Act and other legislation 'affecting all races equally'. All race discrimination in immigration laws should also be abolished: this had been promised by the government a few days before.

The Council's recommendations were widely welcomed. But Dr Connie Mulder, a prominent member of the Conservative Party, who in 1978, as a Cabinet minister, had said under the pass laws and other legislation there should be no African South Africans (see p. 116), condemned the move. If influx control and racial separation were abandoned, 'then we must do away with our own areas, own schools, own facilities ... We must then open everything to blacks, including Parliament.'[35]

Also in September 1985 it was announced that migrant workers from the 'independent' homelands would no longer have to travel 'home' to renew their contracts provided they were still working for the same employer.[36]

In October 1985, although there was no official moratorium on pass raids, the number of people appearing in court was reported to be diminishing and treatment in court was more lenient. In January people were being fined and jailed; in September members of the Black Sash who monitored the courts said that most were cautioned and discharged. An unofficial police source said that police were no longer deliberately going out on pass raids. But the West Rand Development Board was still raiding houses in the Johannesburg area, looking for pass offenders.[37]

Despite the strong hint that the pass laws would be abolished, a leading African road runner, Epraim Sibisi, was arrested in December 1985 by five policemen for not carrying his pass. Mr Sibisi said he was assaulted by one policeman and was held in a police cell overnight. Charges were withdrawn in the morning.[38]

Removals

How many people have been moved from one place to another under the policy of apartheid?

The exact total is not known. The best estimate was made in 1983 by a team of researchers known as the Surplus People Project (SPP). It said that between 1960 and 1983 a total of 3,522,900 removals had taken place. This excludes removals within the homelands, those resulting from agricultural improvement planning, and pass law enforcements. It includes 'numerous instances' of people being moved two, three or even four times.[1]

How many people are still facing removal?

According to the SPP, another 1.8 million people are under threat of removal, and this figure will rise to two million through farm evictions, influx control and 'infrastructural development'.[2]

How many people have been moved under agricultural improvement schemes?

The total is not known: in Natal alone it is thought to number more than one million since the 1950s.[3]

People have had to move because of many different schemes and laws. What are the main removal categories, and how many people have they affected?

The Surplus People Project breakdown is:

Farm – eviction of black tenants from white farms and of redundant workers	1,129,000
Black spots and consolidation – clearing black owned property outside homelands, and fragments of reserves surrounded by 'white' land	674,000
Urban relocation – moving townships in 'white' areas to homelands	670,000

Informal settlements – removal from unauthorized urban settlements	112,000+
Influx control – ejection from 'white' urban areas under pass laws	Incalculable
Group areas – usually intra-city removals due to racial re-zoning	834,000
Infrastructural – relocation due to development schemes; and *strategic* – clearing sensitive areas	23,500
Political – imposed moves, such as banishment and flight from oppression	50,000
Other – moving resettlement areas	30,000
Total	3,522,900

Has the removals policy affected blacks and whites equally?

Three quarters of those moved were Africans and most of the rest (carried out under the Group Areas Act) Coloured and Indian. A total of 2,262 white families were moved under the Group Areas Act from the introduction of the legislation in 1951 to 1981, the Minister of Commodity Development told Parliament in 1983.[4]

What figures on removals has the government made available?

The former Minister of Co-operation and Development, Dr Piet Koornhof, said in May 1984 that almost two million blacks had been 'relocated' but that only 456,860 of these were moved for 'ideological reasons'.[5] In March 1985 the then Minister of Co-operation and Development, Dr Gerrit Viljoen, said that 5,122 Africans were moved from 'white' urban areas to the homelands – thereby, under present law, losing their South African citizenship – in 1984.[6] Dr Viljoen also said that nearly 23,000 Africans were 'resettled' in 1984: this figure appears to include the 5,122 moved to the homelands.[7]

In previous years, information about black removals was refused to Parliament or said to be not known.[8] The Official Yearbook for 1985 gives no figures for removals.

What particular reasons have there been for removals?

The Surplus People Project used 11 different categories:[9]

1. Farm removals, including those due to the abolition of the labour tenancy system (under a 1964 amendment to the 1936 Natives Land

Act) and cash tenancy on white-owned farms. Some farm workers were moved because they became redundant as farms were mechanized; others moved because of dissatisfaction with conditions.

2. Clearance of 'black spots' – properties, often held on freehold by Africans or held in trust by missions, which are outside areas marked for African occupation.

3. Removal from 'badly situated' tribal areas which are carried out to consolidate the homelands into more cohesive units.

4. Urban relocation – removing African townships from areas considered to be in 'white' South Africa into homelands.

5. Removal of 'informal [i.e., unauthorized] settlements' in urban and peri-urban areas.

6. Group Areas Act removals. (See chapter on group areas.)

7. Infrastructural removals – for development of dams, roads, forestry and plantations.

8. Removals for strategic or military purposes.

9. Influx control removals, including implementation of the policy that the Western Cape should employ Coloureds rather than Africans. (The government announced in late 1984 that this policy would be scrapped.)

10. Direct political removals, including banishments.

11. 'Betterment scheme' removals for improving agriculture.

From which provinces of South Africa have people been moved?

All four. The SPP said that the highest number of removals was in the Transvaal (1,295,400 moved with another 605,000 under threat of being moved). The figures for the other three were: Natal (745,500 moved and 622,000 under threat), the Free State (514,000 moved with no figures for those under threat) and the Cape (583,000 moved and 502,000 under threat).

Under which laws do removals take place?

The Surplus People Project says the following laws have been used:

Black Land Act, Number 27 of 1913; Native (Urban Areas) Act, Number 21 of 1923; Black Administration Act, Number 31 of 1927; Slums Clearance Act, Number 53 of 1934; Development Land and Trust Act, Number 18 of 1936; Group Areas Act, Number 41 of 1950 (and various amending and consolidating acts to it); Prevention of Illegal Squatting Act, Number 52 of 1951; Blacks (Abolition of Passes and Coordination of Documents) Act, Number 67 of 1952; Black Resettlement Act, Number 19 of 1954; Black Prohibition of Interdicts Act, Number 14 of 1956; Promotion of Bantu Self-Government Act, Number 46 of 1959; Black Laws Amendment Act, Number 76 of 1963; National States Citizenship Act, Number 26 of 1970; National States Constitution Act, Number 21 of 1971; Expropriation Act, Number 26 of 1975; and the Admission of Persons to the Republic Regulations Act, Number 59 of 1972.

Is removal voluntary or enforced?

Dr Koornhof said in May 1984 [10] that there had been 'an element of force in some removals', but that relocation was now 'development-oriented' and that the government was 'trying not to have to move people by force as far as this is humanly possible'. The year before, in February 1983, he said that removals were carried out with 'compassion and respect for human dignity after deep thought and careful consideration at high government level'.[11] A 1982 government circular said that people involved in removals should be consulted 'on a persuasion basis'.[12]

What methods have been used to persuade people to move?

One community whose case has been documented is that of the Bakwena tribe at Mogopa, near Ventersdorp in the Transvaal.[13] The following steps were taken to achieve their removal:

1. Officials told the tribe that they would be moved from Mogopa to Pachsdraai near Zeerust, which was due to be incorporated into Bophuthatswana. The tribe refused to move and the status quo was preserved.

2. In September 1981 the tribe voted to depose their headman, Jacob More, for failing to adhere to 'democratic principles' and for corruption. The local magistrate refused to accept the decision, saying: 'Jacob More will rule until he dies.' As an agent of the State President, who in law is Paramount Chief of all Africans, he was legally within his rights to make this statement.

3. In February 1982 the Ventersdorp magistrate called a 'resettlement meeting' and repeated that the tribe would be moved to Pachsdraai. The tribe reiterated its opposition.

4. Government officials, Bophuthatswana officials and the deposed headman and some of his allies met behind closed doors to negotiate. The Mogopa people applied to their lawyers to have the meetings held in public. This was not done.

5. On 24 June 1983 Mr More and about 180 families left for Pachsdraai. The tribe's village schools and churches and some houses were demolished by government bulldozers, and water-pumps taken away by

the Ventersdorp magistrate. The bus service to Ventersdorp, 12 miles away, was withdrawn. From June until November a government demolition team camped next to the village.

6. All facilities at Pachsdraai were given to Mr More and his 'planning committee' to allocate. He had lived in one of the poorest mud huts at Mogopa. At Pachsdraai he and his allies lived in houses formerly owned by whites.

7. Pensions were not paid at Mogopa, annual labour contracts not stamped, and the shop-owner's licence to trade was not renewed. In January 1984 the tribe managed to get these matters corrected.

8. In mid 1983 women were approached while the men were at work and told that they had to agree to have numbers painted on their houses. Most refused, but some agreed. Lorries were sent to fetch those who had agreed, and their houses were smashed by bulldozers as they left.

9. The villagers took legal action to have the demolition team removed from their land on grounds of trespass.

10. On 18 November 1983 the Ventersdorp magistrate read the villagers an order in terms of the Black Administration Act of 1927 saying that the tribe should move to Pachsdraai within 10 days and never return. They were told that if they did not move by 29 November they would be moved by force.

11. The villagers' lawyers appealed to the Pretoria Supreme Court to prevent the authorities from evicting them. The application was refused.

12. Church leaders, political groups, students, the Black Sash women's organization and journalists arrived at the village to wait for the removal on 29 November. Trucks arrived but nobody was moved.

13. In the early hours of 14 February 1984 Mogopa was surrounded by armed police. At 4 a.m. Jacob More told the villagers through a loudhailer that they should load their possessions into trucks and go to Pachsdraai. The leaders of the resistance were handcuffed by police and put into police vans. Their possessions were packed by government labourers. People standing outside their houses were reported to have been beaten by police.

14. Outsiders were barred from entering Pachsdraai when the villagers arrived in government trucks.

15. The Mogopa removal was given another twist in September 1985. The Appeal Court ruled that the government should not have moved the residents without parliamentary approval. However, it was not certain whether the people of Mogopa would be able to return to their land – unknown to them until recently, their land was expropriated by the government after their removal, and by that stage all their buildings had been reduced to piles of bricks by the authorities.

The 'Mogopa judgement' was said to be significant for thousands of people still living in 'black spots' as the government would now need Parliament's consent before moving them. This consent is unlikely to be granted under the tricameral system, although the President's Council would have the power to give its approval.[14] *

What facilities does the government provide for people who have had to move?

The 1982 government circular on removals said that in 'border' townships – those in homelands but within commuting distance of 'white' centres – resettled people were provided with water, sewerage systems, electricity and proper roads. In other areas, it went on, rudimentary services such as pit latrines or buckets, temporary huts on loan, or tents were provided. Sources of water were bore-holes, rivers or springs. The water was disinfected if necessary and provided by taps so that it was not necessary to walk more than 250 yards to get it. Clinics, schools, shops, transport facilities and job opportunities should be provided.[15]

However, the Surplus People Project researchers found that one of the largest relocation areas, Onverwacht, established in 1979, with a population of more than 100,000 by the end of 1981, had one clinic, one police station, one supermarket and 19 schools operating a double-shift system for 20,000 pupils. At Botshebelo, with a population of 140,000, there were six doctors, one dentist, 38 community health workers, 800 taps, no hospital and a sewerage system that was being developed, Dr Koornhof told Parliament. In June 1983 a Methodist Church leader said that the same place had one telephone, no electric lights and few qualified teachers.[16]

Is unemployment a problem in resettlement areas?

The SPP found in interviews with more than 1,600 households in 17 removal areas that unemployment averaged 24 per cent in the homelands or on South African Development Trust land. Fifty-five per cent of those who had jobs were migrants living permanently away from home. This figure rose to 71 per cent in the settlements further from 'white' areas. Fifteen per cent of resettled households in the homelands had no breadwinner.[17] Dimbaza, where the film Last Grave at Dimbaza was shot, and which is now claimed to be a showpiece, had an unemployment rate of 35 per cent.[18]

*See chapter on national government.

What is the level of infant mortality in resettlement areas?

A community health worker estimated that 240 out of every 1,000 babies born in resettlement camps died before their first birthday. The infant mortality rate for whites in Cape Town is 10 out of 1,000.

Are removals being halted?

In February 1985 the Minister of Co-operation and Development, Dr Gerrit Viljoen, said that the government had decided to stop the forced removal of Africans pending a review of the resettlement programme. He said that the review could affect hundreds of thousands of Africans living in 20 to 30 rural settlements and another 20 urban areas. Dr Viljoen said, however, that removals would continue if the leaders of the communities agreed.[19] In May 1985 the government issued a list of 52 black townships whose residents would not be removed as planned previously. At least 700,000 Africans were affected. The Black Sash organization described this as 'a fairly major development'.[20]

In February 1985 Dr Viljoen said that the Crossroads squatter camp outside Cape Town could be developed 'provided the masses of squatters co-operate'. But he declined to give an assurance that nobody would be forcibly removed from Crossroads, either to the new township being built at Khayelitsha or back to the homelands. Dr Viljoen's statement to Parliament followed clashes with police in which at least 18 people died which followed rumours that squatters would be forcibly moved.[21]

In April 1985 the government agreed on an 18-month moratorium for illegal Crossroads squatters. Nearly 100,000 people, among them thousands without the legal right to be in the Western Cape, would be allowed to erect homes at Khayelitsha. After 18 months the government would review the moratorium but, according to the Chief Commissioner for Co-operation and Development in the Western Cape, Timo Bezuidenhout, no deportations would take place.[22]

In August 1985 two other communities facing forced removal were reprieved when the people of Driefontein and KwaNgema were given adjacent land that was previously white-owned. This was believed to be the first time since the 1913 Lands Act was passed that Africans have been given the right to live in a rural area outside the homelands or designated townships, and the first time that Africans have been allowed to own land outside of the homelands.

Driefontein attracted international attention in 1982 when the community leader, Saul Mkhize, was shot dead by police at a meeting protesting against the removal.[23]*

*See page 159.

Housing

The houses in which South Africans live range from luxurious ranches through modest farms and apartments to city slums and rural hovels. Are there laws on racial segregation relating to housing?

A number of laws, including the Group Areas Act,* determine that residential areas must be segregated along racial lines. A few areas in 'white' South Africa do have 'mixed' housing, but in the overwhelming majority of areas this is not allowed. Many previously mixed areas have been zoned under the Group Areas Act.[1] In September 1985 an Indian woman who won a £55,000 house with swimming pool in a radio quiz could not move in because the property is in a suburb zoned white under the Group Areas Act. In the 'independent' homelands there are more mixed areas where apartheid legislation no longer applies.

Some housing in South Africa is built by the state or local authorities. Is the standard or provision the same for housing in areas zoned for different racial groups?

In 1983, for example, the government was spending nearly R28,000 (£14,000) on each low-income house for whites, while the Soweto Council was spending R2,000 (£1,000) on each low-income house for Africans.

Is the amount of housing land available to the different racial groups proportionate to their numbers?

About five million Africans, Coloureds and Indians live on under 10 per cent of the area of land allocated to white residential development for 1.6 million whites.[2]

Can all races in South Africa own their homes on the same terms?

Except in a few areas, Africans are currently not allowed to own freeholds outside the homelands. In 1975 the government re-introduced the right of African men, if qualified to be in the area, to buy houses on 30-year leasehold plots. Under the Urban Areas Amendment Act,

*See chapter on group areas.

Number 97 of 1978, qualified Africans were allowed to buy 99-year leaseholds.[3]

The promise of a step towards Africans being allowed full freehold rights in 'white' South Africa was held out in early 1985 by the State President. This did not, however, mean that 'the acquisition of rights to land leads to the acquisition of residential and political rights', he said. The government was 'prepared to negotiate with political leaders of the communities involved on the granting of property rights'. Only those who qualified for 99-year leasehold rights would be able to obtain full individual property rights.[4]

In December 1985, three months after the President's Council recommended it, the government said it would introduce freehold property rights for Africans.[5] All who qualified to have 99-year leaseholds could be granted freehold rights, the Minister of Constitutional Development and Planning, Chris Heunis, said. It did not mean, however, that there would be any change in policy requiring people of different races to live in separate areas. The Black Sash said that about four million Africans would be affected but that 'the majority of Africans still cannot buy land where they choose to live. It is not a dismantling of apartheid.' The government said that legislation would be introduced in 1986 to grant Africans freehold rights.[6]

How many Africans have bought leaseholds?

By the end of July 1985 a total of 34,334 leaseholds had been sold.[7] A big campaign to encourage the purchase of leaseholds was launched, and in August 1985 the leasehold system was extended to 34 more townships in the Cape in places that were previously Coloured labour preference areas where Africans had been discouraged from living. This extension would allow an estimated 152,000 African residents to live in leasehold properties. The government said that the leasehold system would apply throughout the country 'with the exception of a few towns'.[8]

What would happen if an African who had bought a leasehold was disqualified from living in that area?

He would lose the right to occupy the property. He could, however, continue to hold the lease. Disqualification can arise through being sentenced to a fine of more than R500 (£250). Africans can sell, let or bequeath their leasehold rights to any other qualified person. If the rights were bequeathed to an unqualified person, he would have to sell the leasehold: in this case he would be entitled only to the proceeds of the sale. Children of owners of leaseholds can inherit these rights.[9]

Can building societies make loans for Africans to buy leaseholds?

They can now, in terms of a 1978 law; before that it was not allowed.[10]

Is there a housing shortage in South Africa?

Yes. Estimates vary as to the extent: up to 800,000 is one suggested figure.[11] The Official Yearbook for 1983 says: 'The shortage of houses for [Africans] outside the national states is estimated at 420,000 and the present cost of eliminating this backlog is a staggering R3,360 million [£1,680 million].' A total of 50,000 houses was said to be needed for Coloureds in Cape Town, the main area of Coloured population.[12] In September 1985 the housing shortage was said to be so critical that informal settlements which had mushroomed around urban areas house more people than formal townships. The managing director of the Urban Foundation estimated a minimum housing shortfall of 700,000 units. About 1.23 million were living in informal settlements on the outskirts of Durban, 500,000 in Winterveldt, bordering the Witwatersrand, 100,000 in shacks in Port Elizabeth and more than 100,000 in Crossroads, near Cape Town, he said.[13]

How many more houses will be needed by the end of the decade?

In the early 1980s the economic planning branch of the Office of the Prime Minister estimated that $2\frac{1}{2}$ million more homes would be needed by 1990. At 1982 prices, this would cost R4,000 million – 6 per cent of the GDP.[14] Up to 500,000 houses could be required in the homelands by 1988, Parliament was told in 1983.[15]

What is the government's housing policy?

The state is 'responsible for assisting those who cannot buy a house on the open market', according to the Official Yearbook for 1985. In 1982–3 a new policy was announced which involved selling off 350,000 state houses to Africans on the 99-year leasehold scheme, and another 150,000 to whites, Indians and Coloureds. Private enterprise was to be encouraged to enter the housing sphere. Africans should increasingly pay for their housing: 'The sweat capital of the African must come into question and Africans should provide their own housing,' said a deputy minister of Co-operation and Development, Dr G. de V. Morrison.[16] Another deputy minister, Pierre Cronje of the Department of Community Development, said that the government hoped to create 'thousands of little capitalists' among the African population, to help establish 'a broad class of property owners'.[17]

Were there inducements for people to buy the houses being sold by the state?

Discounts of up to 40 per cent were offered, under certain conditions, to those buying within a year of the scheme being announced. People not taking up the offer to buy their own homes were also warned that they might face large rent increases.[18] During 1984–5 much of the Transvaal unrest, in which scores of people were killed, was over rent increases.

Was the policy of selling state houses welcomed?

Not by everybody. One criticism, made by a University of Cape Town expert, Professor David Dewar, was that the shift towards self-help – people earning more than R450 (£225) a month would not qualify for government aid – together with reduced building of sub-economic houses could trap the poor 'in a permanently disadvantaged position'.[19] Another criticism was that selling houses did little to reduce the shortage.

Fewer houses have been built by development boards for Africans: the total of 10,000 in 1982 dropped to 4,000 in 1983, according to the Urban Foundation in October 1985.[20] In November 1985 it was announced that almost half of the R100 million (£50 million) earmarked for upgrading African townships around the country would be spent in the Eastern Cape. The money was part of R600 million (£300 million) announced earlier in the year to combat unemployment.*

What is the usual type of African housing?

Most homes are known as type 51/6 'matchbox': four-roomed houses with outside lavatory, asbestos roof and brick or cement-block walls. Most were without electricity until recently: 16 per cent in 1975, compared to 42 per cent in March 1985, according to a survey of 1,000 African households in urban townships throughout the country.[21]

* See chapter on employment.

How much are leasehold houses sold for?

The selling price in 1985 was said to range between R1,750 (£875) and R2,000 (£1,000).[22]

How much do such houses cost to rent?

The average monthly cost for a Soweto house in 1983 was R40.30 (£20.15) which included house rent, service charges and site rent.[23] In two townships near Durban, Lamontville and Chesterville, violence broke out in April 1983 when rent increases of between 40 and 80 per cent were imposed; the average then in Chesterville was R36.50 (£18.25) a month.[24]

What percentage of the average African wage goes towards rent?

According to a study in *Municipal Engineer* magazine in 1983, nine out of ten African householders earned less than R450 (£225) a month.[25] In 1983 the median wage for an unskilled African was R351 a year, semi-skilled R524, and skilled R849. An unskilled worker would therefore have paid more in rent in Soweto (R483.60 p.a.) than he earned, a semi-skilled worker 92 per cent, and a skilled worker 56 per cent. The large majority of African households have more than one wage-earner, however.

Where are African townships situated?

From the 1950s and 1960s, government policy was to move Africans to townships situated away from 'white' areas. As the policy developed, a number of new townships were established, where possible in areas that are, or could be, incorporated into the homelands, but sometimes still close to major urban commercial and industrial centres. Mdantsane, for example, the second biggest African township after Soweto, is in the 'independent' homeland of Ciskei, yet close enough for workers to commute to East London. The aim was to create a commuter system by extending transport services from the new bantustan towns to the industrial centres outside the bantustans so that Africans need stay only temporarily in the 'white' areas.

What facilities do the townships have?

According to the former Minister of Co-operation and Development, Dr Piet Koornhof, the three Cape Town townships have these facilities:

Langa (33,267 inhabitants): one soccer field, one rugby field and one swimming bath.

Nyanga (48,554 inhabitants): two rugby fields, three soccer fields and no swimming bath.

Guguletu (84,301 inhabitants): three soccer fields, one rugby field and two swimming baths.[26]

Many other townships are also reported to lack facilities comparable to those in white, Indian and Coloured areas.

Squatting

Many people in South Africa live on land they neither own nor rent; some are registered as squatters. How many squatters are there in the country as a whole?

The total is not known. The Department of Community Development said that in 1981–2 there were 48,824 registered squatters.[1] This figure excluded Africans, who are said to be the majority of squatters. The best known African squatter camp is Crossroads, outside Cape Town.

Why have squatter camps sprung up?

Increasing urbanization and a shortage of housing, plus the effects of the influx control laws. In 1960 31.8 per cent of the African population was living in urban areas; by 1980 this had increased to 38.3 per cent. While this drift to the towns went on, housing for African families was frozen in certain 'white' areas, particularly the Western Cape, which was a 'Coloured labour preference area' until late 1984. The pass laws also prohibit spouses and families of migrant workers from living with them in accommodation provided with the job: for this reason, and to escape worse poverty in the homelands, families have often built makeshift accommodation near or in African townships. Conditions in the squatter camps are often very bad: Parliament was told in 1983, for example, that the 900-odd people in the Nyanga dunes were living in tents and plastic-bag shelters. Some 300 had had no toilets for three months or more.[2]

What does South African law say about squatting?

The Prevention of Illegal Squatting Act, Number 52 of 1951, amended in 1955, 1976 and 1977, makes it an offence for people to enter or stay in any land or building, without lawful reason and without the permission of the owner or occupier. Any structure erected can be demolished by court order and people moved if the health or safety of the public is deemed to be endangered. The 1976 amendment made owners of land responsible for ensuring illegal squatting did not take place. Owners convicted of allowing illegal squatting would normally have to demolish any structures at their own expense.[3]

Can squatters' homes be demolished without warning by state officials?

The original Act, and the 1977 amending Act, Number 72 of 1977, allowed for this. The amendment said that illegal structures could be demolished by officials without prior notice.[4]

Can the courts intervene before squatters' homes are demolished?

Under the 1977 Amendment Act, nobody can seek a court interdict against demolition unless he first satisfies the court that he has title or right to the land. This was made retrospective. In terms of proclamations issued in 1957 and 1977, under the Bantu (Prohibition of Interdicts) Act, Africans cannot apply for interdicts against removal orders until after they have complied with the order.[5]

Have squatters' homes been demolished by officials?

Yes. At the Nyanga Bush camp near Crossroads three people were injured in June 1984 when police fired rubber bullets at protesting squatters in demolition raids. In November 1985 three Africans were shot dead by police in Leandra township, about 50 miles east of Johannesburg, during a demonstration against the eviction of 24 squatter families.[6] The same month 20 squatter shacks were demolished in Langa, Uitenhage – scene of the shooting to death by police of 20 Africans on the 25th anniversary of Sharpeville – and 426 families were served notices between midnight and 3 a.m. that a Supreme Court order to evict them would be sought.[7] Crossroads and the nearby KTC camp have also seen a number of demolition raids. Crossroads was described by a deputy minister in the Department of Co-operation and Development as a 'symbol of defiance and anarchy' to be eliminated as soon as possible. All residents of Crossroads with 'Section 10' rights* were to be moved to the new township for Africans being built at Khayelitsha, 25 miles outside Cape Town, and those without such rights – two thirds of Crossroads' population, amounting to 30,000 people – sent back to Transkei or Ciskei.†

Is the government's policy towards Crossroads changing?

In 1983 the executive of the Medical Faculty at the University of Cape Town called on doctors to take a stand against the destruction of squatters' shelters at Crossroads. This was echoed by the head of the Department of Community Health at the University of the Witwatersrand,

*See chapter on pass laws.
†See chapter on removals.

Professor John Gear. There was also criticism of the Department of Health for allowing shelters to be demolished.[8] In February 1985 the government said that Crossroads could be developed as a community, although with diminished size and population.*

By mid 1985, however, government policy appeared to be that all Crossroads squatters – with or without Section 10 rights – would be moved to Khayelitsha, under a moratorium announced in April. The squatters, who started moving that month, were initially housed in tents pitched on concrete slabs until they could rebuild their homes.[9]

By November 1985 about 90,000 squatters were expected to have been resettled at Khayelitsha, leaving about 150,000 squatters at Crossroads. Many more would have to be moved before Crossroads could begin to be upgraded, according to a government official.[10]

* See chapter on removals.

Defence

South Africa has borders with many politically significant states and is in a strategically important position. How much does its government spend on defence, and is this increasing?

The exact total is difficult to determine because of official secrecy and varying accounting methods. In 1985–6 the defence budget rose to R4,274 million (£2,137 million), an increase of 8.1 per cent over the previous year,[1] which had in turn seen a rise of 21.4 per cent over 1983–4.[2] Another estimate[3] puts expenditure at between R4,300 and R5,000 million (£2,150 and £2,500 million) when costs borne by other departments – for instance, housing, building of military bases and health – are included. In 1960–61 the allocation was R44 million (£22 million at today's conversion rate). Apart from 1968–9, it has risen steadily year by year.

How does South African military expenditure compare with that of other countries?

It is about 15 per cent of the government's total budget and 4 per cent of gross national product. This is higher than that of France (3.3 per cent of GNP) and West Germany (3.1), but below that of Britain (5.7) and the USA (6).

Is there concern in South Africa about the level of military expenditure?

There has been concern at the increasing costs of the Defence Force, particularly the price being paid for fighting SWAPO guerrillas in Namibia. The war there is estimated to have cost R547.5 (£274) million in 1984 – R1.5 million (£750,000) per day. The cost of every SWAPO insurgent killed works out at R937,500 (£469,000) in terms of military spending only; if South Africa's total subsidy of an estimated R1,000 (£500) million a year is taken into account, the death of one SWAPO guerrilla costs R1,712,328.70 (more than £850,000).[4]

In June 1985, however, a lower estimate of the cost of the war was given by the head of the Defence Force in Namibia and the South-West African Territory Force, General George Meiring. He said that it was costing about £450,000 a day. The annual cost was about £140 million to South Africa and £30 million to £35 million to the Namibian government.[5]

How large is the South African Defence Force?

Estimates differ because of some government reticence. The latest published figures say that the full-time Defence Force consists of 83,400 men and women: 70,400 in the army, 10,000 in the air force and 6,000 in the navy.[6]

How many people are there in the South African regular army? Is it maintained by conscription or are the troops volunteers?

The army has 17,400 regulars; the rest are conscripts who do two years' service, compulsory for all white males. After their service they go into an active reserve, numbering about 130,000 and known as the Citizen Force, for 12 years, during which they must spend 720 days in uniform. They are then allocated to commando units, a kind of Home Guard, and may spend up to 12 days a year in an army camp up to the age of 55.

The air force has 6,000 regulars and 4,000 conscripts, while the navy has 4,100 regulars and 2,300 conscripts.[7]

The armed forces defend the entire state of South Africa; are the troops drawn from all races?

In the army 5,400 regulars are African and Coloured. Many in the navy are Indian and Coloured. Figures for the air force are not known. In Namibia, most of the 21,000 people in the South-West African Territory Force are African.[8]

Is there apartheid in the Defence Force?

In the army, Coloureds generally serve in a separate infantry battalion, in a maintenance unit, or as drivers, clerks, storemen and military policemen. Their training is segregated. Africans are trained separately from whites as instructors, clerks, infantrymen and medical orderlies. Africans from homelands 'are trained by the South African Army, at the request of their respective governments, with a view to establishing defence forces in their own states'.[9]

In the air force, Coloureds are trained as ground personnel.[10]

There is said to be no segregation in the navy. A spokesman said in 1984: 'On our vessels every man has the same opportunities and facilities on board are shared just as they are in the operational area.'[11] However, the navy's swimming pool at the huge Simon's Town base is segregated: different races use the pool on different days of the week. In January 1984 a Coloured petty officer and a white woman dockyard clerk at Simon's Town were found guilty on an Immorality Act charge.[12]

Is there conscription for blacks?

Provision is made in the new constitution for Coloureds and Indians to be conscripted; this was a major issue in the elections for the new parliamentary chambers. In the 'independent' homelands there are defence forces but, as yet, no universal conscription.

Are immigrants liable for call-up?

In August 1984 white immigrants were made liable and the first were called up in January 1985.[13] Under new legislation, immigrants aged between 15 and 25 years with permanent residence certificates issued before April 1978 would automatically become South African citizens after five years and hence liable to be conscripted.

Are women conscripted?

In September 1983 the then Prime Minister, P. W. Botha, said that the cost of training the 24,000 white women who each year turned 17 and passed their matriculation examinations would cost between R600 and R700 million (£300 and £350 million) and that the country could not afford it.[14] Women can volunteer to train: about 2,000 are in the army.

Does the law make any allowance for conscientious objectors to military service?

Only certain religious objectors are given any alternatives other than military service or jail. The Defence Amendment Act, Number 34 of 1983, covers four categories of objectors:

Religious objectors who decline to serve in combatant capacity: They must wear uniform and perform tasks 'beneficial' to the SADF for the length of the normal call-up (two years continuous service and 720 days over 12 years).

Religious objectors who will not be combatants, perform any maintenance task of a combatant nature or wear uniform: They must serve one and a half times the call-up period while performing maintenance tasks not related to combat. Refusing to do so means a jail sentence for the same period.

Religious objectors who will not perform any service: They must perform one and a half times the call-up period in community, public or municipal service. They cannot take part in politics during this time (which must be continuous service), except to vote. Refusing to perform this kind of service means a jail sentence for the same period.

Non-religious objectors who refuse any type of military service on moral and ethical grounds: They are jailed for one and a half times the length of service – six years' imprisonment. There is no provision for non-religious objectors to do community service instead of serving a jail term.[15]

Is there opposition to conscription?

According to a survey in 1984, more than two thirds of students at the English-language universities of Cape Town and the Witwatersrand opposed conscription.[16] In late 1984 a national campaign to end conscription was launched. One speaker at a Cape Town meeting to oppose conscription was Dr Allan Boesak, patron of the anti-apartheid United Democratic Front. Forty organizations, including the Congress of South African Students, the Institute of Race Relations, the South African Council of Churches and several other church bodies, have endorsed the campaign.[17] In September 1985 four members of the End Conscription Campaign were detained and the homes of other members searched by police. The same day the Deputy Minister of Defence, Adriaan Vlok, said the organization was being used by the African National Congress for its 'evil' aims.[18] The Progressive Federal Party, also in September 1985, called for the end of conscription 'as a matter of urgency'. The use of the Defence Force – particularly the use of the army in African townships in 1985 – was seen by most South Africans as 'an oppressive military extension of the ... apartheid system', the PFP said.[19] The Afrikaans author, André Brink, publicly refused in August 1985 to undergo training or serve in the army after the Defence Act was changed so that people could be called up for duty up to the age of 55.[20]

What legal constraints are there on opposition to conscription?

The South African Council of Churches called on its members in 1974 to ask churchgoers to consider 'whether Christ's call to take up the Cross and follow him in identifying with the oppressed does not, in our situation, involve becoming conscientious objectors'. An amendment to the Defence Act was then passed, making it a crime to suggest to anybody liable for service that he should refuse to comply with his call-up. The penalty was to be a fine of up to R5,000 (£2,500) or six years imprisonment or both.[21]

How many resist or evade conscription in South Africa?

The figure of those evading call-up cannot be determined exactly. One report said that 1,000 objectors to military service were granted political asylum in Britain between 1977 and 1981.[22] Another said that there were at least 300 in Britain by 1983.[23] A third report in August 1985, by the Committee on South African War Resisters, said there were more than 7,000 in Britain, the Netherlands, the US and Sweden. A Dutch government spokesman said at least 300 people had been given asylum because of their opposition to conscription.[24] The National Union of South African Students, most of whose members are English-speaking, estimates that 3,000 to 4,000 youths leave the country every year to avoid military service.[25]

On 22 March 1983, according to the Minister of Defence, General Magnus Malan, 355 men were being held in detention centres in South Africa for refusing to undergo military service. Many jailed objectors are Jehovah's Witnesses (70 in 1983). Several others have been jailed for refusing to serve on 'political grounds'.

The number of people failing to register for service appears to be increasing. General Malan said that 7,589 had not reported for their call-up in January 1985 compared to 1,596 for the whole of 1984. Of the latter, a total of 859 had been found and charged.

A spokesperson for the End Conscription Campaign in Cape Town, Beverley Runciman, said that the rise in the number of men failing to report for service was because more were unwilling to serve in a defence force that supported apartheid. She said that the role of the army in curtailing unrest in the Sebokeng township in the Transvaal in late 1984 was one of the factors behind the increase.[26] In 1985 the army was also used, particularly around Uitenhage in the Eastern Cape, where 20 people had been killed by police during a march to funerals that coincided with the Sharpeville killings, 25 years earlier to the day.

Later in the year as unrest spread, and a state of emergency was declared in a number of districts in the country, the army was used increasingly in black townships. A number of complaints about the army's behaviour were made. At least one serviceman was court-martialled for refusing to go on a patrol which could have been sent into a Durban township. An ECC spokesman said the number of young men refusing to do military duty in townships was increasing.[27]

How strong is the South African Defence Force?

It is the strongest defence force in Africa, according to the International Institute for Strategic Studies in late 1983.[28] Under full mobilization more than 400,000 people could be called up – a figure supported by the military correspondent of the *Cape Times*. The IISS report said that South Africa had 250 Centurion tanks, 1,400 Eland armoured cars, 500 armoured personnel carriers, 1,200 infantry combat vehicles, 313 combat aircraft, at least 10 combat helicopters and 80 other helicopters.

Some countries have banned the sale of arms to South Africa, but its forces are well equipped. Where does South Africa get its arms?

Much weaponry has been manufactured locally since the mandatory arms embargo imposed by the UN Security Council in 1977 after the death in detention of Steve Biko. Some items are bought abroad, despite the embargo. In 1984 four officials of the state-run Armaments Corporation (Armscor) were charged in Britain with making illegal arms purchases. They were granted bail on sureties provided by the South African Embassy, but the government refused to let them return to Britain to face trial after six anti-apartheid protesters took refuge in the British Consulate in Durban and the British government declined to evict them. In 1983 Armscor also launched a drive to sell some of the locally made weaponry abroad. The corporation, normally secretive about its operations, said in the same year that it employed 26,000 people and had a cash flow for procurement of R1,800 million (£900 million) a year.

In 1984 it was reported that Armscor's export turnover was worth R200 million (£100 million) a year. General Malan, speaking at an Armscor function in September 1985, said that South Africa was 95 per cent self-sufficient in military production: the 5 per cent needed from abroad was not in armaments but in tools and technical help.[29] Also during the same month a former South African diplomat said that South Africa could build two atom bombs a year.[30] South Africa has been rumoured to have nuclear capability, and there were reports in the late 1970s that it exploded a device in the South Atlantic.

Has the political influence of South Africa's military leaders increased over the years?

Several political scientists point out that the State President, P. W. Botha, was Minister of Defence from 1966 to 1980, and that the former chief of the SADF, General Magnus Malan, was brought into the Cabinet as

Minister of Defence in 1980. The increasing role in government of the State Security Council (see below), in which the military and security services are strongly represented, has also been noted.

Who are the members of the State Security Council, and what does it do?

According to the secretary of the SSC[31] it includes the Prime Minister (now State President); the ministers of Defence, Foreign Affairs, Justice, and Law and Order; the head of the National Intelligence Service, the chief of the Defence Force, the Director-General of Foreign Affairs, the Director-General of Justice and the Commissioner of Police. Other ministers and senior officials can be asked to attend meetings.

The SSC advises the government on the formulation and implementation of policy and strategy in relation to national security. Through a number of committees it co-ordinates other government departments throughout the country dealing with matters like constitutional affairs, the economy, the military and police, civil defence, community services and cultural activities. There is also a full-time secretariat to support the SSC and the committees, which, among other things, interprets intelligence provided by the police, the National Intelligence Service and the Department of Foreign Affairs.

Has the increasing influence on policy of the military and the State Security Council been criticized?

Professor Deon Geldenhuys of the Rand Afrikaans University said in 1983 that the 'increasing militarization of South African foreign policy ... may well be related to the rising influence of the Defence Force in top-level decision-making'.[32] Professor Gerrit Olivier of Pretoria University said that the Department of Foreign Affairs had, 'by default rather than design', left a gap in the foreign policy field which had been filled by the military in the face of security threats.

Professor Geldenhuys and another RAU lecturer, Dr Hennie Kotze, have also said that the SSC has probably reduced the full Cabinet's decision-making role: 'Apart from the fact that the full Cabinet is only brought into the picture – at the Prime Minister's discretion [now the State President's] – on an *ex post facto* basis, Cabinet discussion of SSC decisions is bound to be further inhibited by virtue of the decisions' carrying the Prime Minister's stamp of authority.' The SSC, they say, is the only Cabinet committee created by law and the only one chaired by the Prime Minister; its task is 'broad enough to embrace virtually every area of government activity at home and abroad'.[33]

There was strong criticism of the Defence Force in May 1985 after two South African soldiers were killed and one captured in Cabinda in northern Angola. The government said that the men were gathering information about the ANC, SWAPO and 'Russian surrogate forces'. The captured commando told a press conference in Angola that the team had planned to attack the Gulf Oil depot in Cabinda. This was denied by the government. The revelation that the army was still operating in Angola, when the government had said some time before that all its troops had withdrawn from the country, drew criticism from a number of South African newspapers.[34]

The involvement in foreign affairs of some military officers has also caused concern, sometimes even to the government. In March 1985 the Minister of Foreign Affairs, Pik Botha, said that about 10 members of the SADF had been dismissed or transferred away from the Mozambique border because of their sympathies for the rebel Mozambique National Resistance guerrillas. South Africa had earlier backed the MNR but withdrew support after the signing of the Nkomati Accord with President Samora Machel of Mozambique. The Accord said that neither country would allow rebel forces to operate within its borders.[35] In May 1985 the Minister of Defence told Parliament that five SADF members had been dismissed on suspicion of being MNR supporters, and that Portuguese-speaking SADF personnel had been transferred away from the border between the two states 'to prevent any suspicion of contact with Mozambique'.

Controversy about the Nkomati Accord and the role of military officers continued in late 1985. The South African government admitted there had been some 'technical violations'. But a diary captured from an MNR base claimed to show that the MNR received substantial support after the Accord was signed and that senior South African officers, including the then chief of staff of the army, General Constand Viljoen, opposed the treaty. General Viljoen denied the allegation. South Africa admitted that it had built a landing strip for the MNR in Mozambique territory and that it had supplied the rebels with 'humanitarian' aid. All this, it said, was intended to encourage the MNR to negotiate with the Frelimo government.[36]

There has also been criticism of the SADF in suppressing black unrest inside South Africa (see p. 152). This criticism was repeated in December 1985 when the SADF was given powers anywhere in the country – not just in areas affected by the 1985–6 state of emergency – to search, seize articles and in some cases to disperse crowds and detain people.[37]

Police

How many police are there in South Africa?

At the end of June 1984 there were 45,660 police. Nearly half were black – 16,680 Africans, 2,764 Coloureds and 1,565 Indians. It is planned to increase the total number of police by 11,000 by March 1987 and to a new total of 85,000 by 1995.[1]

How much is spent on policing in South Africa?

In 1985–6, the police budget was R954.7 million (£477.35 million), up from R796 million (£398 million) for 1984–5 which, in turn, was 41 per cent higher than the previous year.[2] In 1985 the government said that some details of police spending would be kept secret in future.

What powers to enter premises do the police have?

The Criminal Procedure and Evidence Amendment Act, Number 29 of 1955, and the Criminal Procedure Act, Number 56 of 1955, gave judges, magistrates and JPs greater authority to issue warrants allowing the police to enter premises, attend private and public meetings and conduct searches if they have reason to believe an offence is being or is likely to be committed there, or that, as a result of a meeting, security or the maintenance of law and order is likely to be endangered.

In addition, if the police consider the delay involved in getting a warrant would defeat their purposes, they are allowed to proceed without one.[3]

What powers of search and seizure do the the police have?

The Police Amendment Act, Number 70 of 1965, empowered any policeman, at any place within a mile of any South African border, to search without warrant any person, premises, vehicle, aircraft 'or receptacle of any nature' and to seize anything found. This, the Minister of Justice said at the time, was essential for the police to combat the entry of trained saboteurs into South Africa.

Under an amending Act, Number 64 of 1979, the area was extended to within 10 kilometres (6¼ miles) of a border. Another amendment,

Number 24 of 1983, extended the area to the whole country and allowed vehicles to be searched at road-blocks.[4]

Are the South African police armed?

Most white police carry revolvers. The police were armed shortly after the National Party came to power in 1948. They also have a variety of weapons intended for riot control, the most basic of which are truncheons and whips. Teargas and rubber bullets may also be used. Other firearms include shotguns that can fire both light birdshot and heavy buckshot. The R-1 semi-automatic assault rifle using steel bullets and the 9 mm pistol are supposed to be the weapons of last resort.

At the judicial commission of inquiry into the shootings at Uitenhage on 21 March 1985, however, evidence was given that the policemen involved were equipped only with rifles, heavy shotgun cartridges and pistols.[5]

Have many people been shot by the police?

According to government figures a total of 268 adults and 19 juveniles – 287 in all – were killed and 850 adults and 87 juveniles – 937 in all – were wounded in 1984. This included people killed and wounded during the unrest of 1984. Most of those killed and wounded were black. Of the 287 killed, 98 were shot while allegedly trying to escape arrest; the same applied to 345 of those wounded. In 1983 a total of 211 people were killed, compared with 199 in 1982.[6] During the first five months of 1984 the railway police – a separate branch – shot and killed six people and wounded 10.[7]

How many of those shot were alleged to be armed?

Mr Le Grange said that 111 of those killed by the police in 1983 were found to be armed.

How many were shot allegedly trying to escape arrest?

Again according to Mr Le Grange, 124 of those killed and 237 of those wounded in 1983 were attempting to escape arrest.[8]

Under what circumstances are the police legally entitled to fire on someone?

The Criminal Procedure Act says that such force 'as may in the circumstances be reasonably necessary' can be used to overcome resistance or to stop a person fleeing. It goes on to say that the killing of a person who cannot be arrested or stopped in flight by other means than by killing will be 'deemed to be justifiable homicide'.[9] The same Act says that the policeman must be sure or must 'reasonably suspect' that the person he fires on has committed one of 20 named offences or is involved in a 'conspiracy, incitement or attempt to commit' the offence. The designated offences include treason, sedition, murder, culpable homicide, indecent assault, robbery, arson, assault when a dangerous wound is inflicted, breaking into premises, fraud, knowingly receiving stolen property, and escape from lawful custody.

What inquiries are made after a shooting by the police? Who conducts these?

A police spokesman said in late 1982 that 'full investigations are carried out'. A police officer inspects the scene and compiles a report, and the District Commandant and Divisional Commissioner in the area decide whether the use of firearms was justified. If not, a case docket is sent to the Attorney-General, who decides whether to prosecute. This procedure was confirmed by Mr Le Grange to Parliament in March 1983.[10]

What happens when police face prosecution as a result of shootings?

In 1983 17 police were convicted of murder or culpable homicide. Some cases of this kind are outlined below:

● In June 1983 a Natal constable was fined R3,000 (£1,500) and given a suspended sentence of three years after he had opened fire on a truck whose backfiring noise he mistook for gunfire. The constable was allowed to pay the fine at the rate of R100 (£50) a month so that it did not bring hardship to his family. The driver of the truck was killed.[11]

● In February 1984 a white security policeman, Jan Harm van As, was sentenced to 10 years' imprisonment for shooting dead at point-blank range an African detainee, Paris Malatji, whom he was interrogating. Van As was said in court to have forced Mr Malatji to kneel before him, unlocked the safety catch on his gun and held it to the detainee's head to terrify a confession out of him. The gun went off, but the judge could not determine how this happened and therefore rejected the prosecutor's request for a verdict of murder.[12] Van As was released on bail in November 1985 pending an appeal against his conviction. Bail conditions included not leaving Krugersdorp without permission and reporting to the police twice a day.[13]

● In 1984 a constable was cleared of charges arising from the fatal shooting of an African community leader, Saul Mkhize, in April of the previous year. It took place during a meeting to protest against the forced removal of residents of Driefontein. Police said that 500 Africans attacked two policemen who tried to disperse the meeting. Eyewitnesses said that Mr Mkhize had asked the crowd to disperse and that shots were fired after most had done so. Mr Mkhize was shot at a range of about 15 to 20 yards. The court found that the evidence for the defence – that the constable had been attacked and had shot in self-defence – was more probable than the evidence for the state. The judge described Mr Mkhize as 'an arrogant, somewhat impolite man with a strong personality'.[14]

How has the government responded to concern about the number of police shootings?

During a snap debate in the House of Assembly in March 1983 after a mistaken shooting, the Minister of Law and Order, Louis le Grange, rejected a call for a judicial review of police power to shoot: 'I am responsible for a very sensitive portfolio and you cannot expect me to run round excitedly in every situation,' he said. Mr Le Grange told the House that the victim had been shot by plain-clothes policemen in an unmarked car as a result of an 'unfortunate confluence of coincidences' while they were pursuing a dangerous car thief on the run.[15] However, he said that in future police patrol vehicles would have 'positive identification' and that 'police would have to identify themselves before using any force'.[16]

Have there been allegations of police brutality?

Unrest in 1984–5 led to dozens of complaints that police had over-reacted and in some cases provoked further disturbances by their handling of crowds. Some of the cases included:

● The death of a three-year-old girl who had part of her brain blown out when she was shot by a rubber bullet at what was said to be almost point-blank range while playing outside her parents' house in Atteridgeville, Pretoria, in September 1985.[17]

● Among a number of allegations that black girls and women had been raped by police was the statement by the Soweto community leader, Dr Nthato Motlana, that he had treated a teenage girl who said she had

159

been raped by two black policemen in the township's main police station.[18]

● Security force members stoned cars in Duncan Village, East London, in September 1985. One resident who reported the incident to the police said a policeman refused to hear him because they 'did not care about what happened in the township'.[19]

● The Grahamstown Supreme Court granted an urgent application against the police in August 1985 brought by two Catholic priests operating a clinic for unrest victims in Duncan Village, East London. The order prohibited the police from unlawfully harassing, intimidating or interfering with the priests.[20]

● Earlier in 1985 two Progressive Federal Party members of the Cape Provincial Council collected affidavits about police violence near Uitenhage and Cradock. In Cradock a 15-year-old boy was said to have been shot as he ran away from police. The boy died. In Uitenhage a 12-year-old boy was reported to have been shot in his mother's front yard by police passing by in a bus.[21]

These and other cases led the Progessive Federal Party to set up monitoring committees in unrest areas to try to collect allegations of police brutality. Party leaders also called for judicial inquiries into specific cases, notably the shooting in November 1985 of 13 people in Mamelodi township, near Pretoria. By December 1985 the government had rejected all these calls. The government said that people with complaints against the police should lay charges at police stations. Told that many people were afraid to inform the police about fellow-policemen, Mr Le Grange said: 'Many people making allegations against the police are not prepared to have their allegations tested in a court of law ... Because one policeman hits you on the head, there is no reason why you should not complain to one of the 51,000 other policemen.'[22]

Have people successfully sued the police for assault?

Yes. In 1983 a total of 166 people were compensated for assault and R449,235 (£224,618) paid out.[23] In 1984 Mr Le Grange said R83,874 (£41,937) had been paid in out-of-court settlements in 69 cases instituted against him as Minister of Police, including 11 assaults.[24]

Have police been convicted of offences involving violence?

In 1983 a total of 189 policemen were convicted of common assault, 40 of assault with intent to do grievous bodily harm, 14 of culpable homicide, and three of murder. Thirty-one had previous convictions and 31 were expelled from the force.[25]

In March 1985 a white police constable convicted of assaulting a Coloured man who later died was fined R30 (£15). The policeman shouted racial abuse at the man and his white woman companion, challenged him to a fight and knocked him to the ground. The magistrate ruled that the Coloured man, Benito Holmes, suffered brain damage when his body was dropped by an unidentified passerby trying to take him for medical treatment. The policeman was acquitted of culpable homicide but convicted of assault; the R30 fine is lower than many penalties for traffic offences.[26]

How many policemen have died on duty?

In October 1984 it was reported that 941 had died in the previous 70 years. A year later, at least 16 black policemen had been killed since unrest flared in September 1984. The killing of a policeman in Soweto in October 1985 raised fears that police were becoming targets of organized assassination.[27] By December 1985 29 policemen had been killed.

Crime

Some parts of South African society are intensely prosperous while others are extremely poor; there are wide gaps between the extremes of wealth and poverty. It could be argued that some crime reflects the inequalities in a society. How high is South Africa's crime rate?

It is the highest in the Western world, according to a University of Cape Town criminologist, Mana Slabbert.[1] Another study, by Gallup International for the *Daily Telegraph*, said that South Africa was the third most crime-ridden country in the world. (Colombia and Brazil are first and second.) The survey was restricted to white South Africans: experts said that if blacks were included the picture would be even bleaker.[2] In his report to Parliament for the year ending June 1983, the Commissioner of Police, General Johan Coetzee, said that 1,210,178 'offences' (the total for all races) were reported in 1982–3, a 4 per cent increase over the previous year. 'Offences' consist of murder, robbery, rape, and other serious crimes.[3]

Between July 1982 and June 1983 there were 557,100 offences of an economic nature – burglary, robbery, theft – which made them three and three quarter times as numerous as serious violent crime, according to Ms Slabbert.[4]

What kinds of crime are increasing?

Murder has increased from 8,084 in 1981–2 to 8,573 in 1982–3, and burglary from 139,273 cases to 148,766.[5]

What kinds of crime are decreasing?

Rape and robbery were both down slightly between 1981–2 and 1982–3.[6]

The murder rate and high incidence of violent crime in New York are well publicized. Is there anywhere in South Africa with a higher murder rate? What is the most dangerous area in the country?

Soweto 'has the number-one murder rate in the world', according to Brigadier D. J. D. Jacobs, who said that an average of 25 people a week were murdered there in 1984 and 1,219 during the whole of 1985.[7]:

Eighty per cent of the victims were stabbed. In 1983 there were 1,408 murders. Between August and October 1984 a total of 302 rapes were reported.[8]

Are there other areas in South Africa with unusually high crime rates?

The Minister of Law and Order, Louis le Grange, refused to tell Parliament details of violent crime in the Cape Peninsula in 1982. However, the Director of the Cape Town branch of the National Institute for Crime Prevention and Rehabilitation of Offenders said that the city, with only 18 per cent of South Africa's population, accounted for a quarter of the country's crime.[9] The murder rate in Mitchell's Plain, a large Coloured area, increased 700 per cent from 1979 to 1981, while the population rose by only 150 per cent. Robberies increased by 671 per cent, rape by 325 per cent, assault by 315, theft by 278 and housebreaking offences by 252 per cent.[10]

Towards the end of 1984 a social worker reported that wife-battering was the second-highest reported crime in Mitchell's Plain, exceeded only by burglary. It was thought that the actual incidence was even higher, but fear of repeated assault made many women decline to charge their husbands.[11]

Among Coloureds throughout the country, the average homicide rate was reported to be 15 times higher than for whites between 1968 and 1977, according to a study in the *South African Medical Journal*.[12]

The head of the Port Elizabeth murder and robbery squad, Lieutenant-Colonel Eric Strydom, said that in 1983 one person was murdered every 40 hours in his area.[13]

Why is the South African crime rate so high?

Internationally, criminologists have found correlations between environmental factors and crime levels. A number of such factors have been suggested as contributing to the South African crime rate. Among them are:

Overcrowded and inadequate housing, a large population of black workers living in single-sex hostels, an influx to townships from rural areas, and too few police stations (A. P. Khumalo, Chairman of the African Katlehong Community Council).

Unemployment, the high drop-out rate from schools after the 1976 Soweto uprising, the breaking down of extended families, removals to townships outside the cities (such as Mitchell's Plain) under the Group Areas Act, and lack of facilities for child care (Mana Slabbert).

The South African police and courts deal with many offences against legislation peculiar to that country, such as the pass laws. What are the figures for these arrests and convictions?

Pass law *convictions* in the main urban areas rose to 142,067 in 1983, an increase of 42 per cent over the previous year, which itself was up 31 per cent over 1981. The number of *arrests* for pass law offences was also up: there were 206,022 in 1982, an increase of 28.3 per cent over the previous year. The 1982 total amounted to the arrest of 564 people a day or one person every two and a half minutes. The Commissioners' Courts which try these offences 'often deal with cases at the rate of three per minute', according to Mana Slabbert.[14]

Punishment

What offences are punishable by death in South Africa?

The death sentence (carried out by hanging) is mandatory for murder unless there are extenuating circumstances. It can also be imposed for treason, rape, kidnapping, child-stealing, robbery and house-breaking with aggravating circumstances, and for some crimes under the Internal Security Act.[1]

How many people have been hanged in recent years?

In 1984 a total of 115 people were hanged – 14 of them in the week preceding 21 August. Of those executed during the year, 88 were African, 24 Coloured, one Indian, and two white.[2] In 1985 a total of 137 were hanged.

In 1983 two whites, 65 Africans, and 23 Coloureds – a total of 90 – were executed. Sixty-eight were hanged for murder, five for house-breaking with the intent to rob and robbery with aggravating circumstances, 10 for murder and robbery with aggravating circumstances, one for rape and robbery with aggravating circumstances, two for murder and rape, and three for high treason. In the same year 40 people had their death sentences commuted.[3]

A number of people have also been hanged by the 'independent' homelands; at least 69 up to March 1985, 47 of them in Transkei. In Venda, at least five have been executed for ritual murder in the past few years, three of these since December 1984. Hangings have taken place despite a proposal by a judge of the Venda Supreme Court, Mr Justice J. J. Strydom, for a moratorium because of doubts about some evidence produced at ritual murder trials.[4] In Ciskei the homeland got its own executioner, trained by South Africa, in June 1984. The death sentence at that stage had been imposed on seven people, four of them reported to be under the age of 21. Three people were executed in September 1984.[5]

Have numbers of executions varied much over the years?

The figures for South African executions have varied since 1969:

1969–70	80	1978	132
1970–71	80	1979	133
1971–2	56	1980	130
1972–3	55	1981	96
1973–4	43	1982	99
1974–5	57	1983	90
1975–6	61	1984	115
1976–7	90	1985	137

How does South Africa's execution rate compare with those of other countries?

Parliament was told in August 1981 that South Africa hanged more people for a wider variety of crimes than any other 'Western' country.[6]

What is known about the conditions under which executions take place in South Africa?

In August 1981 the Minister of Justice, Kobie Coetzee, refused to answer a parliamentary question on whether more than one person could be executed at one time, how many multiple executions had taken place, how long condemned prisoners had to wait at the gallows before execution, whether they were sedated and how, and how often physical force or teargas was used to forced condemned prisoners to the gallows. Mr Coetzee said he did not want to answer because the questions were 'too gruesome'.[7]

Are there any moves to reassess capital punishment in South Africa?

The government has rejected parliamentary calls for a commission of inquiry, the last time in April 1983. Mr Coetzee said executions had decreased by about 30 per cent 'during the past few years'. Nothing had happened to justify the 're-opening of a closed book' on the merits of capital punishment.

What offences are punishable by whipping in South Africa? How often is corporal punishment used?

Whippings can be imposed for a wide variety of offences, including, under the 1953 Criminal Laws Amendment Act, breaking any law in protest or as part of a campaign against any law. When the Act was being debated it was proposed that 'inciting' or 'procuring' others to commit an offence should be punishable by 15 lashes. Told that under the

Magistrates' Courts Act the maximum number of strokes that could be given was 10, the then Minister of Justice and later State President, C. R. Swart, said: 'What are five strokes between friends?' Ten lashes was nevertheless made the maximum.

Between July 1983 and June 1984 a total of 40,649 people were sentenced to corporal punishment: 1,578 whites, 635 Indians, 13,841 Coloureds and 24,595 Africans. The previous year 40,004 had been similarly sentenced.[8]

Are there any moves to lessen the use of corporal punishment in South Africa?

Two commissions of inquiry into the penal system have recommended moves away from corporal punishment. These proposals have not been accepted by the government, but there is reported to be less frequent use of whippings. However, the Deputy Attorney-General of the Transvaal, Dr J. A. D'Oliveira, has said that 'corporal punishment is at least an alternative to imprisonment. If put to its intended use, it should ease over-crowding of prisons ... Whipping is not more humiliating than imprisonment and will teach a short, sharp lesson.' The amount of force used in whipping was 'very considerable', Dr D'Oliveira said.[9]

In late 1985, however, a new measure to increase the offences for which whipping can be imposed was proposed by the government. One of the more controversial new offences would be public violence which, opposition MPs and a criminologist said, was inspired by opposition to apartheid. Other offences that were due to be included were murder where the death sentence was not imposed, arson or malicious damage to property, and sedition. Whipping would be abolished for homosexuality and bestiality.[10]

Also in 1985, a Pretoria Supreme Court judge, saying that corporal punishment was both 'severe and brutal', laid down a comprehensive set of guidelines on its use by the courts. Whipping was justified only when there were aggravating circumstances in crimes of violence; when there were no such circumstances, it could be used to keep the offender out of prison; whippings should not be handed out with lengthy prison sentences, and should not be used to try to combat a wave of a particular crime.[11]

How long is the typical prison sentence in South Africa?

Between July 1983 and June 1984 81.91 per cent of prisoners served sentences of six months or less.[12] In 1981–2 76.96 per cent served less than six months, while those serving six months to two years made up 10.37 per cent, long-term prisoners totalled 8.64 per cent, and 4.03 per cent were in 'other categories'. These percentages were not markedly different from those of the previous year.[13]

Most prisoners serve only a few months in jail. What offences are they most likely to have committed?

Many would be pass law offenders. The usual sentence for Africans not having the correct documents on them, according to a study of the Johannesburg Commissioners' Courts, is a fine of between R30 (£15) and R90 (£45) or from 30 to 90 days' imprisonment. The criminologist Mana Slabbert has pointed out that many people go to prison because they cannot afford to pay fines. Jailing of pass law offenders for the stated periods would account for statistics which show that 76 per cent of African prisoners serve less than six months, while only 56 per cent of jailed whites serve such a short sentence.[14]

Have there been proposals for alternatives to prison for minor offences?

The National Institute for Crime Prevention and Rehabilitation of Offenders (NICRO) claims that there is increasing support for community service as an alternative to imprisonment. Mr Justice G. Viljoen has said that alternative sentences would be a move towards a more enlightened punitive policy. The Minister of Justice stated in November 1983 that alternatives, shortening of sentences, fines and suspended sentences should be considered.[15]

Are blacks and whites found guilty of similar offences likely to receive similar sentences? In cases involving violence, does the race of the victim affect the sentence imposed?

One recent academic study, *Criminal Justice in South Africa* (1983), included the following findings:

● Sentences for the rape of a white woman were almost twice as severe as when the victim was black. The rapist stood a 50 per cent chance of a heavy sentence if he raped a skilled person or housewife, but a 20 per cent chance if the victim was unskilled or unemployed. A rapist's education was also relevant: the more advanced the education, the more lenient the sentence.[16]

● In 154 robbery cases studied, no white offender received a sentence of more than four years, while 40 per cent of the blacks convicted got more than four years.[17]

One case that aroused attention in 1984 was that of a white man who shot dead a black for apparently stealing the equivalent of 40p left out for the milkman. The white was acquitted and Rand Supreme Court Judge Irving Steyn said that the accused 'deserved a medal for what he did' and 'performed a public service', since a rash of milk money thefts had abated since the killing.[18]

In March 1985 disparity of sentencing was noted when an African from Soweto was fined R400 (£200) with the alternative of four months' imprisonment for placing the ring of a drink can in a parking meter. Two whites charged with the same offence were each fined R50 (£25).[19]

Professor John Dugard of the University of Witwatersrand's Centre for Applied Legal Studies asserted in a paper published in 1985 that 'the racially divided nature of our society promotes an even greater disparity in sentencing than in other societies'. All judges and about 99 per cent of magistrates, he observed, were white; most were 'white Protestant males of conservative outlook, who support the present political/racial status quo (and often the National Party Government) and who have little personal contact with members of the other racial groups except at the master–servant level'. The evidence suggested that whites found guilty of killing or seriously assaulting blacks were punished more leniently than blacks were when they killed or assaulted whites.[20]

Professor Dugard's thesis appears to have been supported in two 1985 cases. In one, five schoolboys aged between 15 and 16 were sentenced to work for 52 consecutive weekends in a hospital after they had been found guilty of culpable homicide for kicking two blacks to death. In the other case, two blacks were sentenced to five and 10 years' imprisonment after they had been found guilty of culpable homicide for stoning a white mother's car and causing the death of her baby.[21]

In 1970 Professor Barend van Niekerk of the University of Natal's law department was charged with contempt of court for writing an article suggesting that blacks were more likely to be sentenced to death than whites. He based his argument on a questionnaire to all South African judges and advocates (barristers): of those who replied, nearly half thought that a black accused was more likely to be hanged than a white. Professor Van Niekerk was acquitted, but the judgement was strongly criticized by lawyers and the press as leaving the way open for further prosecutions for contempt.[22] Professor Van Niekerk has said that since 1911 'more than 150 blacks have been executed for rape, in the vast majority of cases, it would seem, for the rape of a white woman. Not a single white has ever been sentenced to death, let alone executed, for the rape of a black woman.'[23] In late 1985, however, two white men were sentenced to be hanged for raping and burning alive a black woman.[24]

Have questions been raised about the impartiality of the judiciary dealing with cases brought under the state security laws?

Several cases have aroused comment, among them the following:

● The 10-year sentence for treason imposed on Barbara Hogan in October 1982. Professor Dugard noted that people committing similar offences previously had been charged with furthering the aims of the African National Congress under the Internal Security Act and jailed for between one and five years.[25]

● The AWB case. Three members of the extreme right-wing Afrikaner Weerstandsbeweging were given suspended sentences after being found with what Parliament was told was 'a veritable arsenal' of weapons including four AK-47 assault rifles, 4,000 rounds of ammunition, a missile and a smoke grenade. The suspended sentences were contrasted with the 10 years' jail Ms Hogan was ordered to serve, the five years given to an African journalist for having banned literature, and the three years a man received for playing a cassette recording of ANC songs.[26]

● The case of three policemen convicted of giving electric shocks to two suspected cattle thieves and given suspended sentences.[27]

● The 'tea-mug case'. In late 1983 an African was jailed for 18 months for drinking tea from a mug with ANC slogans scratched on it.[28]

● The 'wrong colours case'. In August 1983 an African was sentenced to eight years for having clothes in the yellow, green and black colours of the ANC and with ANC slogans on them.[29]

● The 'nun's tale'. In December 1983 an African nun was imprisoned for four months for having an ANC pamphlet. She was acquitted on appeal.[30]

There has also been some criticism of appointments to the judiciary. Sydney Kentridge, the internationally known advocate who appeared for the family of Steve Biko at the inquest into his death in detention, alleged in 1982 that some judges were put on the bench for political reasons. Professor Dugard, after studying trials of people charged with security offences in the Transvaal between 1978 and 1982, found that 17 per cent of the judiciary heard 84 per cent of the cases, and four judges heard more than half. Three of these were from the Pretoria Bar which, Professor Dugard said, produced most of the 'conservative, executive-minded and formalist' advocates from whose ranks judges are appointed.

The Minister of Law and Order, Louis le Grange, said that suggestions that magistrates were not independent and impartial and therefore should not hear security cases were part of the 'onslaught against South Africa'.[31] On the other hand, two Cape Town magistrates were reported in September 1985 to have refused to hear political cases and resigned after unrest flared in the area. Some prosecutors at the same court in Athlone, a Coloured area, were said to be following suit.[32]

Prisons

How large is South Africa's prison population?

In South Africa the number of prisoners in relation to the total population is extremely high – among the highest in the world, said the government-appointed Hoexter Commission in April 1984.[1] In 1981–2 there were 585.5 people in prison per 100,000 of total population. In comparison, the figure for Britain was 92, for West Germany 91, France 72, Denmark 62, Italy 54, Ireland 35 and Holland 23.[2] During the year ending June 1983, 560,334 people had been in jail out of a total population of 24.8 million – 2.25 per cent.

There is also a disparity between the numbers of black (African, Indian and Coloured) and white prisoners per 100,000 of each group. In 1981–2 the rate for whites was 105, while that for blacks was 1,066 – ten times greater.[3]

Has the prison population been increasing over the years?

According to the Prisons Department in October 1983, the number of prisoners rose by 50 per cent between 1963 and 1975. Between 1970 and 1980 the prison population went up by 12 per cent while the general population rose by only 7 per cent. In the next 20 years the daily average prison population was expected to rise from 106,000 (in 1983), to 170,000, a 62-per-cent increase.[4] The cost per prisoner per day in 1984–5 was estimated at R8.65 (£4.33).[5]

How many of South Africa's prisoners are on remand?

The Hoexter Commission found that during the year ending June 1983, 267,995 (or 47.8 per cent) of the 560,334 prisoners had been waiting for their cases to go to court. Figures for previous years show that generally about half the prison population is awaiting trial.

Are South African prisons overcrowded?

On 30 June 1985 the total prison population was 109,704 in prisons designed to accommodate 80,290. This meant that prisons were 36 per cent overcrowded and was a rise of nearly 5 per cent in a year, according to government figures. Two prisons in December 1983 were 284.9 and 352 per cent overcrowded.[6] Overcrowding, said the Department of Justice's annual report for 1983–4, was 'only a minor problem'. It was dealt with by 'using bunk beds or sisal or felt mats instead of conventional beds'.[7] However, the Hoexter Commission found that 'as a result of a lack of suitable cells, many prisons find it impossible to accommodate hardened criminals in separate cells or two to a cell. It happens quite frequently that 20 or 30 vicious thugs have to spend the night together in one cell.' This often led to gangsterism and cell murders, reported the Commission. In June 1985 Parliament was told that 90 prisoners in Port Elizabeth's North End jail had allegedly been kept in a 15-by-21-foot cell where children had been beaten and sodomized by other prisoners. The toilet of the cell was a pit in one corner.[8]

Are South African prisons adequately staffed?

The criminologist Mana Slabbert said in March 1984 that the ratio of professionally trained staff to inmates was 1:256.[9] In June 1983 only 105 of the 162 approved posts for social workers were filled, according to the Department of Justice's report. In 1981–2 there were only 23 psychologists in the prison service to cater for the daily average prison population of 106,000.[10] The average age of white warders was 21 years in 1983, according to the Department of Prisons, and nearly 53 per cent had less than two years' experience.

Is there apartheid in South African prisons?

Black and white inmates are kept segregated.

What facilities for study do prisoners have?

In 1981–2 nearly 700 prisoners were studying. A total of 1,900 prisoners underwent literacy training.

Have prisoners' studies been restricted?

From 1977 political prisoners were forbidden to take university courses. However, this policy was reversed in 1980.

What work do prisoners do?

The Prisons Act of 1959 said that as far as possible prisoners sentenced to hard labour must be employed on public works, but that short-term prisoners could be hired out for work.[11] Short-term prisoners are often put to work on farms.

Have warders been charged with offences connected with the deaths of prisoners?

In September 1983 six warders were jailed for between one and eight years after three convicts had died and others had been injured at Barberton Prison Farm. The judge described them as 'heroes of the truncheon' after hearing evidence that in temperatures of 35 degrees C. prisoners had been made to load wheelbarrows with gravel and beaten if they flagged. Between December 1982 and September 1983 a total of 11 prisoners died at Barberton, at least four after attacking warders.[12]

In Windhoek in March 1983 a farmer was jailed for six years after the death of a black prisoner working for him. The prisoner had been beaten with, among other things, a crowbar.[13]

From official figures it appears that in the 18 months from July 1982 to the end of 1983, about 25 per cent of people who died in prison suffered unnatural deaths. In the full 1983 year 76 died of unnatural causes and 180 of natural causes. The main cause of unnatural deaths for whites was suicide, while for Africans and Coloureds it was assault by fellow-prisoners.

How many political prisoners are there in South Africa?

The exact total is not known. In May 1985 the government said that there were 509 people serving sentences for offences against the security of the state on Robben Island. All would have been African, Indian or Coloured. An unspecified number of other political prisoners are in jail elsewhere in South Africa, including some whites, who are generally held in Pretoria. Thirty-nine political prisoners, including 17 Namibians, were serving life terms.[14] There are also political prisoners in the 'independent' homelands, but, again, exactly how many is not known.

Are young people and adults convicted on political charges ever imprisoned together?

A boy of 14 was sent to Robben Island in January 1978 after being convicted of sabotage.[15]

Have political prisoners been moved from Robben Island?

They are now being distributed around a number of prisons. Nelson Mandela, the African National Congress leader jailed for life, and a number of others who used to be on Robben Island have been moved to Pollsmoor Prison in the Cape.

Can political prisoners get remission in the same way as ordinary prisoners? Have any been offered conditional release?

There was no remission for 'politicals' before May 1982, but some can now qualify. Up to May 1984 a total of 96 had been granted remission, according to the Prisons Department, though many of these were released only a few weeks before their sentences expired.[16]

In February 1985 the imprisoned leader of the African National Congress, Nelson Mandela, rejected a conditional offer of freedom made to him by the State President, P. W. Botha. In November 1985 there was renewed speculation that Mr Mandela might be allowed conditional freedom, perhaps on condition that he go into exile and not return to South Africa. However, Mr Mandela, who was being treated in hospital in Cape Town at the time, was returned to Pollsmoor Prison after the offer was reported to have been made to him.[17] One white prisoner serving a life sentence, Dennis Goldberg, accepted an offer of release conditional on his renouncing violence – the same offer made to Mr Mandela and some other political prisoners.[18] The Minister of Justice, Kobie Coetzee, said that 22 political prisoners had renounced violence under the terms of Mr Botha's offer: four, all members of the Pan-Africanist Congress, had been freed in addition to Mr Goldberg; the other 17 would be 'credited' by the Department of Prisons, presumably meaning that their renunciation of violence would be taken into account when remission was considered.[19]

A number of Namibian prisoners have been freed. Herman Toivo ja Toivo, a founder member of SWAPO, was released in March 1984, and in November 1985 a total of 22 long-term political prisoners, 16 of them serving life sentences, were freed by the South African-sponsored administration in Windhoek after having been transferred to the territory from Robben Island. The release of the 22 was said by Namibia's justice minister to be a gesture of 'peace and reconciliation' to draw SWAPO into negotiations for a settlement in Namibia. In 1984 the authorities freed 130 SWAPO members detained for more than six years as unofficial prisoners of war in an internment camp.[20]

Mr Botha's offer to release political prisoners also applies to right-wingers serving sentences for violence. Questioned in Parliament in February 1985, the Minister of Law and Order, Louis le Grange, told a Conservative Party MP that conditional release would be considered for members of the Afrikaner Weerstandsbeweging (AWB) and the Wit Kommando.* In November 1985 a member of the Wit Kommando, Massimo Bollo, who had been sentenced to 10 years for attacks on offices of liberal organizations and on two reform-minded academics in Pretoria, was released and immediately deported to Italy.[21]

In May 1985 Colonel 'Mad Mike' Hoare was released from prison after serving less than three years of a 10-year sentence for hijacking. Colonel Hoare and 41 others were convicted of hijacking a plane from the Seychelles, where they had attempted to mount a coup, to Durban. During the trial evidence was offered that senior South African defence and security personnel had known about the coup attempt. The judge found, however, that the government was unaware of it. In February 1984 the Minister of Defence, General Magnus Malan, said that some of those accused in the Seychelles case had been, or still were, employed by the Defence Force. He refused to give any further details.[22]

Have prisoners gone to court to improve their conditions?

In April 1984 Barbara Hogan, serving 10 years for treason,† applied to the Rand Supreme Court to have aspects of her imprisonment improved. She said that she was often denied exercise, was kept alone in a cell surrounded by empty cells, had not had dental treatment until eight months after a tooth had cracked, had had letters removed from her cell, and had problems studying because of difficulties in getting books.[23]

In 1978 eight political prisoners brought a case to court in which they sought a ruling that they could receive newspapers – at that time denied to such prisoners – and magazines and journals of their choice, and that censorship of magazines, letters and visits be limited to that required for prison security. The case was dismissed, but political prisoners were later allowed to hear censored newscasts over intercom systems, and two years afterwards were permitted uncensored local newspapers.[24]

In May 1984 'A category' political prisoners were allowed, for the first time, contact visits from their families – previously conversation had been through a clear plastic panel. In one case, a visit was cut short because a prisoner's mother spoke Sotho and there was, she was told, no Sotho interpreter available: all conversations, the prisons service said,

---

*See chapter on right-wing violence.

†See chapter on punishment.

had to be in a language understood by a warder, who is present at every visit.[25]

In August 1985 the Minister of Justice, Kobie Coetzee, warned that social visits might be curtailed after reports that Mr Mandela had issued a statement through his wife, Winnie, rejecting the idea of a national convention for South Africa. 'No state can permit political propaganda to be issued from prison institutions,' he said. However, the day afterwards an account of a *Washington Times* interview with Mr Mandela was published in South Africa. The reason it was allowed to appear, commentators said, was that the government believed it reflected badly on Mr Mandela, since he was quoted as saying, among other things, that he saw no alternative to violent revolution.[26]

Security Services and Law

What intelligence and political security services have been set up to protect the South African state?

The Special Branch (SB) of the South African Police; the National Intelligence Service (NIS), formerly known as the Department of National Security (DONS), and before that as the Bureau for State Security (BOSS); Military Intelligence (MI); and the Directorate for Security Legislation (DSL). In addition, the State Security Council (SSC) operates at the top level of government.

Has the security service establishment increased in recent years?

The total number of people employed is not known. In 1966 the then head of the SB, General Hendrik van den Bergh, said that the strength of his service had been trebled in the preceding three years. The operations of the NIS are kept secret under the BOSS Act of 1969; Military Intelligence is similarly covered by the Defence Act.

How much does South Africa spend on security? Is this expenditure increasing?

In the 1983–4 Budget, the total sum allocated for security – including defence, justice, the police and prisons – was nearly R4 billion (£2 billion), a rise of 16.7 per cent on the previous year. The portion of this to be spent on the secret services rose by 25 per cent to R92 million (£46 million). This does not, however, include the cost of the SB, which comes out of the police budget and itself rose by more than 4 per cent to about R796 million (£398 million). Police estimated that expenditure on detainees in 1984–5 would increase by more than 53 per cent to R4.7 million (£2.35 million). This spending, however, did not take into account the state of emergency declared later in 1985 in which thousands of people were detained.[1]

Do the security services make public how they spend their money?

The Secret Services Account Act, Number 56 of 1978, allowed for an overall sum of money to be made available without Parliament being told how it was allocated.[2] This was later changed when the press revealed that the Department of Information, which had been running a series of secret projects, had misused large amounts of its secret funds: among other things, this money had been used to finance a pro-government English-language morning newspaper, the *Citizen*. The 'Information scandal' led to the forced resignation of the State President, B. J. Vorster, and the Minister of Information, Connie Mulder, and the prosecution – ultimately unsuccessful – of the Permanent Secretary of the Department, Eschel Rhoodie. After these matters had come to light the Finance Act, Number 101 of 1979, was introduced: secret accounts would be audited by the Auditor-General, and after consultation with the government it would be decided which of the audit reports would be disclosed to Parliament. This Act was followed by the Information Service of South Africa Special Account Act, Number 108 of 1979, which allowed for continuing secret projects of the Information Service (which now falls under the Department of Foreign Affairs) to be financed from the Secret Services Account.[3]

At the beginning of the 1985 parliamentary session a bill was tabled giving the police their own secret account like those held by the Defence Force (which pays Military Intelligence out of its budget), the NIS and the Department of Foreign Affairs. The secret funds given to the police were to be used for 'services of a confidential nature as the Minister of Law and Order may approve as being in the national interest'.[4] The Bill was later passed.

What are the functions of the security services?

These have been officially described as follows:

National Intelligence Service: Introducing the BOSS Bill in 1969, the Deputy Minister of Justice said this service would co-ordinate and complement the activities of the SB and MI. The Official Yearbook for 1983 says that the NIS 'has by law been given the responsibility to identify any threat or potential threat to the security of the state and to report such threat to the Prime Minister [now to the State President] and the State Security Council'.[5] Parliament was told in 1969 that people in this service do not have the power of arrest.

Special Branch: Members of this plain-clothes wing of the police, which deals exclusively with 'political' crime, do have the power of arrest.* The Official Yearbook says of the SB: 'Members of the uniformed branch and of the detective branch with a special interest in and an ability for this type of work are admitted and all members receive the best training in their specific fields.'[6]

*See chapter on detention without trial.

Military Intelligence: This service deals with military matters, but its activities have sometimes overlapped with those of the SB and the NIS.

State Security Council: Having been given information about 'any threat or potential threat' by the NIS, the SSC, according to the Official Yearbook, 'may then order action (whether military, police, or other) or refer the matter to the Cabinet for submission to Parliament'.[7] Some observers believe the SSC is assuming a more dominant role in government.*

The NIS was set up as an intelligence co-ordinating body. Has it gone beyond this role?

According to two defectors and other evidence, it has, among other things:

● Been behind a plot to discredit the former British Liberal Party leader, Jeremy Thorpe, involving allegations that Mr Thorpe had a homosexual affair with a man named Norman Scott. Mr Thorpe was later charged with conspiracy to murder Scott and acquitted.[8]

● Used a double to frame the anti-apartheid campaigner Peter Hain for a bank robbery in London. Mr Hain was acquitted.[9]

● Paid a former vice-president of Bishop Abel Muzorewa's United African National Congress in Zimbabwe a total of R400,000. South African business interests were said to have supplied the money because they wanted James Chikerema to promote continued links between South Africa and Rhodesia (as it then was) after independence.[10]

● Intercepted the mail of the Progressive Federal Party MP Helen Suzman.[11]

● Tapped telephones of the right-wing Herstigte Nasionale Party.[12] In January 1970 the party's first leader, Dr Albert Hertzog, was fined R50 (or 25 days' imprisonment) on a charge arising from a statement he made about the then BOSS.[13]

● Kept files on a number of political figures and nearly every important South African writer, including Laurens van der Post, André Brink, Nadime Gordimer and Etienne Leroux.[14]

● Kept files on a number of overseas people, including Harold Wilson, Jimmy Carter and Tiny Rowland, head of Lonrho.[15]

● Maintained some links with both the CIA and British Intelligence organizations.[16]

● Been involved, according to a mercenary leader, Colonel Mike Hoare, in an attempt to stage a coup in the Seychelles.[17]

● Maintained killers on its staff. The former head of the then BOSS,

*See chapter on defence.

General Hendrik van den Bergh, told a commission of inquiry: 'I have enough men to murder if I said "kill". I don't care who the victim is. That is the kind of men that I have.'[18]

South Africa has a wide range of security laws: what contingencies do they cover and what sanctions and penalties do they provide for?

The principal security laws, detailed in later chapters, allow for people to be 'banned' and detained without trial, for meetings to be prohibited, and for organizations to be declared unlawful.* In addition to these laws, there are a number of other Acts which deal with security. These include the following:

Public Safety Act: Allows for a state of emergency in a specified area or over the whole country for up to 12 months. It was under this Act that states of emergency were declared in 1960 and 1985.† Emergency regulations can be used to suspend most laws.

Indemnity Acts: The first, Act 61 of 1961, barred people detained during the 1960 state of emergency following the Sharpeville shootings from bringing court actions for unlawful detention. It also said that no court action could be brought against the government, or against people acting on its authority, for any act or statement dating from after the Sharpeville killings that was intended to prevent or suppress disorder, restore order or public safety, preserve life or property, or terminate a state of emergency. The second, Act 13 of 1977, passed shortly after the Soweto uprising began, said that no court action could be brought against the state or any of its officials acting 'in good faith . . . to prevent or terminate internal disorder'.

Post Office Act: Allows for mail to be intercepted if it is suspected of containing evidence of a crime or potential crime.

Protection of Information Act: Allows for the State President to declare any place or area a 'prohibited place'. Anybody there or nearby 'for any purpose prejudicial to the security or interests of the Republic' can be jailed for up to 20 years. A similar sentence can be imposed on anyone disclosing, or compiling for disclosure, to any hostile state, agent, or organization or supporter thereof, information on a wide range of subjects: armaments, defence, prohibited places, anti-terrorist activities, etc.

Intimidation Act: Anyone intimidating another person by threat or assault is liable to a fine of up to R20,000 (£10,000) or a jail term of up to 10 years or both.

---

* See separate chapters on detention without trial, banning orders, banned gatherings, and unlawful organizations.

† See chapter on detention without trial, and state of emergency.

Demonstrations in or near Court Buildings Prohibition Act: Bans demonstrations within 500 metres of court buildings on weekdays without permission. Penalty: a fine of up to R1,000 (£500) or one year's imprisonment or both.

Explosives Amendment Act: Lays down a maximum of three years in jail for people causing an explosion so as to endanger life.

General Laws Amendments Acts: Have been used to alter many of the security laws described previously. Among other matters now covered, it is forbidden to undergo training for sabotage abroad, or to advocate changes in South Africa that would involve the help of foreign governments.

Dangerous Weapons Act: Unless licensed, possession of a weapon which could cause bodily injury, or possession of an object that could be mistaken for a firearm, is an offence. One possible penalty is whipping.

Prohibition of Disguises Act: Makes it an offence to wear disguise intending to commit an offence.

With all these laws in force, how 'free' is South Africa compared to other countries in the world?

South Africa is joint fifth from the bottom in the world when it comes to observing human rights, according to the *World Human Rights Guide* by Charles Humana. The listings are based on the rights and freedoms detailed in the UN International Convention on Civil and Political Rights. They include freedom of movement and of peaceful political opposition, freedom of speech, religion, marriage and divorce, prompt trial on the basis of innocence until guilt is proved, the right to form independent trade unions, to buy and drink alcohol, to practise homosexuality, and to make use of contraception and early abortion.[19]

Is common law, as well as the 'security' laws, used against political opponents of the government?

Charges of treason have been, and are again being, brought against people the government considers politically radical. In 1956 a total of 156 people of all races were arrested to face treason charges in the wake of an 'assembly of the people' and the drawing up of the Freedom Charter under the aegis of the Congress Alliance. The number was whittled down over the years that followed and in March 1961 the remaining 30 were all acquitted.[20]

More recently, treason charges have been laid against supporters of the A N C. In April 1985 46 people, most of them leaders or supporters of the United Democratic Front, were due to answer charges of treason.[21] In December 1985 12 on trial in Pietermaritzburg were freed when treason charges against them were dropped. One legal observer believes there is a growing tendency for the authorities to make use of common law rather than the security laws, with the aim of 'normalizing' the legal process.[22]

Unusually, 16 of the 46 on treason charges in 1985 were granted bail in May of that year. The Attorney-General of Natal had earlier refused them bail under a provision of the Internal Security Act, but the Natal Judge President granted the bail application, subject to stringent conditions, and strongly criticized the Act for impinging on the freedom of the courts – one of the few recent occasions when a judge has commented on security laws.[23]

Detention without Trial

Is detention without trial a longstanding feature of South African law?

A number of Acts passed since the establishment of the Union in 1910 give police this power. During the Second World War, for example, two men later to achieve high office in South Africa – B. J. Vorster, who became successively Minister of Justice, Prime Minister and State President, and Hendrik van den Bergh, who was head of the Special Branch and later of BOSS – were detained for their alleged pro-Nazi sympathies under an emergency law passed in 1940.

Detention without trial is often introduced as an emergency measure in wartime. Are there laws in South Africa permitting such detention in peacetime?

Although South Africa has not been formally at war since 1945, the government has long warned about the need to counter what it now calls a 'total onslaught' against the country. To this end, legislation for detention has been introduced in, among others, the Public Safety Act, Number 3 of 1953; the General Law Amendment Act, Number 39 of 1961; the General Law Amendment Act, Number 37 of 1963; the Criminal Procedure Amendment Act, Number 96 of 1965; the General Law Amendment Act, Number 62 of 1966; the Terrorism Act, Number 83 of 1967; the Internal Security Amendment Act, Number 79 of 1976; the Criminal Procedure Matters Amendment Act, Number 79 of 1978: and the Internal Security Act, Number 74 of 1982.

Legal powers to detain without trial also exist in the 'independent' homelands of Transkei, Bophuthatswana, Venda and Ciskei.

When was detention first made use of on a large scale?

The government took this action after the Sharpeville shootings on 21 March 1960, when 69 Africans protesting at the pass laws were killed by the police. On 30 March a state of emergency was declared throughout most of the country, the armed forces placed on standby and 11,727 people detained – 98 whites, 36 Coloureds, 90 Indians and 11,503 Africans.[1] The emergency regulations governing detentions were Proclamations R90 and R91 of 1960, under the Public Safety Act of

1953, which gave magistrates and commissioned police officers the power to detain anybody 'if considered desirable in the interests of public order or of the person concerned, or if the person was committing or suspected of intending to commit an offence ... or if the person was thought to have information relating to such an offence'.[2]

How were those detained during the 1960 state of emergency eventually dealt with?

Some were released in May and June, but about 400 stayed in detention until the state of emergency was lifted on 31 August. Many detainees were never charged with any offence, but there was also a large number who were charged and convicted for incitement, taking part in riots or possessing dangerous weapons. Among them were some people who had helped to organize anti-pass-law demonstrations, including Pan-Africanist Congress leader Robert Sobukwe, who was jailed for three years for inciting others to campaign against the pass laws, and Albert Luthuli of the African National Congress, who was fined £100 for burning his pass.[3] Many of these leaders were 'banned'* after being released from prison. After Mr Sobukwe's sentence was up, he was held in jail for another six years under new legislation (see below).

Did the lifting of the 1960 state of emergency mean an end to new legislation extending the scope of detention without trial?

Several laws dealing with detention without trial were passed between the end of the emergency and 1982, when the Internal Security Act, Number 74 of 1982, consolidated much security legislation. Among them:

The General Law Amendment Act, Number 39 of 1961, allowed for detention for 12 days.[4]

Another General Law Amendment Act, Number 37 of 1963, provided for detention of up to 90 days or until 'in the opinion of the Commissioner of Police' the detainee had replied satisfactorily to all questions. Detention orders could be, and were, re-imposed after 90 days: according to the Minister of Justice in 1965, since the introduction of the Act a total of 147 people had been held for between 90 and 179 days, and 13 for more than 180 days.[5]

This law, which became known as the '90-Day Act', was in due course replaced by the '180-Day Act', officially known as the Criminal Procedure

*See chapter on banning orders.

Amendment Act, Number 96 of 1965. The new law provided for the detention of 'potential state witnesses' for six months or until relevant criminal proceedings were finished.[6] As with the 90-Day Act, re-detention was allowed; people could be held in solitary confinement; no visitors were permitted except a magistrate once a week; and no court of law could order a detainee's release. A detainee who refused to give evidence in court could be given repeated jail terms of up to 12 months. People charged with a serious offence could be refused bail on an order of an Attorney-General. If no evidence was produced in court in 90 days, the person could apply to a judge in private chambers to be released.[7]

The 1963 General Law Amendment Act (Number 37) also provided that people convicted of certain political offences could, after serving their sentences, be held in continued detention without further trial if the Minister of Justice thought that on release they were likely to further any of the aims of communism. This part of the Act was used to detain Robert Sobukwe, the PAC leader, and became known as the 'Sobukwe Clause'. Originally the clause was meant to be reviewed by Parliament every year, but in 1964 the minister himself was given the right to extend its operation. He used this power to hold Mr Sobukwe for another five years until May 1969, when he was released and confined to Kimberley under a banning order. Mr Sobukwe died in 1978, still banned.[8]

The Sobukwe Clause was repealed in the Internal Security Amendment Act, Number 79 of 1976, but was revived in the same Act to allow for preventive detention 'for a specified period' and appears, in similar form, on the statute book still.[9]

The General Law Amendment Act, Number 62 of 1966, allowed 'terrorists' to be detained for up to 14 days for interrogation. A judge could extend this period. This provision was replaced by a new one included in the Terrorism Act, Number 83 of 1967, under which a total of 4,140 people had been held by 1 June 1982, when the detention clause was again superseded by one under the Internal Security Act, Number 74 of 1982.[10]

In many legal systems people who have not been tried are assumed to be innocent until proven guilty. Is this always the case in South Africa?

Under the Terrorism Act the onus of proving innocence was put on the accused, who could be detained indefinitely. The Act was also made retrospective to 27 June 1962, when, the Minister of Justice told Parliament, terrorists first began training.[11] In 1982 this Act was superseded by the Internal Security Act (see below).

The 1982 Internal Security Act now governs most detentions. What are its provisions?

The Act identifies various categories of detention, lays down procedures and conditions for these, re-defines a number of offences, and modifies earlier provisions relating to sentencing and the onus of proof: [12]

Preventive detention: Sections of previous laws allowing for preventive detention are echoed in the Act. It is now subject to review by a committee of three appointed by the State President on the recommendation of the Minister of Justice. Detainees may make representation in person to the committee, two of whose members must be lawyers. If the committee endorses the action of the Minister of Law and Order, the detainee cannot pursue the matter any further, though the case can be reviewed again six months later. If, however, the committee finds against the minister, he is not obliged to free the detainee. In such a case the papers will be referred to the Chief Justice (or an appeal judge designated by him), who can set aside the minister's decision only if he is satisfied that the minister exceeded his powers, acted in bad faith or based his decision on incorrect considerations.

This review procedure has been called 'ineffectual and cosmetic', a judgement based in part on the record of reviews between 1977 and 1982, which resulted in recommendations for release in only nine out of 366 cases.

Detention of witnesses: The Attorney-General has unrestricted power to hold state witnesses until court proceedings have ended or for six months if no proceedings are started. There is a distinction in law between 'political' offences and serious common-law crimes; the decision of the Attorney-General to detain witnesses for non-political cases is subject to confirmation by a judge in chambers. There is no such review in political cases.

Detention for interrogation: Like the Terrorism Act, the ISA allows a person suspected of involvement in terrorist activities to be held indefinitely for interrogation. Detainees should be visited not less than once a fortnight by a magistrate and district surgeon. They will also be visited 'as often as possible' by an Inspector of Detainees, appointed by the Minister of Justice. People can be detained under the ISA by a senior police officer, but the Minister of Law and Order must give his written authorization for any detention in excess of 30 days. After six months the police must provide 'adequate' reasons why the detainee should not be released. A review committee looks at the detention after six months, but the minister is not bound to follow a recommendation that the detainee be released. There is no appeal against the minister's decision.

Onus of proof, etc.: Under the old Terrorism Act a person had to prove innocence 'beyond a reasonable doubt'. Under the ISA the onus of proof is no longer so severe: a presumption created by law may be rebutted with proof 'on a balance of probabilities'. There are no minimum sentences and offences relating to terrorism, subversion, sabotage and communism are more precisely defined.

Under the Internal Security Act detainees seem to have more protection than before. Have the safeguards satisfied critics? Have they been effective?

Civil rights groups, lawyers, and academics maintain that detention without trial is still open to abuse. In support of this, the provisions of the ISA and the minister's directives on the treatment of detainees have been compared with the circumstances surrounding the death in detention of Dr Neil Aggett in February 1982:

Visits by magistrates: A magistrate trying to see Dr Aggett was denied access by the police.

Visits by the Inspector of Detainees: He was refused access to Dr Aggett by the police.

Interrogation: The directives say that a detainee shall be treated 'in a humane manner' and not 'assaulted or otherwise ill-treated or subjected to any form of torture or inhuman or degrading treatment'. A fellow-detainee testified to the inquest that he saw Dr Aggett being beaten and forced to perform strenuous physical exercise. Immediately before his death, Dr Aggett himself said he had been severely ill-treated and assaulted.

Sleep: The directives say that a detainee 'shall be afforded ample opportunity to sleep'. Dr Aggett was kept in the interrogation rooms for one stretch of 62 hours.

Exercise: The directives say that a detainee 'shall be afforded ample opportunity . . . to do physical exercise'. In Dr Aggett's case an exercise yard was said to be 'not available'.

Limit of detention: The directives say investigations 'shall be concluded as rapidly as possible so as to limit the period of detention to the minimum'. A security police major said he was quite happy to detain Dr Aggett for more than a year to extract a statement from him.[13]

Dr Aggett was not the first person to die in detention. How many deaths have there been?

At least 69 people had died in detention in South Africa from 1963 until the end of September 1985. In addition, a number have died in the 'independent' homelands – three in five weeks in late 1985 in Ciskei. All were from the township of Ginsberg, near King William's Town, home of Steve Biko, who died in detention in 1977. One of the three was aged 15.[14] At many of the inquests there have been allegations of ill-treatment and torture. Among the officially stated causes of death have been 'suicide', 'fell out of seventh-floor window', 'fell from the tenth-floor window while being interrogated', 'slipped in the showers', 'slipped down the stairs', and 'natural causes'.[15]

The families of a number of detainees who died while in the custody of the Special Branch have sued for damages. Among them are the following:

● In 1979 the state paid the widow of Joseph Mdluli a total of R15,000 (£7,500 at today's conversion rate) and covered her legal costs. Four policemen were charged over the death of Mr Mdluli but were found not guilty.[16]

● In an out-of-court settlement, also in 1979, the family of Steve Biko was paid R65,000 (£32,500) and legal costs.[17]

● The family of Tshifiwa Muofhe, who died while detained in the 'independent' homeland of Venda, settled out of court for R150,000 (£75,000) in 1983. The inquest magistrate found that two Venda security policemen had inflicted the injuries which had caused Mr Muofhe's death. Later the Venda Chief Justice found them not guilty of murder and said that the injuries occurred when the police were trying to prevent Mr Muofhe from escaping.[18]

● In Namibia in January 1985 the South African government paid out R58,000 (£29,000) to the widow of Jona Hamukwaya who died within hours of being detained by the Koevoet (Crowbar) unit of the security police. One witness at the inquest said he saw the detainee being 'beaten like a snake'. This was the first settlement of damages against Koevoet, who have repeatedly been accused of atrocities against Namibian civilians. A further eight victims of Koevoet assaults were paid a total of R33,000 (£16,500).[19]

How many people have been detained under security legislation?

Precise figures are difficult to get, but the most reliable estimates are:
    Internal Security Act: From 1 January to 31 October 1985 the Detainees'

Parents Support Committee (DPSC), perhaps the most authoritative monitor, said that 1,633 people had been detained. This was about 600 more than the 1,100 detained in the whole of 1984, which, in turn, was the largest number of detentions in any year apart from 1960–61, when the Sharpeville shootings took place and a state of emergency was declared, and 1976–7, the time of unrest after the Soweto uprising.[20]

State of emergency*: From the declaration of the emergency on 22 July to the end of 1985 the police said that 6,733 people had been detained under emergency laws. However, non-police estimates put the total at 7,006 from the declaration of the emergency until 28 November 1985. The regulations allowed for detention of up to 14 days which could be renewed.[21]

Homelands: Figures here are even more difficult to obtain, but the DPSC said in November 1985 that over 1,846 people had been held in Transkei since May. The head of the Transkei security police, General Leonard Kawe, said it was an 'exaggeration' to say that more than 1,000 people had been held in September and October.[22] Figures are also difficult to get for Ciskei, but in one incident alone in September 1985 a total of 2,900 people were detained all at once for holding an illegal gathering.[23]

Political arrests: The DPSC estimated that 25,000 people had been arrested for public violence and other alleged political offences between September 1984 and the end of November 1985.[24]

What has been the government's reaction to criticism of detention without trial and deaths in detention?

The Minister of Law and Order, Louis le Grange, said in 1982, after the death of Ernest Dipale while in Special Branch custody, that 'you won't get much information if you keep a detainee in a five-star hotel or with a friend'.[25] His predecessor, J. T. Kruger, told a 1977 National Party congress, on hearing that Steve Biko had died: 'His death leaves me cold.' [26]

What is known about conditions under which detainees are held?

Claims that detainees are tortured have been made since the introduction of detention without trial in 1963 and were widely repeated after the proclamation of the state of emergency in July 1985. A study released in September 1985 by the University of Cape Town's Institute of Criminology, funded by the Ford Foundation, gave these figures based on a sample of 176 people:

*See chapter on state of emergency.

- 83 per cent claimed some form of physical abuse.
- 75 per cent reported being beaten, including punches, hitting, kicking, slapping and assault with implements.
- The next three most frequently reported forms of physical abuse were forced standing, maintaining abnormal body positions, and forced exercises.
- A quarter said they were subjected to electric shocks, 18 per cent to strangulation and 14 per cent to suspension.
- Nearly 80 per cent claimed they were held in solitary confinement.
- Most were interrogated for between six and eight hours while 6 per cent said they were interrogated for 16 to 24 hours.

The study concluded: 'The results provide clear and definitive evidence that physical torture occurs on a widespread basis and constitutes a systematic and common experience for those detained for interrogation purposes under South African security legislation.' [27]

Have the courts intervened in cases of detention?

Until late 1985 the courts generally said that they were powerless to intervene. In September 1985, however, the evidence of a Port Elizabeth district surgeon, Dr Wendy Orr, led the Eastern Cape Supreme Court to order an injunction restraining police from assaulting detainees from two prisons. Another four judgements restricted police from assaulting detainees or ordered magistrates and district surgeons to visit detainees to investigate reports of torture and report back to the courts. In Natal the Supreme Court ordered the release of four people detained under the Internal Security Act because the police did not show that their reasons for detaining them were consistent with the Act. Observers, including Professor Dugard, saw the judgements as a sign that the judges were asserting their independence and as a response to criticism that the courts had not been active enough in curbing abuse of state power. [28]

Also in late 1985, three detainees applied to the courts to challenge the 'unnecessarily harsh' rules applying to emergency detainees. Soon after the application was brought, the rules were changed to allow detainees access to selected reading matter – previously only the Bible had been allowed – and to buy food from prison shops. [29]

Have judges visited detainees? What have they said?

Some have. The Judge President of the Cape, G. G. A. Munnik, said he had received no complaints of maltreatment or assault during visits to Internal Security Act detainees. The Judge President of the Eastern Cape,

Dante Cloete, also speaking in late 1985, said judges in his division had seen 'hundreds' of detainees and he personally had received only one complaint of an assault.[30]

What medical attention can detainees receive?

Until late 1985 detainees were seen only by district surgeons, who are employed by the state. In October it was announced that the South African Medical Association would appoint panels of private doctors in various regions of the country who would be available to district surgeons if a second opinion was needed. It was also reported that the government had agreed to MASA's request that a detainee should be able to choose a doctor from the panel if the detainee wanted an opinion other than that of the district surgeon. Critics pointed out, however, that detainees still had a restricted choice.[31]

Banning Orders

Some people in South Africa have their freedom restricted by banning orders. What is a banning order?

It is a document signed by the Minister of Law and Order (formerly by the Minister of Justice) which, typically, prevents a person from

attending 'any gathering, or any particular gathering, or any gathering of a particular nature, at any time, or during any period, or on any day, or during specified times or periods';

setting foot on any 'educational institution', harbour, airport, newspaper or publisher's office;

leaving the magisterial district to which he or she has been confined by the minister;

writing anything for publication;

being quoted by any newspaper or magazine.

In addition, a banning order often requires that the person

report regularly, usually once a week, to the police;

resign from any public body or office or organization specified by the minister;

remain at home from 6 p.m. to 6 a.m. every day and from 6 p.m. on Friday to 6 a.m. on Monday (known as a house-arrest warrant).[1]

What legislation gives the Minister of Law and Order the power to ban?

The Internal Security Act, Number 74 of 1982, and before that the Suppression of Communism Act, Number 44 of 1950 (and as amended at least six times over the years). The power to ban belongs to the minister alone. He does not have to apply to the courts for a banning order.

Was banning under the Suppression of Communism Act used only against communists?

In April 1966 the then Minister of Justice, B. J. Vorster, said, 'You don't have to be a communist to be banned under the Suppression of Communism Act.' Several members of the old Liberal Party, which was strongly anti-communist, were banned under the Act in the 1950s and 1960s. Hundreds of others whose links with communism were never established in a court of law were also banned. In reply to queries about such individuals, successive ministers said that the banned person 'in the opinion of the minister' was furthering the aims of communism.

Is there any appeal against a banning order?

Under the old Suppression of Communism Act, there was no appeal to a court. In the mid 1970s Mr Vorster was quoted as saying that it was 'the easiest thing in the world' for a banned person to appeal in the courts against an order on the grounds that the government had acted *mala fide*. There have, however, been no successful appeals. Under the 1982 Internal Security Act a review board was set up under the auspices of the Department of Law and Order to hear appeals against the minister's decisions. To date no appeal has succeeded. Several people banned under the Act have refused to use the appeals procedure, believing, in the words of one that this would 'lend legitimacy to the government's system of banning'.[2]

How long are banning orders in force?

In the early 1950s banning orders were often issued for two years and later most were for five years. All could be renewed, as many were. Under the Internal Security Act, orders can be reviewed every 12 months.

How many people have been banned, and how many are banned now?

It has been calculated that by the end of 1978 a total of 1,378 people had been banned. About 15 people were banned in December 1985: six had been held under the Internal Security Act or emergency regulations and were served with banning orders on their release. One, however, was still in detention when the banning order was served. A number of others, believed to be about 172, are 'listed', which means they may not be quoted by the media in South Africa. Of those, 22 were in prison in late 1985, 89 were in exile and 21 were dead.[3]

Who is currently banned?

The most famous is Mrs Winnie Mandela, anti-apartheid campaigner and wife of the imprisoned African National Congress leader, Nelson Mandela. The Reverend Beyers Naude, a former minister of the Dutch Reformed Church and head of the banned Christian Institute, was 'unbanned' in late 1984 after seven years. Others include trade unionists who are banned, said Minister of Law and Order Louis le Grange in September 1983, because of links with the ANC.

About 60 banning orders were allowed to lapse in July 1983.

Can there be additional restrictions on the freedom of Africans?

The Native Administration Act, Number 38 of 1927, empowered the Governor-General (later the State President) to order any African tribe, section of a tribe or individual member to move from one place to another and not to leave any stated area for a specified time. The Native Administration Act, Number 42 of 1956, gave the government power to serve banishment orders without prior notice and barred courts from issuing interdicts suspending banishment orders. The government stated in April 1985 that a total of 194 individuals and four groups of Africans totalling 11,508 people had been served with banishment orders since the introduction of the legislation. On 5 April 1985 three individuals and 4,082 Africans in groups were currently subject to the orders. These figures excluded the homelands, whose governments also have powers to banish people. At least 14 men had died in banishment up to 1978, according to the Institute of Race Relations.

The government said that the orders were made against people 'responsible for disturbing the public order'. Investigations have found that most were banished for opposing the establishment of black local authorities and the issuing of passes to women.[4]

What happens to people who break their banning orders?

They are charged in court. This has happened in a number of cases: the usual penalty for a first offence is a suspended sentence, with a jail term for any further infringement.

How are banning orders most frequently broken?

One of the most common offences is attending a 'gathering'. The original Suppression of Communism Act defined a gathering as 'any gathering, concourse or procession in, through, or along any place, of any number of people having a common purpose, whether such purpose is lawful or unlawful'. This definition was changed in 1962 so that the minister could ban people from a gathering which did *not* have a 'common purpose'. In effect this means that a banned person cannot meet more than one other person at any one time.[5]

What have the courts considered to be a 'gathering', as far as banned persons are concerned?

In 1964 a banned Rhodes University lecturer, Terence Beard, went to a party given by a colleague. He sat alone in the kitchen throughout the evening, according to evidence given in the case, while guests came one by one to see him as the party continued in another room. He was arrested and charged with breaking his banning order by attending a gathering. Although he had not been in the company of more than one other person at a time, he was found guilty on the grounds that he and the other party-goers had a 'common purpose'.

More recently, in July 1983, Peter Jones, a colleague of the late Steve Biko, was found guilty of breaking his banning order by attending a party given for workmen who had renovated his office.[6]

In late 1985 Mrs Mandela defied several of the conditions in her banning order over a stretch of time. In August she returned to Soweto after her house in Brandfort in the Orange Free State to which she had been banned was petrol-bombed. She said that security police were behind the attack.[7] The same month she held an illegal press conference at her lawyer's office in central Johannesburg to say that the time had passed when South Africans of all races could settle their differences through a national convention. She also rejected President Reagan's offer of $10,000 to rebuild her home and adjoining clinic damaged in the petrol-bomb attack.[9] In October she addressed a memorial service for an executed ANC member, Benjamin Moloise, in central Johannesburg. Police were said to be investigating.[10] In December she attended the funeral of 12 black victims shot by police in Mamelodi, near Pretoria. She also addressed about 4,000 of the 50,000 people who had come to the funeral.[11]

Just before Christmas 1985 Mrs Mandela's banning order was changed when she was no longer banished to Brandfort but allowed to live anywhere except in the Johannesburg/Roodepoort areas. She was also allowed to attend social gatherings which were not political gatherings, and no longer had to report regularly to the police. The same day as the banning order was amended, she was removed by security police from her home in Soweto. Two days later she returned to Soweto and was arrested with some violence. She was later released on bail. Her lawyers also appealed against the ban on living in Soweto and barring her from politics. Just before New Year's Eve, after a visit to her husband in Pollsmoor Prison, she was again arrested as she tried to make her way back to Soweto. She was again given bail.[12]

Banned Gatherings

What kinds of meetings or gatherings are banned in South Africa?

Meetings are banned if the Minister of Law and Order or a magistrate considers they might seriously endanger the public peace.[1] Individual meetings may be banned, or a blanket prohibition may be put on a certain kind of gathering, or meetings held by a particular organization.

All open-air gatherings except sports meetings have been banned for several years. All indoor assemblies dealing with boycotts of schools and universities were banned in March 1985. In September 1985 the ban was extended to forbid meetings advocating work boycotts. Meetings of at least 64 named organizations are also banned.[2] In September the ban on open-air meetings received a legal setback when the Transvaal Supreme Court said the proclamation banning open-air meetings failed to reveal 'a degree of reasonable lucidity' and was therefore invalid. Legal sources said the court ruling did not apply to bans on specific meetings or on specific organizations.[3]

Among meetings recently banned were:

● Virtually every organization affiliated to the United Democratic Front was banned in October 1985 from holding meetings in African, Coloured and Indian areas of the Western Cape.[4]

● An academic conference to be held at the University of Cape Town in November 1985 on the role of the UDF in South Africa's future was banned.[5]

● The annual congress of the National Union of South African Students due to be held at the University of Cape Town in December 1985 was banned. It was moved elsewhere.[6]

● A fancy-dress dance to raise money for an education and care centre in the Coloured area of Mitchell's Plain, near Cape Town, had to be cancelled on police orders.[7]

Gatherings have been banned at various times since the early 1950s.

In one recent case the magistrate of Wynberg, in the Cape, banned at 2 p.m. one day a meeting of the United Democratic Front due to be held at 8 p.m. the same day. The ban was imposed on the grounds that 'in the opinion of' the magistrate there was reasonable apprehension of a disturbance of the peace. The UDF sought a judge in chambers who, at 6.30 p.m., 'unbanned' the meeting on the grounds that there had been many meetings of the UDF in the past without disturbance. The meeting went ahead peacefully as before.

What legislation is used to ban meetings?

The main law dealing with meetings used to be the Riotous Assemblies Act, Number 17 of 1956, but this has now been superseded for most purposes by the Internal Security Act, Number 74 of 1982. The ISA's section on gatherings makes similar provisions to those of the earlier Act, but adds that a person can be detained for 48 hours 'if the actions of such person are deemed to lead to a state of public disturbance or disorder'. If the police think further detention is necessary, application must be made to a magistrate, who can give permission for a further 14 days' detention.[8]

How does the law define a gathering?

The original Riotous Assemblies Act, Number 17 of 1956, said that a gathering was a 'public' assembly of twelve or more people. However, in 1974 the word 'public' was deleted from the Act, and when its successor, the Riotous Assemblies Act, Number 30, became law in the same year, the definition was changed to 'any number of people'.[9]

What activities connected with banned gatherings have been made illegal?

The original Riotous Assemblies Act said it was an offence to 'convene, preside at, or address' a banned meeting. The General Law Amendment Act, Number 39 of 1961, added that it was an offence to 'encourage, promote, or by means of threat cause the assembly or attendance' of a banned meeting. It was also forbidden to 'advertise or in any other way make known' such a meeting. In 1974 the new Riotous Assemblies Act made attendance a criminal act.[10]

In September 1976 the editor of the Durban *Daily News* was arrested at a cocktail party and charged under the 'advertising' section of the Act. On 25 September the government had banned a meeting to celebrate the coming to power of Frelimo in neighbouring Mozambique. That afternoon's *Daily News* carried a news report giving details of the gathering: this was held to be advertising a prohibited meeting, and the editor and his senior assistant editor were later found guilty.

Are gatherings at particular places banned?

Under the 1962 General Law Amendment Act, the minister has prohibited meetings other than religious services on the steps of the Johannesburg City Hall and in the Grand Parade in Cape Town – both favoured sites for protests. The Gatherings and Demonstrations Act, Number 52 of 1973, has been used to ban demonstrations and gatherings in the vicinity of Parliament, which includes the Anglican Cathedral and the city campus of the University of Cape Town – again both often the scene of protests. Exempt were religious services, funerals and official functions, or those permitted by the Chief Magistrate of Cape Town.[11]

In 1984 a University of the Western Cape theology student tried to use the prohibition on gatherings on the Grand Parade to lay a charge against the State President, P. W. Botha, saying that permission had not been sought from the chief magistrate to hold a gathering when Mr Botha was inaugurated as State President. The Attorney-General declined to prosecute, saying that the Minister of Law and Order, who was present at the ceremony, was entitled to give permission for such a meeting.[12]

Are the same laws used to control gatherings of all racial groups, or are African gatherings subject to additional restrictions?

Proclamation R 268 of 1968 made it an offence throughout the country 'except with official permission, to hold, preside at, or address any gathering in a Bantu area at which more than 10 Africans are present'. Exempt are church services, weddings, funerals and sports meetings. This proclamation re-introduced similar measures put into effect during the Defiance Campaign of the early 1950s.[13]

Can particular people be banned from attending gatherings, even when the gatherings themselves have not been banned?

Under the Suppression of Communism Act, Number 44 of 1950, and the 1954 amending Act, the minister could prohibit people 'listed' as 'communists', or those deemed by him to be furthering any of the aims of communism, from attending particular gatherings. In terms of the 1954 amending Act, he did not have to give reasons or give the 'listed' people an opportunity to defend themselves. The playing of recordings of speeches by people barred from gatherings was made an offence.[14] The 1982 Internal Security Act, which largely superseded this legislation, contains similar provisions.

People banned under the Suppression of Communism Act (and now under the Internal Security Act) may not attend *any* gatherings, even social ones. In practice this has been taken by the courts and the Special Branch to mean meeting more than one other person at a time.*

*See chapter on banning orders.

Unlawful Organizations

There are a variety of political organizations in South Africa. Are all of them legally permitted to operate?

A number of organizations have been banned* since 1950, including the following: the Communist Party of South Africa, the African National Congress, the Pan-Africanist Congress, the Congress of Democrats, Umkonto we Sizwe (Spear of the Nation) and Poqo (military wings of the ANC and PAC respectively), the Yu Chi Chan Club, the African Resistance Movement, the National Committee for Liberation, the South African Defence and Aid Fund, the Christian Institute, and a number of Black Consciousness organizations: the Black People's Convention, South African Students' Organization, South African Students' Movement, Union of Black Journalists, Black Community Programmes, Soweto Students' Representative Council, Association for the Educational and Cultural Advancement of the African People, Black Women's Federation, National Youth Organization, Border Youth Organization, Eastern Province Youth Organization, Natal Youth Organization, Transvaal Youth Organization, Western Cape Youth Organization, Medupe Writers' Association, Zimele Trust Fund, and Siyazinceda Trust Fund. The latest organization to be banned was the Congress of South African Students (COSAS) in late 1985. The governments of 'independent' homelands have also banned a number of organizations: Transkei, for example, prohibited virtually all Black Consciousness groups about the same time as South Africa in October 1977 and, in 1984, banned COSAS, the UDF and the Azanian Students' Organization.

Can people of all races join any lawful political party?

From 1968 to June 1985, racially mixed political parties were banned and membership was a criminal offence under the Prohibition of Political Interference Act, Number 51 of 1968. The law also barred anybody from helping a party which had any number of members belonging to another 'population group' or addressing any party meeting at which all or most of those present belonged to another population group.[1] This legislation

---

*Most laws empowering the government to ban organizations – the Suppression of Communism Act, the Unlawful Organizations Act and the 1976 Internal Security Act, for example – have now been incorporated into the 1982 Internal Security Act.

was abolished in June 1985. Three white parties in the House of Assembly –the National, Conservative, and New Republic parties – and another without parliamentary representation, the Herstigte Nasionale Party, said, however, that they would not admit black members despite the repeal of the law.

What happened when non-racial political parties were made illegal in 1968?

The non-racial Liberal Party decided to dissolve itself rather than split up into separate parties for whites, Coloureds, Indians and Africans. The Progressive Party (now the Progressive Federal Party) decided to shed its black membership 'under protest and under compulsion', and become a 'whites only' party. Neither the governing National Party nor the then official opposition United Party had any black members.[2]

However, the Prohibition of Political Interference Act was widely ignored, particularly in later years. For example, during the campaign leading up to the 'whites only' referendum on the new constitution in November 1983 Chief Gatsha Buthelezi, the Chief Minister of KwaZulu, spoke to a meeting of the Progressive Federal Party calling for a 'no' vote. Neither he nor the party was prosecuted.

The law was also openly disregarded during the elections for the new Coloured and Indian houses of Parliament in 1984, when the supposedly 'Coloureds only' Labour Party campaigned for election to the Indian chamber. The party was said to have circumvented the Act by having two members of the Indian house elected as independents while still belonging to the party.[3]

In November 1984 the Progressive Federal Party voted to open its ranks to all races, despite the Act. In January 1985 the party decided to start a branch in Lenasia, a predominantly Indian area near Johannesburg. An official said that Indians and Coloureds had shown interest in joining.[4] In August of the same year a branch in the Coloured area of Ravensmead, Cape Town, was formed.[5] Also that month, the PFP, amid some controversy at its annual congress, decided that it would participate in elections for the Coloured House of Representatives and the Indian House of Delegates, but would not rush in if it appeared that the party's credibility would be destroyed.[6]

Despite the repeal of the Act, the Inkatha movement, a largely Zulu-based organization headed by the Chief Minister of KwaZulu, Gatsha Buthelezi, was, by late 1985, not open to all races.[7]

Announcing in 1985 that the law would be repealed, except for the clause prohibiting political parties from receiving money from abroad, the government said that 'changed circumstances', particularly the new tricameral Parliament, meant that the Act was no longer serving its original purpose of protecting the various population groups.[8]

Which law was used to ban the Communist Party? Were other organizations affected as well?

The Suppression of Communism Act, Number 44 of 1950, made specific provision for the party to be banned. It also made communism a criminal offence, and said that any other organization furthering the achievement of any of the aims of communism could be declared unlawful by proclamation.[9] Organizations or people could ask a court to declare banning invalid on only three grounds: that the government acted in bad faith, *ultra vires*, or without applying its mind to the issue.

How does the law define communism?

The Suppression of Communism Act said:
 ' "Communism" means the doctrine of Marxian socialism as expounded by Lenin or Trotsky, the Third Communist International (the Comintern) or the Communist Information Bureau (the Cominform) or any related form of that doctrine expounded or advocated in the Union [later the Republic] for the promotion of the fundamental principles of that doctrine and includes, in particular, any doctrine or scheme –

 (a) which aims at the establishment of a despotic system of government based on the dictatorship of the proletariat under which one political organization is recognized and all other political organizations are suppressed or eliminated; or

 (b) which aims at bringing about any political, industrial, social, or economic changes within the Union by the promotion of disturbance or disorder, by unlawful acts or omissions or by means which include the promotion of disturbance or disorder, or such acts or omissions of threat; or

 (c) which aims at bringing about any political, industrial, social, or economic change within the Union in accordance with the directions or under the guidance of or in co-operation with any foreign government or any foreign or international institution whose purpose or one of whose purposes (professed or otherwise) is to promote the establishment within the Union of any political, industrial, social, or economic system identical with or similar to any system in operation in any country which has adopted a system of government such as is described in paragraph (a); or

 (d) which aims at the encouragement of feelings of hostility between the European and non-European races of the Union, the consequences of which are calculated to further the achievement of any object referred to in paragraph (a) or (b).'[10]*

Has the legal definition of communism been criticized?

The Johannesburg Bar said that the objects of 'communism', as defined, 'include many liberal and humanitarian objects which are advocated and cherished by persons who are very far from being communists. These provisions have no legal bounds and . . . are a complete negation of the liberty of the subject as guaranteed by the rule of law.'

Which law was used to ban the African National Congress and the Pan-Africanist Congress?

The Unlawful Organizations Act, Number 34 of 1960, was introduced exactly a week after the Sharpeville shootings and on the day when many blacks stayed away from work in response to the ANC's and PAC's call for a day of mourning. The new law said that if these two bodies were considered to threaten or be likely to threaten the safety of the public or the maintenance of order, they and all subsidiary branches and committees could be declared unlawful organizations. This was done when the Act was promulgated. Similarly, the Act provided that any organization set up to carry on, directly or indirectly, any activity of an unlawful organization could also be banned.[11]

The Congress of Democrats, a white organization grouped with the ANC in the Congress Alliance, was also banned under this Act in 1962.[12]

What means did the government use to ban the guerrilla groups Umkhonto we Sizwe and Poqo?

Under the General Law Amendment Acts of 1962 and 1963, more power was given to the government to ban organizations. In terms of the 1963 Act, the State President could declare that any organization or group existing since 7 April 1960 – when the Unlawful Organizations Act was promulgated – was an organization which had been banned. Umkhonto and Poqo were both declared illegal, as were the Yu Chi Chan Club and the African Resistance Movement.[13]

The South African Defence and Aid Fund, established during the 1960

*This section was deleted in the 1982 Internal Security Act.

state of emergency to help political detainees, was similarly banned in 1966.[14]

Under what Act were the Black Consciousness groups banned?

The Internal Security Amendment Act, Number 79 of 1976, which replaced the Suppression of Communism Act, also allowed for groups to be banned. This was used on 19 October 1977 against the Black Consciousness groups.[15]

What happens to the funds of groups declared unlawful?

The law provides for the property and assets of banned groups to be liquidated and taken by the government.[16]

Can fund-raising by organizations be prohibited or restricted?

The Fund-Raising Act, Number 107 of 1978, allows the government to prohibit the collection of funds by an organization. A ban of this kind was placed on the Federation of South African Trade Unions (FOSATU)* in June 1980. Prohibition can be imposed if the Minister of Health, Welfare and Pensions deems it to be 'in the public interest'. No appeal to the courts is allowed.[17]

Under the Affected Organizations Act, Number 31 of 1974, a body can be banned from obtaining overseas funding if the State President declares it to be an 'affected organization'. A body is considered to be 'affected' if it is deemed that 'politics were being engaged in by or through the organization with the aid of or in co-operation or consultation with or under the influence of an organization or person abroad'.[18]

What are the penalties for contravening the Affected Organizations Act?

Up to five years' imprisonment or a fine of R10,000 (£5,000) on first conviction, doubled on second conviction, for soliciting, receiving or bringing into the country foreign money. Obstructing an officer inquiring into an organization which might be declared 'affected' carries a maximum one year's imprisonment or R600 (£300) fine or both.[19]

*See chapter on trade unions.

Which organizations have been declared 'affected'?

The National Union of South African Students in 1974 and the Christian Institute in 1975, two years before it was banned outright.

Is it legal for any South African political party to receive overseas funding?

No. This is banned under the Prohibition of Political Interference Act.

Passports and Visas

The freedom to travel abroad using a passport from one's own country is a recognized human right. What is South African policy?

Passports are issued at the discretion of the Minister of Home Affairs (formerly the Minister of the Interior). Successive ministers have said that the granting of a passport is 'a privilege not a right'.

Are many South Africans refused passports?

In 1984 the government said that the previous year nine Coloureds, 20 Indians, 25 Africans, and seven whites had been refused passports. In 1982 a total of 99 people had their applications turned down.[1]

What kinds of people are refused passports?

Most of those who have been refused passports have been recognized as opponents of government policy. Among them are the following:
  ● Hassan Howa, former Chairman of the non-racial South African Council on Sport (SACOS), was refused a passport for the ninth time in 1984.[2]
  ● In 1983, Saths Cooper, Vice-President of the Black Consciousness AZAPO organization, had his application turned down for the seventh time since 1969.[3]
  ● Bishop Desmond Tutu, then General Secretary of the South African Council of Churches and later to become winner of the 1984 Nobel Peace Prize, was denied a passport to attend a United Nations conference in Geneva in 1983. In 1982 the Bishop's application to the Transvaal Supreme Court to have his passport returned had been dismissed. The minister said the passport had been withdrawn because it was not in 'the public interest' for the Bishop to have one, as 'he had vigorously propagated an economic boycott against South Africa while he was overseas'. At various times the Bishop was granted temporary documents, valid only for a particular trip, to travel abroad.[4]
  ● In November 1985 a magistrate ordered that Dr Allan Boesak's passport should be returned to him after it had earlier been confiscated. But the Minister of Home Affairs, Stoffel Botha, ordered the following day that the passport should not be returned. Dr Boesak appealed to the Cape

Town Supreme Court for the return of his passport, but this was refused in December.[5]

● In late 1985 the government refused passports to two separate groups of students from Stellenbosch University and Nederduitse Gereformeerde Kerk clerics who wanted to travel to Zambia to hold talks with the African National Congress. Government sources said that anybody planning to hold meetings with the ANC would be prevented from leaving the country. Later, however, one of the NGK clerics did travel to Zimbabwe for a World Council of Churches meeting and he, with Bishop Desmond Tutu and others, was reported to have held talks with the ANC.[6]

Has anyone ever been granted a passport, but then been prevented from leaving the country?

After his release from Robben Island, where he had been held for six years in preventive detention after completion of sentence, Robert Sobukwe, the Pan-Africanist leader, was confined to Kimberley under a banning order.* He applied to the Ministry of the Interior for permission to leave the country. This was granted, but the Ministry of Justice refused to waive his banning order so that he could leave the magisterial district to which he had been confined. Had he attempted to leave, he would have been charged with breaking his banning order. Mr Sobukwe applied to the Supreme Court for the impasse to be resolved. He lost and remained in South Africa until his death in 1978.

Can someone who has been refused a passport legally leave South Africa?

An exit permit can be applied for. This allows the holder to leave, but removes all right of return. Several former political prisoners and others involved in political activity have been given exit visas. It is an offence to leave the country without a valid passport or travel document.[7]

Can all women married to South Africans enter the country freely?

Under the Immigration Regulation Amendment Act, Number 43 of 1953, no women born outside the country who married South African Indians after 10 February 1953, nor their children if minors, could enter the country without special permission. Women married before that date, and their children, could enter until February 1956. This policy was

*See chapters on detention without trial and banning orders.

partially relaxed in 1978, when about 100 wives and their children were allowed to come from India to join their husbands in South Africa. Later, however, a succeeding minister ruled that this concession applied only to people married before January 1977.[8]

Are there restrictions on foreigners wishing to visit South Africa?

Entry is controlled under the Aliens Act, Number 1 of 1937, and the Admission of Persons to the Republic Regulation Act, Number 59 of 1972. Visas are not normally required by British visitors, but citizens of the USA and some European countries do have to have them. The Admission of Persons Act prevents the entry of 'undesirable' people and permits the removal of people who become 'undesirable'.[9] Under the Aliens Act, nobody who was not 'likely to become readily assimilated with the whites' could enter South Africa for permanent residence unless given special permission.[10]

In September 1985 the government said that it would abolish discriminatory aspects of its immigration laws. Legislation to be introduced in the 1986 parliamentary session would remove any differentiation based on race from the Aliens Act.[11]

The move to abolish apartheid for immigrants came at a time when figures showed that the number of immigrants was decreasing and the number of emigrants increasing. Between January and April 1985 the net gain of people was 5,011 – a drop of nearly 40 per cent over the same period in the previous year. In July 1985 there was a net outflow of 299 – the first time outflow had exceeded inflow for seven years. Professional and technical workers accounted for the largest percentage of those leaving.[12]

What kinds of people have been refused admission to South Africa?

The most notable recent case was that of the American civil rights leader and contender for the Democratic Presidential nomination, the Reverend Jesse Jackson. He was denied a visa in January 1985, although he had visited the country in 1979.[13] The Reverend Martin Luther King was denied permission to enter the country in the 1960s. Jacobo Timerman, author of a book about his detention without trial in Argentina, and of another critical of the Israeli invasion of the Lebanon, was refused a visa in 1983. He had been due to give an academic freedom lecture at the University of the Witwatersrand.[14] A number of journalists from overseas papers have also been barred from entering the country.

In mid 1985 a leading defender of human rights, Cardinal Paulo Arnas of Brazil, had his visa withdrawn when the government discovered that he was due to address a meeting organized by the End Conscription Campaign.[15] During the same period, nine Irish and a British anti-apartheid activist were refused admission to South Africa. The group, who had been invited by the South African Council of Churches, were held in Johannesburg airport's transit lounge and sent home.[16]

Right-wing Violence

Have any opponents of apartheid in South Africa met violent deaths which have been attributed to the Right?

A number have died in incidents which families, friends and others have blamed on the Right:

● A banned political scientist, Dr Rick Turner, was gunned down in front of his children as he answered the front door to his house in Durban in January 1978.

● A Durban lawyer and former Robben Island political prisoner, Griffiths Mxenge, was found stabbed to death on 19 November 1981.

● Mrs Victoria Mxenge, also a lawyer and Mr Mxenge's widow, was shot and hacked to death by four men outside her home in Umlazi, Natal, on 1 August 1985.

● The charred bodies of four missing officials of the Cradock Residents' Association, an affiliate to the UDF, were found near Port Elizabeth. They were Matthew Goniwe, Fort Calata, Thomas Mkhonto and Sicelo Mhlawuli.[1] At the funeral of the four men Dr Allan Boesak said: 'The people believe the police murdered these four men, and I believe them.'[2]

Have opponents of apartheid been killed outside South Africa?

Those who have been killed outside South Africa include:

● Abraham Tiro, a former Black Consciousness student leader, killed by a parcel bomb while in exile in Botswana in the early 1970s.

● Joe Gqabi, representative of the ANC in Zimbabwe, shot dead in Harare in August 1981.[3]

● Ruth First, academic, anti-apartheid activist, and wife of Joe Slovo, who was thought by the government to be a mastermind of ANC guerrilla attacks, killed by a parcel bomb in Maputo, Mozambique, in 1982.[4]

● Jeanette Schoon, a former banned person married to an ex-political prisoner, killed with her daughter by a parcel bomb in Angola in 1984.[5]

Have any other opponents of apartheid died in suspicious circumstances?

Three trade unionists died in two separate car accidents in 1982 and 1983; a cleric just elected Chairman of the anti-apartheid Border Council of Churches was killed when his car overturned in 1982; and the son of a worker for the South African Council of Churches died when the family car overturned, also in 1983.[6] The suspicion has been voiced that not all car deaths are accidents because several prominent South Africans are known to have had their cars tampered with. Recent incidents include the following:[7]

● A bomb was attached to the car of the Anglican Dean of St George's Cathedral in Cape Town, the Very Reverend Edward King, in March 1983.

● The General Secretary of the African Food and Canning Workers' Union, Jan Theron, had the tyres of his car tampered with in 1983.

● Dr Allan Boesak, President of the World Alliance of Reformed Churches and a prominent Coloured opponent of apartheid, also had his car tampered with in the same year. Dr Boesak and his family have also received a number of telephoned death threats.

Have there been many attacks and threats against opponents of apartheid?

In 1979 a man was jailed for six years for firing shots into the flat of Colin Eglin, who was then Leader of the Opposition. In August 1982 a man with a machine gun threatened Mana Slabbert, the Cape Town criminologist who was at that time married to Mr Eglin's successor, Dr Frederick van Zyl Slabbert. In the same year the house of Dr Nthatho Motlana, Chairman of the Soweto Committee of Ten, was stoned, and a van belonging to Winnie Mandela, anti-apartheid campaigner and wife of the jailed ANC leader Nelson Mandela, was tampered with.[8]

The minister of Law and Order, Mr Louis le Grange, told Parliament in 1984 that between September 1983 and June 1984 a total of 43 incidents 'which can be regarded as vandalism' were reported to police. Forty complaints had been investigated and suspects questioned, but there had been no arrests. Later in 1984 Mr Le Grange said that he was not unduly worried about right-wing radicalism but 'more worried about radicalism on the Left'.[9]

Incidents in 1985 included the following:

● The home of Mrs Mandela in Brandfort, to which she had been confined under a banning order, was fire-bombed in August. She held the security police responsible.[10]

● Two teargas canisters were thrown into the grounds of the home of the PFP member of the provincial council, Di Bishop.[11]

● An anonymous group calling itself the Vigilante Action Group claimed responsibility for a fire that destroyed offices of seven organizations linked to the UDF in Cape Town in October.[12]

● The home of Dan 'Cheeky' Watson in Port Elizabeth was destroyed in an explosion. Mr Watson attracted prominence in the 1970s by breaking sports apartheid and playing for an African rugby team. More recently, the family business was exempted from an almost total boycott by Africans of white-owned shops in Port Elizabeth. Two Africans who were in the Watson home at the time of the explosion were seriously injured.[13]

● An attempt was made to petrol-bomb the offices of the South African Council of Churches in Johannesburg.[14]

In addition, the London offices of the banned African National Congress were bombed in March 1982. South African agents were widely held to be responsible.

Have many people been caught and prosecuted for violence against opponents of apartheid?

There have not been many prosecutions, and of these very few have resulted in prison sentences. Exceptions to this were the case of the man who fired into Mr Eglin's flat, and that in which the two former members of the Afrikaner Weerstandsbeweging (AWB – see below) were jailed for 15 years under the Terrorism Act in June 1983. According to court evidence, they had planned the assassination of the Prime Minister, P. W. Botha, the General Secretary of the South African Council of Churches, and Dr Boesak, had plotted to spread syphilis germs at the Sun City holiday complex in Bophuthatswana and to spread nails on the road leading to it, had spoken of destroying multi-racial hotels, and had made and collected weapons and hoarded explosives stolen from a mine.[15]

In June 1983 the leader of the Afrikaner Weerstandsbeweging, Eugene Terre'Blanche, was fined R300 (£150) and given two suspended sentences for possessing an AK47 assault rifle, 362 rounds of ammunition and a revolver. One of his co-accused in that case was among those earlier jailed for 15 years under the Terrorism Act.[16]

What is the Afrikaner Weerstandsbeweging?

The AWB (its name means 'Afrikaner Resistance Movement') is a white supremacist group formed in 1972 in reaction to the policy of dialogue with black Africa adopted by the then Prime Minister, B. J. Vorster. It first came to prominence in 1979 when members tarred and feathered a professor. AWB members are sometimes armed and wear jackboots and swastika-like emblems. P. W. Botha ordered police investigation into the group after members heckled him at a meeting in Pretoria on the new constitution. Mr Terre'Blanche and one of the men jailed for 15 years are former policemen.[17]

What is the AWB's attitude to law and order?

At the end of April 1985, AWB leader Eugene Terre'Blanche told a rally of 2,000 people in Pretoria that there should be no restrictions on the police in combating black unrest. 'If you cannot protect us and cannot keep order, the AWB will maintain the order,' he said. The rally ended in a 'march of gratitude' to police headquarters where a letter was handed over saying: 'The AWB is at all times at your disposal for the maintenance of law and order and the protection of our people.'[18] No arrests were made, although the march was a contravention of the ban on outdoor demonstrations; the following day a number of blacks were arrested while holding a demonstration outside the United States Consulate in Johannesburg.

Are there suspicions that police are involved in right-wing violence?

Certain cases have aroused such suspicions. A bullet fired into the home of a Durban lecturer was found to be identical to the kind used by police. In another case, two security policemen were named by a former colleague as being responsible for sending an acid-impregnated T-shirt to the daughter of banned editor Donald Woods. The same former security policeman, Donald Card, identified a member of the Special Branch as the person who smashed the windscreen of a car belonging to the author and former Liberal Party leader, Alan Paton.

There have been burglaries at the offices of organizations opposed to apartheid. Has police involvement ever been alleged?

Cases have included one in March 1983 at the offices of the General Workers' Union in Cape Town, when only union documents were stolen. The caretaker of the building made a sworn statement to the police giving them the registration number of a van used by three whites who had allegedly entered the union's offices. Later that week the van was seen in a 'police only' parking bay outside Caledon Square police station. The police said this was a 'coincidence'. The Minister of Law and Order, Louis le Grange, said that the registration number given to the police was 'probably false'.[19]

Have any serving policemen been convicted of harassing opponents of apartheid?

No.

Have there been allegations that the parliamentary Right encourages violence?

The Conservative Party under Dr Andries Treurnicht has been the subject of such charges, which it denies. However, a Potchefstroom University professor, J. van Tonder, says that Dr Treurnicht and a senior party official, Dr C. P. Mulder, have been 'fanning the flame of violence, intentionally or unintentionally'.[20]

In September 1985, amid unrest in many parts of the country, Dr Treurnicht called on the government to 'unleash' the security forces. 'Keeping our security forces on a leash and allowing them to use only birdshot and rubber bullets has had serious consequences,' he said.[21]

Guerrilla Attacks

Why are guerrillas operating in South Africa?

The main black nationalist group, the African National Congress, says that it has turned to armed struggle against the government because it has no alternative: that decades of pleading for a non-racial state and years of non-violent protests against apartheid were ignored and the ANC banned. The government says that the ANC is manipulated by communists and that the blacks' political future lies in the homelands. In late 1984 and 1985 there were government suggestions that talks could be held with the ANC if it renounced violence. The ANC said this could occur only if the government abandoned apartheid and freed political prisoners.

What is the homeland leaders' attitude towards the ANC?

It is banned (as in 'white' South Africa) in all the 'independent' home-lands. Some leaders' views are ambivalent: they support the goal of black liberation but oppose the ANC's tactics. The Transkei Prime Minister, Chief George Matanzima, for example, said in April 1983: 'We believe in non-violence while they [the ANC] believe in violence.'[1] The KwaZulu Chief Minister, Chief Gatsha Buthelezi, who had earlier conducted some talks with overseas representatives of the ANC, said in March 1983 that the ANC 'have now become opponents of black people'.[2] In late 1985, the Zulu King, Goodwill Zwelithini, warned that Zulus would rise in their thousands to drive out the exiled ANC leadership if it tried to set foot in South Africa. Speaking at the same rally, Chief Buthelezi accused the ANC of turning 'black brother against black brother'.[3]

What is the ANC's attitude to the homeland leaders?

The ANC regards them as 'sell-outs' and refuses to recognize them as genuine leaders. It is reported that the jailed ANC leader, Nelson Mandela, has several times been offered release from prison on condition that he is confined to Transkei. He has always refused.

How strong are the ANC guerrilla forces?

The South African Defence Force estimates that the ANC has up to 7,000 guerrillas. US intelligence reports estimated in 1983 that between 1,000 and 2,000 were inside South Africa.[4] Up to 8,000 blacks are reported to have left South Africa in the wake of the Soweto uprising to join the ANC; and Professor Mike Hough of Pretoria University's Institute for Strategic Studies said in late 1982 that about 20 people a month were leaving the country for insurgency training.[5] As unrest flared in many parts of the country from September 1984, a number of people were believed to have left for training.

How strong is black support for the ANC inside South Africa?

Funerals both of ANC guerrillas killed in South Africa and of unrest victims, and memorial services of ANC activists hanged in Pretoria have attracted large crowds. The sight of ANC flags, as well as those of the Communist Party, which works closely with the ANC, has become increasingly common at funerals. At one in December 1985, at Queenstown in the Eastern Cape, people carried wooden models of submachine guns and revolvers, acting out battles in which whites were killed.[6]

Opinion polls also confirm support for the ANC. In March 1985 56 per cent of blacks polled by the *City Press* newspaper in Johannesburg supported the ANC.[7] In a survey conducted by the London *Sunday Times* in August 1985 of blacks in Johannesburg and Durban – two of the country's main urban areas – 49 per cent said Nelson Mandela, in jail since the early 1960s, would make the best president for South Africa. Second was Bishop Desmond Tutu with 24 per cent. Chief Gatsha Buthelezi received 6 per cent.[8] Chief Buthelezi's low showing appears to be confirmed by another poll released in October: on the Witwatersrand he won support from 11 per cent, against 29 per cent for the ANC and 13 per cent for Bishop Tutu. In Natal–KwaZulu the survey conducted by the Institute of Black Research found that the anti-Buthelezi camp – the ANC, UDF and Bishop Tutu – outpointed him by 37 to 34 per cent, leading to the conclusion that 'even in his own territory Buthelezi represents a minority'.[9]

Opinion polls vary on some of the strategies being pursued by the ANC and other organizations. One, in May 1985 among adult Africans on the Witwatersrand, conducted by the Human Sciences Research Council, found that only 20.8 per cent supported international economic boycotts of South Africa, while 67.3 per cent supported further foreign investment.[10] However, two other polls – which were not conducted by the government-funded HSRC – found different opinions. The London *Sunday Times* poll said that 77 per cent of blacks thought other countries were right to impose economic sanctions unless South Africa agreed to get rid of apartheid.[11] The Institute for Black Research (IBR) poll said that 73 per cent of the urban blacks interviewed supported some form of disinvestment – 49 per cent wanted conditional and 25 per cent total disinvestment – while 26 per cent favoured investment.[12]

On the armed struggle, 36 per cent in an IBR survey and 43 per cent in the *Sunday Times* approved, while 54 and 52 per cent respectively opposed violence. The IBR poll said that 66 per cent approved of strikes, boycotts of white businesses and protests against high rents and unequal education. Sixty-two per cent disapproved of attacks on blacks who worked for the system, such as community councillors and homelands authorities – an almost daily feature of the 1984–6 unrest – while 28 per cent approved.[13]

Is there support among white South Africans for negotiations with the ANC?

A survey of white opinion on the ANC conducted by the government-backed Human Sciences Research Council and released in late 1984, at a time when there were hints that talks could be held with the banned organization, said that 42.9 per cent of whites favoured these talks while 43.9 per cent opposed them. The amount of support for direct negotiations surprised observers.[14]

In March 1985, however, another opinion poll, conducted for the Afrikaans newspaper *Rapport*, came to a different conclusion. Whites were asked: 'Do you think some form of negotiation between the government and certain black leaders of South Africa is necessary?' A total of 16 per cent said that the ANC should be involved. Other black leaders the respondents thought should be included were those who worked within the system, including homeland leaders (70 per cent), and the UDF and AZAPO (38 per cent). (The total exceeded 100 per cent because more than one answer to the question could be given.)[15]

What is the ANC's strategy for armed struggle?

Its leaders say that it attacks military and security targets and tries to avoid civilian deaths, but that it is impossible for civilians to be completely unaffected by an armed struggle. Academic observers like Tom Lodge and Professor Gwendolen Carter of Indiana University in the USA have said that the ANC has embarked on an 'armed propaganda' struggle.[16]

In June 1985 an ANC conference in Zambia appeared to signal intensification of the armed struggle when it urged:

- Workers to sabotage machinery in factories.
- Black policemen to 'turn their guns against their masters'.
- The townships to be made 'ungovernable'.

The ANC said it was not embarking on a terror campaign against whites, but it was difficult to know who ranked as a civilian when 'so many whites in South Africa have guns'. The campaign was directed at military targets which included the police, army, community councillors and white farmers who support the Defence Force.[17]

The South African forces are well armed and trained. Are they winning the war against the ANC or are both sides inflicting damage?

By mid December 1985 there had been 122 guerrilla attacks, nearly three times the 44 recorded in 1984, according to the Institute for Strategic Studies in Pretoria. These do not include the dozens of attacks on individual black policemen and community councillors. From 1976 to the end of September 1985 there were 355 reported insurgency attacks for which the ANC's armed wing, Umkhonto we Sizwe, was mainly responsible. These included attacks on police stations (18 since 1976), murder of policemen or state witnesses (13), murder of civilians (17) and, during the first nine months of 1985, a total of 42 sabotage and attempted sabotage incidents.[18]

In September 1985 the Minister of Law and Order, Louis le Grange, said that since 1976 a total of 196 'terrorists' had been arrested and 73 killed in clashes with police.[19]

The South African government has initiated 'reprisal' raids on alleged guerrilla bases outside South Africa: 42 people were killed in a raid on Maseru (Lesotho) in December 1982, while four were killed in a similar raid on Maputo (Mozambique) in October 1983, and at least 16 killed in a raid on Gaborone (Botswana) in June 1985. In all these incidents, people said not to be ANC activists were killed. In December 1985 nine people, three of them said not to be ANC members, were killed in a raid by unknown men in Lesotho.

The ANC's armed struggle escalated at the same time with landmine explosions near the borders with both Zimbabwe and Botswana in which nine whites were killed. South Africa increased pressure on neighbouring states not to harbour ANC supporters.[20] In January 1986, during a South African blockade of Lesotho, a miltary government less hostile to Pretoria was installed in a coup. ANC members were expelled by the new rulers. The blockade was then lifted.

The Churches

Can all South Africans worship at any church they choose?

The 'Church Clause' of the Native Laws Amendment Act, Number 36 of 1957, allowed the Minister of Native Affairs (later of Co-operation and Development) to control the presence of Africans at services in 'white' areas. They could be barred from any service if he thought they were 'causing a nuisance' or if he thought it 'undesirable' for them to be present. The Act said that the minister could impose the ban if the local authority agreed, if the church concerned had been given reasonable time to make representations, and if the minister had considered the availability or otherwise of alternative facilities.[1] However, opposition to this clause was so widespread that it was never invoked.

What is government policy now on mixed worship?

In March 1978 the minister said that churches could decide for themselves about the following organizational matters:

Black attendance at church services in 'white' areas;

Services for blacks in church buildings controlled by a white congregation;

Arranging and conducting other church activities for blacks in members' homes or other church buildings;

Arranging and conducting other bona fide church meetings or conferences attended by blacks and whites.

The minister said that permits would be needed for large gatherings such as a series of evangelical services or congresses lasting more than a day. No facilities could be erected for blacks without approval.[2]

What churches are represented in South Africa?

There are three white Dutch Reformed churches:

The Nederduitse Gereformeerde Kerk (NGK), which is the largest with 1.7 million adherents (81.9 per cent).

The Nederduitsch Hervormde Kerk (NHK) with 246,000 members (11.9 per cent).

The Gereformeerde Kerk (GK), also known as the Dopper Kerk, with 128,000 members (6.2 per cent).

There are also branches of the NGK for blacks:

The NG Kerk in Afrika (NGKA) for Africans
The NG Sendingskerk for Coloureds
The Reformed Church in Africa for Indians

About 1.1 million Africans belong to the NGKA, 678,000 Coloureds to the Sendingskerk, and 4,000 Indians to the Reformed Church in Africa.

The main English-speaking churches are the Anglican Church of the Province of South Africa, with 456,000 white members, the Methodists (414,000 members), the Presbyterians (129,000) and the Catholics (393,000). In addition, 120,000 people are Jewish.[3]

Africans have about 3,000 independent churches with a total membership of nearly five million, though some have only a handful of members. Eleven million Africans are Methodist, 700,000 Lutheran, 800,000 Anglican, 360,000 Presbyterian and 1.6 million Catholic.

Churches with Coloured members include the Lutheran (95,000 members), Anglican (351,000), Methodist (140,000), Congregational (170,000) and Catholic (264,000).

More than 512,000 Asians are Hindu and 154,000 Muslim. A total of 21,000 are Catholics, while smaller numbers belong to other Christian churches.[4]

What are the churches' attitudes towards mixed worship?

The 'English' churches do not practise any colour bar, although most churches are predominantly attended by one racial group.

The Dutch Reformed churches appear to be moving away from strict segregation after years when blacks were not allowed into 'white' churches. However, incidents involving the exclusion of blacks are still reported:

● In 1983 an NHK minister was reported to have refused to conduct a funeral service because blacks were attending.[5]

● In December 1984 six people who went to an NHK church to mourn the death of a farmer from Randfontein, Transvaal, were told that they were 'not allowed to enter the white people's church'. The minister, the Reverend Douw Steyn, said if people of other races wished to attend a 'white' funeral service, the family of the deceased had to make an application that would be approved or rejected on merit by the church's governing body. Other races had attended funerals 'on numerous occasions, but in this case no application was received'.[6]

● Also in 1984, in Krugersdorp, Transvaal, the local NGK submitted a petition with 513 signatures opposing an application by the Pentecostal

Church for 'people of colour' to be allowed to attend its services. The town council rejected the application.[7]

What are the churches' attitudes towards the Immorality Act and the Mixed Marriages Act?

The Cape Synod of the NGK asked the government in 1936 to prevent mixed-marriages and to introduce apartheid. In 1983, however, the Synod said that the Acts contradicted the scriptures. The other two Dutch Reformed churches have also accepted that these laws should be scrapped. The English churches oppose the Acts.[8]

In 1983 the Sendingskerk decided that it would solemnize mixed marriages, would recognize such unions as bona fide, and would help and protect couples if they were prosecuted.[9] The Presbyterians have also adopted this policy.

Can the clergy work freely among all races?

White churchmen need permission to live in areas allocated to race groups other than their own.[10] In 1984 Dr Nico Smith, an NGKA cleric later to be involved in controversial talks with the banned African National Congress, was given permission to live in the African township of Mamelodi. The same year the Right Reverend Stephen Naidoo was appointed Catholic Archbishop of Cape Town. It was reported that he would continue to live in an Indian area of the city.[11]

Have the security laws been used against clergy and church groups?

The Christian Institute, a non-racial interdenominational organization, was declared an 'affected organization' in May 1975 and barred from receiving funds from overseas. In 1977 it was banned under the Internal Security Act, as was its director, Dr Beyers Naude, a former NGK minister, and senior colleagues. A number of other clerics have been banned and/or detained, including Father Cosmas Desmond and the Reverend David Russell (banned), the present leader of the Labour Party, the Reverend Alan Hendrickse (detained) and the Reverend Allan Boesak (detained).

Archbishop Denis Hurley was charged with contravening the Defence Act when he alleged misconduct by the Defence Force in Namibia. The charges were withdrawn in February 1985, when the prosecutor said that the defendant had been 'misquoted'. However, the Archbishop said that he stood by his allegations.[12]

In late 1985 the Transkei government said that it would introduce a bill to prevent churches in the territory from being members of the World Council of Churches. The WCC has been strongly attacked by the South African and Transkei governments for its support of revolutionary groups, particularly the ANC and SWAPO.[13]

Have other religious organizations been investigated by the government?

The South African Council of Churches was investigated by the government-appointed Eloff Commission in 1981–3. The then head of the Special Branch, Lieutenant-General Johan Coetzee, recommended a total ban on foreign funding of the SACC. The Commission itself said that the law controlling donations to welfare organizations should be extended to cover the SACC. It claimed that the Council pursued 'strategies of resistance' to government policies and identified with the 'liberation struggle', in which it shared with other organizations 'the common aim of achieving radical socio-economic changes in South Africa'.[14]

Have there been attempts to discredit clergy who oppose the government?

Towards the end of 1984 the *Star* of Johannesburg published allegations that a Coloured church leader, the Reverend Allan Boesak, was having an affair with a white woman. The paper said that the information had been collected by a 'dirty tricks department' of the security police. In March 1985 Dr Boesak was exonerated of any impropriety by his church. At the same time the second-in-command of the security police, Brigadier Johan van der Merwe, admitted that 'in certain circumstances' it was in the interests of the police to disseminate false information to discredit leaders of 'subversive' organizations. He added one proviso: the false information should not affect the morals of the community which the security police served.[15]

In November 1985 the former Anglican Dean of Johannesburg said that the police had offered to withdraw a charge against him of contravening the law against homosexuality if he became a police informer. He refused, was fined in court and resigned as Dean.[16]

The Press

Is it generally agreed in South Africa that the country has a free press?

The government says that the South African press is 'the freest in Africa'. The South African Ambassador to Britain, Dr Denis Worrall, said in November 1984 at a Cambridge Union debate: 'You have a free press in South Africa.' On the strength of that statement, the *Cape Times* quoted extensively from the speech given during the same debate by the banned former editor of the *Daily Dispatch*, Donald Woods.[1] Police were subsequently reported to be investigating a charge against Tony Heard, the editor of the *Cape Times*, under the Internal Security Act: if found guilty, he could be jailed. A year later Mr Heard had not been brought to court. He was, however, charged in November 1985 shortly after he had published an extensive interview in the *Cape Times* with the president of the banned African National Congress, Oliver Tambo. Security police told Mr Heard that he had violated Section 56(1)(P) of the Internal Security Act prohibiting the printing without government permission of 'any speech, utterance, writing or statement' of a banned person. The penalty is a maximum jail sentence of three years. There is no option of a fine. Mr Heard did not seek permission to publish and chose to test the public's right to be informed on what he considered to be a matter of great importance: the views of the ANC. Mr Heard had interviewed Mr Tambo in London a few days before publication of the article; security police later issued him with a subpoena for the tape-recording of the interview.[2]

Dr Worrall said at Cambridge that the editor of the *Cape Times* and others 'would all say they run a free press'.[3] Many editors, however, do not agree. A former editor of the *Star* has said that editing a newspaper in South Africa is 'like walking blindfold through a minefield'. The present editor of the *Star*, Harvey Tyson, said in March 1985 that rating press freedom in the United States at 100, Britain at 80, and Israel at 50, South Africa had a rating of 40.[4]

Which laws affect the press in South Africa?

In addition to common law, at least 100 statutes bear on what may or may not be printed in South Africa. Among the most important are the following:

Affected Organizations Act: Stops newspapers from appealing for, or even accepting, funds from overseas for organizations declared 'affected' and thus prohibited from getting money from abroad.

Armaments Development and Production Act: Bans papers from publishing material that could be construed as incitement to strike at armaments factories.

Atomic Energy Act: Much information on atomic energy may be published only with official permission. The penalty for contravention is a fine of up to R10,000 (£5,000) or up to 20 years' imprisonment or both.

Defence Act: In effect says that 'no person shall publish ... any information relating to the composition, movements or dispositions' of the South African Defence Force. During the South African invasion of Angola in 1974, no details were allowed to be published inside the country, although the rest of the world's press was writing about it.

Gatherings and Demonstrations Act: Bans demonstrations in the vicinity of Parliament in Cape Town. Newspapers may not report that a gathering of this kind is planned.

Internal Security Act: Covers a multitude of prohibitions including aiding banned organizations, quoting banned people, and 'furthering the achievement of any of the objects of communism', which, as newspaper lawyer Kelsey Stuart has said, is a wide offence, as many of the objects of communism are also the objects of perfectly legal organizations.

Official Secrets Act: Makes it an offence to publish 'any sketch, plan, model, article, note, document or information relating to munitions of war or any military, police or security matter ... in any manner or for any purpose prejudicial to the safety or interests of the Republic'. The maximum penalty is 15 years' imprisonment.

Police Act: Anybody who publishes 'any untrue matter' about the police or an individual policeman without having 'reasonable grounds' for believing the statement is true is guilty of an offence. The onus of proof is on the publisher. The penalty for contravention is a fine of up to R10,000 (£5,000) or five years' imprisonment or both.

Prisons Act: In effect prohibits the publication of any material on prisons without official approval.

Riotous Assemblies Act: Prohibits notice of a banned meeting being published; bans publication of a speech made by a banned person; makes it an offence to report a speech that could incite public violence; stops publication of speeches that could lead to boycotts or strikes; and – in terms of this Act and at least four others – makes anybody 'engendering feelings of hostility between the European and other races' liable to a fine of up to R2,000 (£1,000) or imprisonment of up to two years or both.[5]

*State of Emergency:** Sweeping powers to control the press were con-

*See also chapter on state of emergency.

tained in regulations gazetted for the state of emergency declared on 21 July 1985. The Minister of Law and Order could specify any newspaper or journal which systematically published 'subversive' material, preventing further publication. Shortly after the declaration of the emergency the police said that it intended to ensure that the free flow of information was not inhibited but that 'dramatized versions, slanted truths and half-truths' would not be allowed.

On 2 November 1985 a number of restrictions were introduced. They said that no foreign or local journalist could ''make, take, record, manufacture, reproduce, publish, broadcast or distribute, or take or send to any place ... any film ... or any photograph, drawing or other representation or any sound recording' of any incident of unrest or 'any conduct' of the security forces. This had the effect of prohibiting all but officially approved television coverage of the conflict. Only accredited journalists were allowed to report on unrest. They had to report first to commanding police officers and could be ordered to leave the area of unrest or be confined to a particular spot for police reports. Penalties for contravention included confiscation of equipment, a fine of up to R20,000 (£10,000) or imprisonment of up to 10 years without the option of a fine.

Have newspapers been prosecuted?

Perhaps the most famous case was the Prisons Act trial brought against the *Rand Daily Mail* and its then editor, Laurence Gandar, after publication of three articles by a former political prisoner, Harold Strachan, detailing assaults, electric shock treatment and generally poor prison conditions. Strachan was later jailed again for making the statements and three warders were convicted of various offences in relation to the articles. The editor, a reporter and the paper itself were all found guilty of having failed to take reasonable steps to prove that the information printed was correct. The case is estimated to have cost the *Rand Daily Mail* more than £100,000. Many newspapers have been deterred by this case from publishing anything on prisons that has not been released by the Commissioner of Prisons himself. *Die Volksblad*, a government-supporting newspaper, was fined for printing a picture of Dimitrio Tsafendas, the killer of the former Prime Minister, Dr Hendrik Verwoerd, in 1983.[6] The *Star* was found guilty, also in 1983, of publishing a picture of a woman convicted of murder.[7] In October 1984 a cameraman working part-time for Britain's Independent Television News (ITN) faced two charges in Cape Town of contravening the Prisons Act by filming Pollsmoor Prison and Robben Island without authority from the Commissioner of Prisons. He was fined R300 (£150).[8] Provisions of the Prisons Act do appear to have been eased slightly. In May 1984 the Minister of Justice, Kobie Coetsee, said that there had been an informal agreement for nearly two years between the press and the Prisons Department. The Department regarded the right to comment fully on information about prisons before publication and to have its comments published with equal prominence as adequate 'verification' in terms of the Act.[9]

The Prisons Act, while meant to deter the press, has also caught at least one tourist. In March 1985 Mrs Jean Morris, visiting Pietermaritzburg from Britain, was arrested after she photographed two policemen raising the flag outside a police station. She was later released.[10]

In 1983 the *Rand Daily Mail* and the *Sunday Times* were fined under the Official Secrets Act for revealing details of the National Intelligence Service's activities during a coup attempt in the Seychelles.[11] The *Star* was also found guilty of quoting a banned person, Oliver Tambo.[12] In addition, three Afrikaans newspaper editors were found guilty of various offences in 1983.[13]

Have any newspapers been banned in South Africa?

The first bannings took place during the 1950s. The (South African) *Guardian* was banned under the Suppression of Communism Act in 1952, as were two of its successors, *Advance* (1954) and *New Age* (1962). The magazine *Fighting Talk* was banned in 1963.

More recently, in October 1977, the *World* and *Weekend World*, which circulated widely among blacks, particularly in Soweto, were banned, as was the Christian Institute publication *Pro Veritate*. In late 1980 a strike closed the black-read *Post Transvaal* and *Weekend Post*: when they were due to reappear they were both refused re-registration in terms of the 1962 Newspaper and Imprint Act.

In August 1984 the *Windhoek Observer* was banned under the Publications Act. The ban was lifted, however, a fortnight later by the Publications Appeal Board.[14]

Have the security laws been used against individual newspaper editors?

There were a number of cases in the 1950s. The editors and staff of the *Guardian*, *New Age* and *Spark* were banned under the Suppression of Communism Act, as were three editors of the Liberal Party paper *Contact*, Patrick Duncan, Ann Tobias and Jill Jessop. The Cape Town weekly *Torch* editor, Joan Kay, and the founder and editor of *Africa South*, Ronald Segal, were also served with banning orders.

More recently, in October 1977, the editor of the *World*, Percy Qoboza, was detained and his paper banned on the same day. Donald Woods, editor of the *Daily Dispatch*, which had campaigned vigorously over the death in detention of Steve Biko, was banned under the Internal Security Act later that same day.

Have the security laws been used against individual journalists? Have the police acted against journalists reporting the news?

In 1977 at least 12 black journalists were detained without trial. Two were banned in 1978, one in 1980, six in 1981, and two white student journalists in 1982. Between 1973 and 1981 more than 73 black journalists were detained. In addition, the Union of Black Journalists was banned in 1977, and at least five leaders of its successor, the Media Workers' Association of South Africa, have also been banned.[15]

Towards the end of 1984 at least 14 journalists were subpoenaed to answer questions relating to unrest around the country. The subpoenas were issued in terms of Section 205 of the Criminal Procedures Act, Number 51 of 1977, which requires the person subpoenaed to answer questions before a magistrate relating to a particular incident. The penalty for refusing to answer is a maximum prison term of 12 months which may be repeated if on completion of sentence the person still refuses to answer.[16]

Among those subpoenaed were the editors of the three Cape Town newspapers, the *Cape Times*, the *Argus* and *Die Burger*, who were ordered to hand over to the police photographs of student unrest at the University of the Western Cape in September 1984. The police intention, according to one of the editors,[17] was to identify students from the photographs and prosecute them.

Journalists have also been injured by the police while reporting unrest. In August 1984 four were hurt as policemen with *sjamboks* (whips) charged a crowd outside a Johannesburg civic centre. The police said that it was 'bad luck' that journalists had been injured.[18] Several incidents of assaults on journalists were reported during the 1985–6 state of emergency. Two photographers, one of them the internationally known Peter Magubane, were shot by police, and journalists were sometimes attacked by black crowds either because they were seen to be part of the system or because their equipment was mistaken for police gear.[19] In Cape Town in September 1985 three journalists were *sjambokked* by police while the correspondent for *The Times* was injured by birdshot fired by police.[20] In October 1985 four black journalists were beaten up by soldiers in Soweto.[21] A number of other complaints of assault were made.

Have journalists been charged with offences arising from their work?

Cases in recent years include the following:

● Patrick Laurence was sentenced to 18 months' imprisonment, suspended for three years, in 1973 for attempting to publish an interview in the London *Observer* with the banned Pan-Africanist Congress leader, Robert Sobukwe.

● Since 1960 about a dozen journalists have been charged under Section 83 of the Criminal Procedure and Evidence Act, Number 56 of 1955, for refusing to disclose their sources of information. Sentences have ranged from eight days to six months for those found guilty.

● Several journalists have been found guilty of possessing banned literature. Some were jailed, including a banned *Sowetan* journalist, Joe Thloloe, who was sentenced to 18 months for having a document of the banned PAC in April 1983. He was later acquitted on appeal after serving some of the sentence on Robben Island.[22]

● Allister Sparks, a correspondent for the *Observer* and *Washington Post*, was charged for quoting a banned person in 1983. His wife and another journalist, Bernard Simon, a correspondent for the *Economist* and *Financial Times*, were charged with defeating the ends of justice. These charges were later dropped.[23]

● In late 1984 a correspondent for the *Windhoek Observer* was charged under the Official Secrets Act when she revealed that the security police were opening her mail. She had complained to the Windhoek postmaster about this; some days later she opened an envelope addressed to her and found inside a letter to the postmaster from the security police ordering him to tamper with her mail. The letter, which had apparently been sent to her inadvertently, was covered by the Official Secrets Act and she was charged. Later, however, the charges were dropped.

● In 1985 police were investigating six matters in connection with reports published in the *Eastern Province Herald* of Port Elizabeth. One of the reports stated that two men had been arrested by the security police, whereas in fact the arrests had been made by the CID. As a result of this error a charge under the Police Act was being considered, even though the report had been corrected the following day.[24]

● During the 1985–6 state of emergency and widespread unrest, a number of journalists were arrested: nine were held during an attempted march on Pollsmoor prison in Cape Town in August 1985, although charges were later dropped; the same month a three-man crew working for the American television network CBS were arrested for 'disobeying the police'; and an Agence France-Presse photographer was detained under the Internal Security Act after taking a photograph of a soldier standing guard outside the Witwatersrand Military Command in central Johannesburg.[25]

Has action been taken against newspapers and journalists in the 'independent' homelands?

Several journalists have been detained without trial in Transkei and Ciskei. In April 1980 the Transkei government banned the *Daily Dispatch*, the main newspaper selling in the area, for what it called 'false reporting' and detained two of its reporters. The ban was later lifted.

Which political parties do South Africa's newspapers support?

Afrikaans papers all support the ruling National Party, except for *Die Afrikaner*, which backs the Herstigte Nasionale Party, and *Die Patriot*, published by the Conservative Party. Many English papers favour, to a greater or lesser extent, the official opposition Progressive Federal Party. However, the *Citizen*, originally funded covertly by the government, is pro-National Party.

South Africa's press is subject to various laws. Is it restricted in any other ways?

The majority of newspapers are subject to decisions of the Media Council, which has a stringent code of conduct. Like its predecessors, the Council was set up as newspaper proprietors' preferred alternative to government-appointed statutory body. The Media Council is similar to Britain's Press Council, but has wider powers.

Some newspapers are increasingly practising self-censorship. Journalists on the *Daily Dispatch*, for example, have said that stories likely to annoy the leaders of the Ciskei and Transkei 'independent' homelands are frequently spiked by the editor.[26] In mid 1985 the *Daily Dispatch* was forced to apologize in a front-page editorial for calling Nelson Mandela and other jailed political leaders 'criminals' after a 10-week boycott of the paper called by the United Democratic Front. The UDF said the boycott had caused a 30 per cent drop in sales.[27] In 1984 the Pietersburg *Northern Review* refused to print a picture of the popular band Juluka because one of the people shown was white and another black, and they had their arms around one another's shoulders.[28]

A former Professor of Journalism at Rhodes University, Les Switzer, has said that the English press is being increasingly co-opted by the state, and that 'few editors in the past 15 years have fulfilled their editorial responsibility of ensuring adequate reporting of news which is of real importance to the total population'.[29]

The Minister of Constitutional Development and Planning, Chris Heunis, said in 1984 that a new media 'style' would be needed under the country's new constitution. This should be 'a media style that will emphasize common matters and consensus opportunities ... rather than conflict'.[30]

The *Rand Daily Mail*, known internationally as the most vocal opponent of apartheid among the South African press, was closed by its board at the end of April 1985, allegedly because its financial losses were too high for the company to bear any longer. President P. W. Botha greeted the announcement that the *Mail* would close by saying that he was glad that a new spirit of national unity was prevailing in South Africa.

Radio and Television

Who controls radio and television in South Africa?

The government controls broadcasting through the South African Broadcasting Corporation. The controlling Board consists of from five to 15 members, all appointed by the State President. It reports to the Minister of Foreign Affairs and Information.[1]

How many radio and television stations does the SABC run?

From January 1986 the SABC was due to run an English service and an Afrikaans service; a serious music station, Radio Allegro; six regional stations (similar to Radio Two); Radio Orion, a nightly music station; Radio 5, a 'youth-orientated' service; nine services in the vernacular for Africans; Radio Lotus for Indians in Natal; and an external service.

There are four television stations: TV1 in English and Afrikaans for whites; TV2 and TV3 for Africans in different languages; and TV4, a light entertainment channel intended for all races. All radio and television stations carry commercials.

Bop-TV also broadcasts from Bophuthatswana and can be received in some parts of the Witwatersrand. In May 1984 Ciskei said it would establish a television network.

In 1983 the SABC had an income of R316 million (£158 million) while in 1984 it lost R1.6 million (£800,000), forcing it into cutbacks in both radio and television services.[2]

When was television first introduced in South Africa?

Full transmission began in January 1976. In the 1950s and 1960s the government had resisted calls for the introduction of TV. One Minister of Posts and Telegraphs (then responsible for the SABC), Dr Albert Hertzog, called it a 'little bioscope' and said once: 'Friends of mine recently returned from Britain tell me that one cannot see a programme which does not show black and white living together, where they are not continually propagating a mixture of the two races.' The year after Dr Hertzog was dismissed as Minister of Posts and Telegraphs the government appointed a commission of inquiry into the desirability of introducing TV. It reported in favour in November 1970.[3]

Do SABC programmes and news bulletins give balanced coverage of current affairs?

A study made when a series of by-elections was taking place in April and May 1983 showed the following allocation of time in TV reporting of political news: National Party 79.1 per cent, Conservative Party 8, Progressive Federal Party 5.2, New Republic Party 4.9, and Herstigte Nasionale Party 2.8. In *Election Review*, a by-election round-up following the late-night news, the PFP was not mentioned once during the fortnight studied. The National Party was allotted 57 per cent of the time.[4] Only two of the 20 cabinet ministers did not appear on TV during the period under review. Cabinet ministers or deputy ministers appeared on the TV news 94 times, with one bulletin referring to 10 ministers. The Prime Minister appeared or was quoted 17 times.[5]

During the run-up to the referendum on the new constitution in November 1983 the National Party, which advocated a 'yes' vote, was given nearly 400 per cent more air-time than the PFP, which was campaigning against the constitution, and 500 per cent more than the Conservative Party, which also advised a 'no' vote. The actual referendum result corresponded remarkably closely with the broadcast coverage preceding it:[6]

	TV coverage	Voting
Yes	67%	65.95%
No	32.5%	33.53%

During the unrest of 1985, there was widespread criticism that the SABC was playing down news and that overseas television viewers were seeing more of the violence of both protestors and police than South Africans. The SABC's director-general said that the corporation was satisfied that it was not underplaying the unrest, but would not offer 'the perpetrators of violence and terrorism any opportunity to propagate their views and actions to a wider public'. It felt no need to succumb 'to the misplaced ... obligation to sensationalize or to publish and be damned'.[7]

Does the SABC censor music?

In the 1960s the SABC banned the Beatles' records from all its stations after John Lennon's remark that the group was 'more famous than Christ'. In 1985 the SABC said it would no longer play any music by Stevie Wonder because of his support for the ANC. Six months later, however, the ban was relaxed: an SABC spokesman said the corporation had made its point that it objected to 'blatant politicization of music', but his records would again be played on the air.[8]

Apart from censoring South African television coverage of unrest, has overseas TV been curtailed?

In November 1985 the government banned all filming in areas affected by the state of emergency declared in July.* The prohibition meant a news blackout of public disturbances, boycotts, assaults on people and property, and the conduct of the security forces, unless approved by the Commissioner of Police. The Foreign Correspondents Association in South Africa said the ban was 'a severe form of censorship' in 'an attempt to prevent news of South Africa's social conflict from reaching the outside world'. There was an immediate drop in overseas pictorial coverage of unrest: the South African Ambassador to Britain, Denis Worrall, said later in November that criticism in the British media had been 'toned down' and that he was 'fairly happy' with news coverage after the restrictions were imposed.[9]

*See chapters on the press and state of emergency.

Books

What kinds of books have been banned in South Africa?

All kinds: *Black Beauty* and *The Return of the Native* were once embargoed;
Tennessee Williams's *A Streetcar Named Desire*, Ernest Hemingway's
Across the River and into the Trees, John Steinbeck's *The Wayward Bus* and
Robert Graves's *I, Claudius* have all been banned. Works by South African
writers which have been prohibited include Nadine Gordimer's *Burger's
Daughter*, André Brink's *Dry White Season* and *Looking on Darkness*,
Etienne Leroux's *Magersfontein, O Magersfontein*, and a wide range of
books by black South Africans. Many political publications have also
been banned.

Under which law are books banned?

The main law involved in book banning is the Publications Act, Number
42 of 1974, as amended, but there are also a number of other Acts
under which material can be prohibited.

What are the guiding principles of the Publications Act?

The introduction says: 'In the application of this Act, the constant
endeavour of the population of the Republic of South Africa to uphold a
Christian view of life shall be recognized.' [1] According to the Act, a
publication is 'undesirable' if it or any part of it

'is indecent or obscene, or is offensive or harmful to public morals;

'is blasphemous or is offensive to the religious convictions or feelings
of any section of the inhabitants of the Republic;

'brings any section of the inhabitants of the Republic into ridicule or
contempt;

'is harmful to the relations between any sections of the inhabitants
of the Republic;

'is prejudicial to the safety of the State, the general welfare or the
peace and good order . . .' [2]

Who is responsible for banning books?

Three bodies are involved with censorship, dealing not only with books, but with any 'publication or object, film, public entertainment or intended entertainment'. The Directorate of Publications is an administrative body. It sets up a number of committees to which items are referred and which have the power to declare them 'undesirable'. A Publications Appeal Board is at the top of the structure to review censorship decisions.[3]

How many censorship committees have been established, and what is the qualification for membership?

By 1983 a total of 1,000 *ad hoc* committees had been set up,[4] mainly in the two largest cities of Johannesburg and Cape Town. Committees consist of at least three members, selected from a list compiled every three years by the Minister of Home Affairs. They must be, 'in the opinion of the minister', through 'educational qualifications and knowledge fit to perform the functions entrusted to the committees under the Act'.[5]

How do committees go about deciding whether books are 'undesirable'? Do they give reasons for their decisions?

No evidence is heard by the committees, which simply read books submitted and decide whether they should be banned. Committees must furnish reasons to the Directorate of Publications for their decisions. The Directorate informs interested parties, on request, of the reasons.[6]

When a committee is considering a ban, can the public object?

No. The Act as amended in 1977 makes it an offence to 'prejudice, influence, or anticipate' a decision of the Directorate or a committee.[7]

What exactly are the committees' powers in terms of banning publications?

In most cases a committee's ban means that a publication may not be imported or distributed.[8] However, they can also ban the importation of all works from a specific publisher or dealing with a particular topic. In addition they can ban *possession* of an 'undesirable' publication or object, but such decisions must be confirmed by the Publications Appeal Board. A ban on a periodical may include all subsequent issues – *Playboy*, for example, is banned in this way.

How does the Publications Appeal Board review committee decisions?

Anybody financially affected by a decision, the person who originally referred the item, the Directorate of Publications or the Minister of Home Affairs can ask the Appeal Board to review a decision, whether a committee has banned a publication or passed it.[9] The Board can appoint a committee of experts to advise it and other experts can be consulted. In 1982, for example, advice was sought from an unnamed African leader, theologians, and an authority on explosives. Another committee of three political scientists has been established to advise the Board about how not to hamper research on 'communism' and similar ideologies.[10]

Do people appealing against a ban appear before the Board?

They have the right to appear before the Board or to be legally represented. They can question witnesses directed to appear by the Board, but can bring forward evidence only with the Board's consent. The Board must give full reasons for confirming or setting aside a committee's decision.[11]

Can the Appeal Board's decisions be challenged in the courts?

The original Act said that a decision by a committee, the Directorate or the Board could not be subject to an appeal to a court. This was challenged in 1979 and the Appellate Division did allow a person found guilty of producing an 'undesirable' publication the right to discover the reasons for the banning and to produce counter-reasons. The Publications Amendment Act, Number 44 of 1979, negated this judgement. Anything found 'undesirable' by a committee would therefore be 'undesirable' by legal definition, and a person later prosecuted for having produced the offending item would not be able to question in court the validity of the committee's decision.

There is, however, some limited access to a special division of the Supreme Court. But there is no right of further appeal on questions of law to the Appellate Division.[12]

Has there been criticism of the appeals system?

It has been pointed out that, while anybody can complain about a publication, only a limited number of people can lodge an appeal: the person who originally complained, the Directorate of Publications itself, the Minister of Home Affairs, and anyone who has 'a direct financial interest' in the publication. This, it is said, reduces the number of appeals in political cases, as many producers of political literature do not have a 'direct financial interest' in it.[13]

Who proposes items for banning?

Members of the public or customs officers can ask the Directorate of Publications to arrange for a committee to examine any 'publication or object'. The Directorate itself can also submit anything it thinks 'undesirable'.[14] Professor André du Toit of the Department of Political Philosophy at the University of Stellenbosch reported in March 1983 that less than 6 per cent of items were submitted by the public. More than 80 per cent of them came from the police and customs officials.[15]

This was confirmed in a recent study by Gilbert Marcus of the University of the Witwatersrand. He found that between 1976 and 1982 police and customs officials submitted from 78 to 84 per cent of all publications and objects each year.[16] In 1982–3 members of the public submitted 78 of the 1,808 publications, publishers 113 and the Directorate itself 88.[17]

What kind of material is submitted for banning?

According to Professor Du Toit, nearly 50 per cent is political material. Using official statistics, he found that pornography made up 2.9 per cent of items submitted, light reading matter 16.5 per cent, works with 'possible literary merit' 4.9 per cent, and political material 49.3 per cent (having increased from 25.1 per cent between 1975 and 1979).[18]

The trend to refer 'political' publications may be increasing. In 1982–3 a total of 1,070 out of 1,808 publications – just under 60 per cent – were submitted to committees for being 'possibly prejudicial to the security of the state', according to the Department of Internal Affairs.[19]

How many of the items submitted for banning actually end up banned?

In 1982–3 a total of 931 items, just over half of those submitted, were declared 'undesirable', while 859 were passed.[20] The proportion of items banned has stayed at roughly 50 to 55 per cent since 1980. A former editor of the *Rand Daily Mail*, Ray Louw, has estimated that 30,000 publications were banned from the introduction of censorship up to the end of 1983.

What kinds of political publications have been banned?

As well as books, a large amount of other printed material dealing with political topics has been banned. Pamphlets and booklets about the role of the uniformed police and the Special Branch were declared 'undesirable', while a booklet giving legal advice to detainees was banned because it advised them to commit perjury rather than refuse to testify in political trials.[21] A report on Namibia by the Southern African Bishops' Conference, alleging misconduct by Defence Force members, was banned in 1983.[22] A pamphlet containing an interview with a conscientious objector was declared undesirable because, the Appeal Board said, it created distrust in South Africa's war effort in Namibia and because it 'sides with the enemy'.[23] Four other publications on conscientious objection have also been banned.[24]

The Freedom Charter, drawn up by the ANC and other organizations in 1955, has caused censorship problems: although the Board said that the Charter was 'not necessarily undesirable', censorship committees have banned publications solely because they quoted or reproduced the document.[25]

Possession of certain books can also be illegal in terms of the Internal Security Act, Number 74 of 1982, although the books do not necessarily have to be banned under the Publications Act. In 1984 a Soweto woman was found guilty of possessing *Island in Chains* by Indres Naidoo (a former Robben Island political prisoner) and Albie Sachs (a South African exile), published by Penguin Books in 1982. The ISA says that publications 'published or disseminated by, on behalf of, or under the direction or guidance of an unlawful organization' cannot be legally possessed. The Soweto woman was sentenced to 18 months in jail, 12 months of which were suspended, after the magistrate found that *Island in Chains* had been published 'in the interests' of the banned African National Congress, which was the same as 'on behalf of' it. The whole sentence was suspended on appeal.[26]

Are publications banned indefinitely, or can bans be reviewed?

Members of the public or the Directorate of Publications itself can apply for a review two years after the original ban. Appeals against these new decisions can be made to the Board in the usual way.[27]

Can publications be subject to controls short of outright banning?

A 1978 amendment to the Publications Act allowed the Appeal Board to 'impose such conditions as it might see fit' on the presentation or distribution of publications. This can be done by controlling the selling, hiring or lending of a publication – for instance, access to it may be restricted to people of specified age groups. The Board can also prohibit a publication from being displayed in public, or control the way it is displayed.[28]

The covers of books can be banned as 'undesirable'. One recent case involved a novel by Wessel Ebersohn, *Store Up the Anger*, which is loosely based on the death in detention of Steve Biko. The offending dustjacket showed a picture of a black man reflected in a pair of sunglasses worn by a white man.[29] Coincidentally or not, one of the security policemen called to testify at Mr Biko's inquest always appeared in dark glasses. Universities, research bodies and some individuals have access to banned publications by permit from the Directorate of Publications.[30]

Have any books been 'unbanned'?

Leroux's *Magersfontein, O Magersfontein* was unbanned by the Appeal Board as a result, said André Brink, of 'the near-unanimous revolt of the Afrikaner literary establishment'. *Burger's Daughter* by Nadine Gordimer, which was banned in the second half of 1979, was unbanned three months later, after the lifting of the prohibition on Brink's *Dry White Season*. These two works were judged to be so badly written that they would not offend anyone. (Conversely, the ban on *Looking on Darkness* was upheld because a committee of literary experts found it 'wholly devoid of literary merit'.[31]) The longstanding ban on *Lady Chatterley's Lover* was eventually reversed, and in January 1983 the Appeal Board lifted the ban imposed the year before on Athol Fugard's play *Master Harold and the Boys*.

Some non-fiction political books have also been unbanned. In December 1984 books written by the presidents of Mozambique, Zambia and Tanzania were allowed to be read by South Africans: President Samora Machel's *Mozambique: Revolution or Reaction*, banned in 1977; President Kenneth Kaunda's *Zambia Shall Be Free*, and a jointly written book, *Africa's Freedom*, whose co-authors include President Kaunda and the President of Tanzania, Julius Nyerere, and which had been banned in 1964.[32]

Is censorship becoming more liberal?

A number of writers and observers think so. André Brink, for one, attributes part of the change to the replacement of former Judge Snyman as Chairman of the Appeal Board in 1979. Brink also cites the revolt of the Afrikaner literary establishment over the ban on *Magersfontein*, and the threat of *zamizdat* publication by some writers, himself included: 3,000 copies of his *Dry White Season* were distributed before the Directorate of Publications discovered its existence and banned it.[33]

At least one National Party MP, Hendrick Coetzer, has appealed for 'more maturity' over censorship and for less attention to be paid to 'the immature and illiterate and sanctimonious elements among us'. The new Chairman of the Appeal Board, Professor J. C. van Rooyen, has also said that the criterion of the 'likely reader' is becoming more important in deciding whether books should be banned. This seems to have led to the unbanning after 14 years of Jonty Driver's *Elegy for a Revolutionary* and the lifting of the embargo on J. M. Coetzee's Booker Prize-winning *Life and Times of Michael K*.

Film and Theatre

What kinds of films and plays have been banned in South Africa?

The films *A Taste of Honey*, *Lolita*, *1900*, Fellini's *Satyricon*, *A Clockwork Orange* and *Streamers*, Athol Fugard's play *Master Harold and the Boys* and hundreds of others considered to deal too explicitly with sex, violence and politics.

Under which law are films and plays banned?

The Publications Act, which covers any 'publication or object, film, public entertainment or intended entertainment'. 'Film' is defined to include film cassette, tape cassette and videotape. Films made or imported by the South African Broadcasting Corporation – the state-controlled organization that runs radio and television – and all government departments are exempt from the Act.[1]

How is censorship of films and plays carried out?

Film and theatre censorship works in basically the same way as for publications. The same bureaucracy – the Directorate of Publications, *ad hoc* committees set up by the Directorate, and the Publications Appeal Board – decides what can be shown in South Africa. However, unlike publications, *all* films 'intended to be exhibited in public' must be seen and passed by a committee.[2] Plays and other 'public entertainments' may be staged without prior permission, but at any point a complaint can be made to a committee, which must then decide whether to give or withhold approval. Thus a play can be banned before going into production, simply on the basis of the script.

Are films shown in private exempt from censorship?

Not if the film was originally 'intended to be exhibited in public'. Amateur films, slides and tape recordings can be made and screened without approval in private, but need permission for showing in public, even in members-only clubs.

Can films and plays be censored or restricted although not banned outright?

Cuts can be ordered in films before they are approved. Age restrictions for audiences can also be imposed. Both cuts and age restrictions are made frequently.[3] *Streamers*, for example, was first banned and later passed for viewing by people below the age of two and over the age of 21.[4] South Africa's first home-produced striptease video, *Dreamwife*, was banned in 1984 but released a year later with two cuts and restricted to viewers of under two or over 18.[5]

Before plays are approved, the likely audience is considered. Thus an experimental theatre like the Market in the centre of 'white' Johannesburg has been allowed to present 'political' plays which may not be performed in the African townships.[6]

In 1985 there were strong protests from the right wing about a production of Strindberg's *Miss Julie*, in which the African actor John Kani appeared with a white actress, Sandra Prinsloo. Complaints, particularly about a love scene, were made to the Minister of Home Affairs and the Appeal Board, which ruled that only people over 16 could see the play. Approval had to be sought from the Board if the production was to move from the Baxter Theatre in 'white' Cape Town.[7]

Are many films banned?

In 1982–3 a total of 121 films were banned, 659 approved conditionally (age restrictions, cuts or both) and 609 passed without conditions. Of the 79 films taken on appeal, 26 were rejected, 48 approved with conditions and five without conditions.[8] A video series of *Roots*, based on the book by Alex Haley, was banned in 1984 as harmful to race relations and likely to be 'an encouragement to violence'.[9]

In late 1984 security police in Johannesburg seized 33 video cassettes belonging to Britain's Independent Television News. The cassettes included footage of rioting in black townships. protests and meetings against apartheid, and coverage of the funeral in December 1982 of some of the 42 people killed in a South African commando reprisal raid against alleged ANC guerrillas in Lesotho.[10]

Are many 'public entertainments' banned?

In 1982-3 nine were examined, of which four were approved unconditionally and five conditionally.[11]

In 1982 Athol Fugard's play *Master Harold and the Boys* was banned because of 'excessive crude language'. However, in January the following year the Appeal Board lifted the ban, saying that the 'crude language' was 'contextually justified' and that the play spoke 'eloquently about black–white relations and perhaps more aptly about a master–servant relationship in South Africa'.[12] Production of Fugard's *Sizwe Bansi is Dead* (about the pass laws) and *The Island* (about Robben Island) has also been prohibited at various times.

Are theatre and film posters subject to censorship?

Changes have been ordered in a number of cases. In the 1950s and 1960s, for example, posters for *The King and I* were altered to show Deborah Kerr in the arms of a shadow. The original showed her being embraced by Yul Brynner playing the King of Siam: Siamese are Asians and the poster was thus thought to be contravening the Immorality Act. The poster for the film *Oceans II* was changed to eliminate the black Sammy Davis Jnr, shown walking with two white actors.

Have playwrights been subject to other sanctions besides censorship of their work?

In June 1982 the Reverend Mzwandile Maqina of Port Elizabeth, author of *Give Us This Day*, *Trial* and *Dry Those Tears*, was banned under the Internal Security Act. Thus none of his plays could be performed. A number of other black playwrights have been dealt with in the same way.

The 'Poet Laureate of Soweto', Ingoapele Madingoane, whose dramatic readings of poems have been performed in township community halls, was arrested in January 1984 and his material confiscated. He was charged with 'possession of undesirable publications'.[13]

The two internationally acclaimed actors John Kani and Winston Ntshona were detained without trial in Transkei in the mid 1970s while performing two Athol Fugard plays, *Sizwe Bansi is Dead* and *The Island*, and were forbidden to put on the plays in the territory.

Is film and theatre censorship becoming more liberal in South Africa?

As with publications, there has been some liberalization in recent years. In 1983 a number of bans were set aside, notably those on Fugard's play *Master Harold and the Boys* and on a series of films (shown earlier on British television) based on short stories by Nadine Gordimer.[14] *Under Fire*, a film about the Sandinista revolution in Nicaragua, was also unbanned, even though a censorship committee had warned that it 'could sow seeds of revolution where fertile ground existed among blacks who felt that they were victims of an unjust and oppressive regime'.[15]

Besides books, films and public entertainments, the censorship laws refer to 'objects'. What objects have been banned?

T-shirts with the slogan 'Halt All Apartheid Tours' were banned in February 1983, when an unofficial West Indies cricket team was touring South Africa.[16] Clothing in the colours of the ANC has been considered illegal. T-shirts and posters commemorating the death in detention of Steve Biko have been proscribed, as has a T-shirt with the slogan 'Free Mandela', despite a Publications Appeal Board decision that a call for the release of the jailed ANC leader was not in itself a reason for finding something 'undesirable'.[17] A pocket badge and a T-shirt bearing a clenched-fist motif were banned in 1985.[18]

A number of records, including one by the South African-born singer Miriam Makeba, have also been prohibited.

State of Emergency

A state of emergency was introduced in some parts of South Africa in July 1985. What did the emergency regulations say?

Among the offences promulgated were:

Verbally threatening harm to another person or preparing, printing, publishing or possessing a threatening document;

Failing to comply with any order or direction issued under the regulations;

Hindering any officer in the performance of his duties;

Destroying or defacing any emergency regulations;

Disclosing the name or identity of anybody arrested under the emergency regulations before the name has been officially confirmed;

Making statements calculated to subvert the government or legislature;

Inciting people to resist or oppose the government and causing fear, panic or alarm or weakening public confidence;

Advising or inciting people to stay away from work or to dislocate industry.[1]

What were the penalties for contravening the regulations?

A prison sentence of up to 10 years and/or a fine of R20,000 (£10,000).[2]

What powers did the security forces have?

Among other powers they could:

Search people, premises and vehicles, and seize any article that could be used in a crime;

Seal off any area to control entrance and departure;

Control traffic;

Close off any public or private place, including businesses;

Remove any person from a particular place if needed to preserve public order;

Control all essential services and all installations related to these services;

Order curfews during which people might be on the streets;

Control, regulate or prohibit the distribution of news or comment on the emergency regulations or the conduct of any security officer in terms of the regulations.[3] *

Was there any redress against abuse of these powers by the security forces?

The regulations said that no civil or criminal proceedings could be brought against the state, the State President, Cabinet minister, anybody in the service of the state or 'any person acting by direction or with the approval of' a state official dealing with the emergency, the safety of the public or the maintenance of public order. This meant that no person could apply to the courts for an interdict to set aside any emergency regulation. Nor could any person who was assaulted, robbed or tortured in detention bring a case against any officer acting under the emergency powers.[4]

In how many areas was the emergency declared? How many people were affected?

The original emergency decrees affected 36 districts, including Johannesburg and Soweto, the mining towns of the East Witwatersrand, Port Elizabeth and other towns in the Eastern Cape where there had been unrest for some time.[5] In late October the emergency was lifted in six districts but, less than a week later, it was extended to Cape Town and seven surrounding districts in the Western Cape and Boland. At this stage it was estimated that more than nine million people – about a third of the population – were living under a state of emergency. This included the 'independent' homeland of Transkei, whose 26 magisterial districts have been under a state of emergency since 1960 apart from a brief period around 'independence' in October 1976.[6]

In December 1985 the emergency was lifted in eight areas, several of them small towns where there had been little unrest. The State President, P. W. Botha, said that 'the revolutionary climate . . . is fast losing momentum'.[7]

How did the 1985–6 emergency regulations differ from previous ones?

The last emergency in South Africa was in 1960, a week after Sharpeville; there have also been emergencies in Transkei (see above), Ciskei,

*See chapter on the press.

Bophuthatswana, Venda and QwaQwa. Some emergency decrees have been incorporated into the ordinary law of the land of South Africa and the homelands. The 1985–6 emergency differs from the 1960 in these respects:

● *1960:* The power to detain was given to the Minister of Justice, magistrates and commissioned officers above the rank of lieutenant – a fairly senior position.

● *1985: Any* member of the police, army, railway police and prisons department could order detention.

● *1960:* The Minister of Justice could direct any organization to discontinue functioning during the emergency.

● *1985:* Legislation passed since 1960 allows for organizations to be banned without the need for an emergency to be proclaimed.*

● *1960:* The Minister of Justice was given the power to prohibit meetings.

● *1985:* Laws passed since 1960 allow for meetings to be banned and gatherings to be dispersed without the need for a state of emergency to be proclaimed.[8] †

Did the state of emergency have the desired result of ending unrest?

The South African Institute of Race Relations said in December 1985 that 992 people had been killed since August 1984, of whom 483 had died since the state of emergency was declared[9]; by the end of the year the death toll was more than 1,000.

Across the country the death rate in political violence (including accidental deaths and unknown causes) more than doubled: 1.66 average deaths a day before the emergency was declared to 3.41 after the proclamation.[10] But in the Port Elizabeth–Uitenhage area the rate had been cut from an average of 0.56 deaths to 0.17 after the emergency was declared, while on the East Witwatersrand the rate was down from 0.47 to 0.17.[11] In early November 1985 the government ordered new curbs on the press ‡ which meant that death records were drawn largely from official police reports which journalists could not verify independently: from the introduction of the curbs the death rate was said to have gone down from 3.41 to 1.5 a day.[12]

Unrest reports were still being issued every day five months after the emergency was declared. The commander of the police counter-insurgency unit was reported in November 1985 to have said: 'The

* See chapter on unlawful organizations.
† See chapter on banned gatherings.
‡ See chapter on the press.

campaign has spread to country towns . . . Incidents of rebellion in many townships are the first in their existence . . . The objective is to create . . . liberated areas in the black townships, from where the terrifying war can be spread to the cities and white suburbs, to bring about the downfall of the government.'[13]

By the end of October 1985 unrest over the previous year had resulted in damage of at least R100 million (£50 million).[14]

Was there unrest outside the areas declared to be emergency zones?

In August 1985 there was an outbreak of rioting in African and Indian townships around Durban in which at least 70 people died. After attacks by Africans on Indian areas, and at least one attack in revenge by Indians on Africans, followers of Chief Gatsha Buthelezi sent out vigilante patrols: police reported finding 17 severely mutilated bodies, arousing speculation of attacks on young Africans by Buthelezi supporters.[15] An opinion poll in September 1985 showed that 56 per cent of Africans questioned blamed police instigators and 20 per cent Buthelezi supporters for starting the trouble.[16]

In addition, eight areas in Cape Town and the Boland, which had not been affected by the July emergency proclamation, had to be declared emergency zones on 26 October 1985 after serious rioting broke out, in which at least 30 people were killed.[17] Unrest and deaths were also reported from a number of other areas, notably East London, where no emergency had been declared.

Was the unrest aimed mainly at whites? Were many whites killed?

Much of the unrest was aimed at symbols of what is often called 'the system' – white authority – and at blacks regarded as collaborators. By the beginning of November 1985 the police said about 1,920 private homes and the homes of 460 black policemen had been destroyed; 615 schools damaged; at least 3,300 buses destroyed by fire; 3,140 private vehicles and 1,600 police vehicles set alight; 525 shops and factories, 180 development corporation buildings, 25 churches, 15 clinics and 75 off-licences destroyed. Also by November 1985 232 blacks had been killed by rioters, as were 15 members of the security forces, 14 policemen, one soldier and 10 development corporation officials. By December 1985 a total of 29 policemen had been killed.[18]

Several homes belonging to black MPs were attacked, among them the one Indian minister in the Cabinet, Amichand Rajbansi, and a KwaZulu MP, Francis Dlamini, who was shot dead.[19]

A number of blacks were reported to have been killed in fighting between supporters of the United Democratic Front and Black Consciousness organizations, notably AZAPO.[20] Black criminals are also said to have molested people in the name of the 'liberation struggle', some demanding protection money from householders after claiming to be members of the banned COSAS movement.[21]

No whites were reported to have been killed in emergency areas, although at least three had died since the unrest began in September 1984.[22]

The emergency regulations allowed for detention without trial. What did the regulations say?

While under the Internal Security Act, Number 74 of 1982, detentions had to be ordered by a commissioned police officer, the emergency regulations allowed 'any policeman, soldier, railway policeman or prison officer of any rank' to arrest 'without warrant any person to keep law and order'.[23] Detention was limited to 14 days unless extended by the Minister of Law and Order.

While in detention, people were forbidden to sing or whistle, make unnecessary noise, cause unnecessary trouble or be a nuisance. Anybody committing these offences could be sentenced by any prison officer to solitary confinement, deprivation of one or more meals a day and, if the detainee was a boy under the age of 14, six strokes.[24]

Detainees were allowed to read only the Bible or 'another holy book of religion'. They were not allowed to study or receive food and tobacco. They were, however, entitled to 'exercise in the open air for at least one hour a day, weather permitting'.[25]

In August 1985 some regulations were slightly relaxed: detainees would be allowed reading matter other than the Bible, provided they had permission to study, and could have outside medical attention, provided they had permission from the official medical officer.[26]

What is known about conditions for detainees?

In August 1985 the regulations were amended to allow people to be held 'at any place outside a prison'. It was thought that this may have become necessary because of overcrowding in existing prisons.[27] The Department of Prisons, saying that its jails were 36 per cent overcrowded before the influx of detainees, coped by transferring prisoners to less crowded institutions and using 'stacked beds' or bunks. 'A high standard of health and hygiene is maintained,' a spokesman said.[28]

One detainee who was held for 101 days said that she was questioned for only 30 minutes in that entire period and left, like others, for 23 hours each day in a single-person cell.[29]

In October 1985, after two detainees brought an urgent application to the Rand Supreme Court, regulations were changed to allow detainees to buy food from prison shops and to receive selected reading material.[30]

In November 1985 a number of detainees went on hunger strike in protest at being held for more than 14 days, the initial detention period allowed under the emergency regulations. A few days after news of the hunger strike came out, the prisons department said that it would not release any further detailed information about it because it was not in the interests of 'the administration of discipline and good order in prisons'.[31]

How many people were detained under the state of emergency?

From the declaration of the state of emergency to 28 November 1985 a total of 7,006 people had been detained. Of these, 5,777 had been released and 1,229 were still detained.[32] A police spokesman said in September 1985 – a year after unrest broke out – that more than 14,000 people had been arrested before the state of emergency was declared.[33] The same month figures compiled by the Detainees Parents' Support Committee showed that 45 out of 80 office-bearers of the United Democratic Front – 56 per cent – were out of action because of death, trials or detention.[34]

Were there allegations that emergency detainees were tortured?

A number of allegations were made, both in courts and outside. Among them were:

● A Port Elizabeth district surgeon, Dr Wendy Orr, brought an urgent application in September 1985 to the Supreme Court alleging 'systematic' assault and abuse of emergency detainees. In 153 cases injuries to detainees could not have been inflicted lawfully. In 60 cases detainees had facial injuries, eight had perforated eardrums, 26 had weals and blisters consistent with quirt blows on 'unusual' parts of their bodies and four were not injured on admission but were later found to have injuries consistent with assault. The court granted an urgent interdict restraining the police from assaulting detainees.[35]

● The Detainees Parents' Support Committee said in October 1985 that detainees were sexually harassed, physically abused, assaulted, given electric shocks to the genital areas, held in solitary confinement, denied visits by relatives and threatened with death.[36]

● An African woman told journalists that while in detention she had been hit repeatedly with a telephone directory, had her head covered with a canvas bag and been given electric shocks.[37]

● Amnesty International said in August 1985 that detainees had been hooded, beaten, partially suffocated and given electric shocks. Others had been threatened with summary execution with guns held against their foreheads. There were also charges that the 'helicopter torture' was being used: this involves handcuffing the victim by the wrists and ankles, hanging him upside down on a pole placed behind the knees, spinning him around and beating him.[38]

● Two Progressive Federal Party MPs said in November 1985 that during a visit to emergency detainees in two Witwatersrand prisons 11 of 14 young people claimed they had been assaulted.[39]

Have there been allegations of brutality by the security forces in curbing unrest?

A number of allegations have been made, among them:

● A 70-year-old Cradock woman said in an affadavit presented to the State President, P. W. Botha, that she had been raped by two white soldiers. In another, a woman said she had been *sjambokked* while in bed with flu and that her daughter, who was eight and a half months pregnant, was whipped across the stomach when she tried to intervene. Another woman from Graaff-Reinet said her 20-year-old son was shot while entering a neighbour's house, having been told earlier by police: 'Botha has said we can kill you like flies.'[40]

● Three people, two of them boys aged 12 and 16, were killed in the Coloured township of Athlone, near Cape Town, in October 1985 in what was described as a 'Trojan Horse' police ambush. A lorry carrying armed police hidden in wooden boxes twice drove past a barricade, inviting stone-throwers to attack it. When, on the second occasion, stones were thrown, police emerged from the boxes and opened fire with shotguns, killing three. The Progressive Federal Party said that it had been told of other occasions when police used unmarked vehicles.[41]

● In scenes shown around the world on television, police armed with whips dispersed demonstrators at the University of Cape Town and thousands of others in Athlone who were trying to march on Pollsmoor prison, where Nelson Mandela was being held.[42]

● Thirteen people were killed in November 1985 in Mamelodi, near Pretoria, amid allegations that police had fired tear-gas canisters from a helicopter, had assaulted innocent people and had not given a warning before opening fire on a crowd.[43]

An opinion poll of Africans on the Witwatersrand in October 1985 said that 90 per cent of those polled were opposed to the military presence in the townships and 89 per cent felt threatened by it. Of those polled, 77 per cent said they felt threatened by the police. A month earlier another poll found that 70 per cent opposed police handling of the unrest and 61 per cent believed the police were against all blacks, whether involved in disturbances or not.[44]

What has been the government reaction to allegations of brutality in detention centres and townships?

In September 1985 the army announced that an office would be set up to handle complaints of military 'excesses' in support of police.[45] It was later reported that few complaints were received because of fears of victimization if people did complain. The Minister of Law and Order said in October 1985 that assaults on detainees were 'inexcusable'.[46] In December 1985 the head of the police counter-insurgency unit, Major-General Burt Wandrag, said that rioters were often accompanied by their legal advisers and photographers in attempts to formulate complaints against the police. The riots were 'skilfully planned in advance' and the tendency 'is now for women, many of them pregnant, and children to form the front line of rioters. Should they become casualties, the fact is exploited by the domestic and foreign news media to the advantage of the rioters.'[47] All security force members had been indemnified against court action when the emergency was first proclaimed. In November 1985 the indemnity was extended to security forces throughout the country – not just those in emergency districts.[48]

The police said children formed the front line of rioters. Were many children affected by the unrest?

Many youngsters were arrested by police. Among others, there were: 745 in Soweto early in the emergency;[49] 40, the youngest aged 10, in a Worcester, Western Cape, township in November 1985;[50] and a 12-year-old detained at 2 a.m. from his Soweto home in October 1985.[51] The exact total of detained children is not known; nor is the number of children killed in the unrest.

The unrest was accompanied by widespread school boycotts. In some areas regulations were promulgated to say that no pupil could be outside a classroom on any school day from 8 a.m. to 2 p.m. without written permission, while people who were not pupils or did not work at schools were not allowed to be in the immediate vicinity of educational buildings.[52] The Soweto police chief said in August 1985 that all children found on the streets during school hours would be arrested, regardless of age. If they were not registered at school, 'it will be up to their parents to prove it,' he said.[53]

Concern was expressed at the effects of unrest and detention on children. A conference in Johannesburg organized by Concerned Social Workers highlighted some abuses: children at a pre-school centre in Soweto had been tear-gassed; a four-year-old was killed by a police rubber bullet while playing in her yard; children as young as six were being kept in detention; and young children were being left alone after their parents had been arrested.[54]

Nearly 1,000 people had died in the unrest by mid December 1985. Were funerals affected by emergency regulations?

A number of restrictions were imposed on black funerals in emergency areas at the end of July 1985. Open-air services were banned, only one person could be buried at a time, only ordained ministers could speak during the service and they were not allowed to 'defend, attack, criticize, propagate or discuss any form of government, any principle or policy of a government' or the state of emergency or the actions of the security forces. Mourners were not allowed to travel in a vehicle and had to follow a route designated by the police. Loudspeakers, banners and flags were banned at funerals.[55] The curb on funerals came 10 days after the funeral of four UDF leaders in Cradock, killed in mysterious circumstances near Port Elizabeth, at which flags of the banned South African Communist Party were displayed.[56] In a number of cases after the funeral curbs were introduced, the prohibitions were reported to have been ignored.

Did unrest in South Africa also extend to the 'independent' homelands?

A number of incidents were reported, particularly in Transkei and Ciskei. In Transkei a night curfew was imposed two days after South Africa's state of emergency was proclaimed; a sweeping ban was put on the funeral of a Transkeian who died in South Africa; and a number of people were detained under security laws: one estimate put the figure as high as 1,000.[57] A curfew was also imposed in Zwelitsha in Ciskei; three pupils were drowned in a river while trying to escape after being dispersed from a school and assaulted by Ciskeian police; and curbs were put on funerals.[58] A number of detentions and deaths of Ciskeian citizens were also reported. In Lebowa a student leader died after being beaten by the homeland police.[59] Bophuthatswana's president called an emergency session of Parliament to give him greater control over educational institutions: he could close any of them and bar any student 'in the public interest'.[60]

Blacks also boycotted white-owned shops in protests during the emergency. How effective were they?

In Port Elizabeth, among the first cities to be affected by a boycott, turnover went down by between 30 and 100 per cent in some businesses in the city's predominantly black shopping area.[61] A number of businesses were reported to have closed permanently. In East London and Queenstown the Manpower Department gave shopkeepers and restaurateurs blanket exemption to allow short-time work, permitting working hours and wages to be reduced by up to 80 per cent, as boycotts took effect.[62] Other boycotts had similar effects in a number of other towns and cities.

Did the state of emergency end the process of reform promised by the government?

A number of changes were promised in the months after the emergency was proclaimed in July 1985. They included restoring South African citizenship to Africans previously deemed nationals of the 'independent' homelands, the phasing out of the pass laws, freehold rights for Africans, Africans to be represented on the President's Council and some relaxation of social segregation.*

On the other hand, the state of emergency aroused widespread international criticism. France recalled its ambassador, banned any new French investment in South Africa and led a call in the United Nations Security Council for mandatory sanctions against South Africa. The resolution was vetoed by the United States and Britain. A resolution calling for voluntary sanctions was adopted, with the USA and Britain abstaining.

Later in the year the Commonwealth Conference in Bermuda adopted a tougher line on South Africa, with Britain virtually alone in resisting calls for sanctions.

*See chapters on the homelands, pass laws, housing, national government and social segregation.

South Africa responded to this international pressure by making contingency plans to repatriate 1.5 million foreign workers if sanctions were imposed.

International concern was also felt at South Africa having to postpone repayment of some of its international debts: at first until the end of 1985, then until March 1986, while one report said that Pretoria was trying to get debts rescheduled until 1990.[63]

A study by the University of Cape Town's Institute of Criminology in late 1985 said that the government's reform process and use of security laws, including the state of emergency, were linked. 'Highly repressive state measures, with detention as a central device, constitute part of the reform package and should not be understood as a hangover from earlier authoritarian periods,' it said. 'The purpose remains, as before, entirely political; detention without trial is a method aimed at destroying internal political opposition.'[64]

Bibliography and Sources

Abbreviations used in the references are shown in parentheses.

Books and Pamphlets

Brink, André, *Mapmakers*, Faber & Faber, London, 1983

Davenport, T. R. H., *South Africa: A Modern History*, 2nd edn, Macmillan, London, 1978

De Klerk, W. A., *The Puritans in Africa*, Penguin, Harmondsworth, 1976

Desmond, Cosmas, *The Discarded People*, Penguin, Harmondsworth, 1971

Dugard, John, *The Denationalization of Black South Africans in Pursuance of Apartheid*, Centre for Applied Legal Studies Occasional Papers 8, University of the Witwatersrand, Johannesburg, 1984

Horrell, Muriel, *Laws Affecting Race Relations in South Africa 1948–1976*, South African Institute of Race Relations, Johannesburg, 1978 (*Laws 1948–76*)

Horrel, Muriel, *Race Relations as Regulated by Law in South Africa 1948–1979*, South African Institute of Race Relations, Johannesburg, 1982 (*Laws 1948–79*)

Laws 1948–76, see Horrell

Laws 1948–79, see Horrell

Lewin, Julius, *Politics and Law in South Africa*, Merlin Press, London, 1963

Marquard, Leo, *The Peoples and Policies of South Africa*, 3rd edn, OUP, London, 1962

National Union of South African Students, *The Ciskei*, Cape Town, 1983

South Africa 1983 and *1985*, Official Yearbook of the Republic of South Africa, Chris van Rensburg Publications, Johannesburg, 1983 (*Yearbook 1983* or 1985)

South African Review, vol. II, Ravan Press, Johannesburg, 1984

Streek, Barry, and Richard Wicksteed, *Render Unto Kaiser: A Transkei Dossier*, Ravan Press, Johannesburg, 1981

Stuart, Kelsey, *The Newspaperman's Guide to the Law*, 2nd edn, Butterworth, Durban, 1977

Survey of Race Relations in South Africa, South African Institute of Race Relations, Johannesburg (*Survey*, various editions)

Total War in South Africa, Allies Press [London, 1984]

Walker, Eric, *A History of Southern Africa*, 3rd edn, Longman, London, 1962

Walshe, Peter, *Church versus State in South Africa*, C. Hurst & Co., London, 1983

Yearbook 1983, see *South Africa 1983*

Newspapers, News Agencies, Magazines, Journals and Radio Stations

Agence France-Presse, Paris (AFP)

Argus, the, Cape Town

Associated Press (AP)

Beeld, Johannesburg

Business Day, Johannesburg
Cape Times, Cape Town (*CT*)
Capital Radio, Umtata
Citizen, the, Johannesburg
City Press, Johannesburg
Daily Dispatch, East London (*DD*)
Daily Express, London
Daily Telegraph, London
Deurbraak, Cape Town
Die Burger, Cape Town (*Burger*)
Eastern Province Herald, Port Elizabeth (*EPH*)
Economist, the, London
Fair Lady, Cape Town
Finance Week, Johannesburg
Financial Mail, Johannesburg (*FM*)
Financial Times, London (*FT*)
Guardian, the, London
Index on Censorship, London
International Herald Tribune, Paris (*IHT*)
Journalist, Southern African Society of Journalists, Johannesburg
Lawyers for Human Rights *Bulletin*, Johannesburg
Natal Mercury, Durban (*Mercury*)
Natal Witness, Pietermaritzburg (*Witness*)
Observer, the, London
Pace, Johannesburg
Pretoria News, Pretoria
Rand Daily Mail, Johannesburg (*RDM*)
Resister, London
Reuter
SASPU Focus, South African Student Press Union, Cape Town
South African Digest, Pretoria (*SAD*)
South African Hansard, House of Assembly, Cape Town (*SA Hansard*)
South African Law Journal, Pretoria
South African Newsletter, London
South African Press Association (*SAPA*)
South African Radio, Johannesburg (*SA Radio*)
Sowetan, the, Johannesburg
Star, the, Johannesburg
Sunday Express, Johannesburg (*Express*)
Sunday Star, the, Johannesburg
Sunday Telegraph, London
Sunday Times, Johannesburg (*ST*)
Sunday Times, London
Sunday Tribune, Durban (*Tribune*)
The Times, London (*Times*)
Washington Post, Washington, DC (*WP*)
Weekly Mail, Johannesburg (*WM*)
West Africa, London

References

Introduction

1. T. R. H. Davenport, *South Africa: A Modern History*, 2nd edn (Macmillan, 1978), p. 5
2. *Guardian*, 5 March 1985
3. Eric Walker, *A History of South Africa*, 3rd edn (Longman, 1962), p. 72
4. *Times*, 13 August 1984
5. André Brink, *Mapmakers* (Faber & Faber, 1983), p. 15
6. W. A. de Klerk, *The Puritans in Africa* (Penguin, 1976)
7. *SA Hansard*, June 1984, cols. 9836–7
8. *Star*, 16 October 1985
9. *Guardian*, 1 November 1985
10. *SA Digest*, 4 October 1985
11. Capital Radio, 7 November 1985
12. *Cape Herald*, 19 October 1985
13. De Klerk, *The Puritans in Africa*, p. 98

Race Classification

1. *Laws* 1948–76, p. 16
2. ibid.
3. *Laws* 1948–76, pp. 16–19
4. ibid.
5. ibid.
6. ibid.
7. *RDM*, 23 July 1983
8. ibid.
9. ibid.
10. *RDM*, 23 July 1983
11. ibid.
12. ibid.
13. *Laws* 1948–76, pp. 16–19
14. ibid.
15. ibid.
16. *CT*, 8 February 1985
17. *Argus*, 9 February 1985
18. AP, 6 April 1984
19. *RDM*, 23 July 1983
20. *ST*, 4 November 1984
21. *Argus*, 27 August 1984
22. *Guardian*, 5 March 1985
23. ibid.
24. AP, 10 March 1985; *ST*, 3 March 1985
25. *ST*, 3 March 1985
26. SAPA, 13 October 1985

Sex across the Colour Line

1. *Star*, 28 November 1984
2. ibid.
3. *Times*, 26 April 1985
4. *RDM*, 16 April 1985
5. ibid.
6. ibid.
7. *Guardian*, 12 July 1984
8. *RDM*, 16 April 1985
9. AP, 29 October 1985; *ST*, 3 November 1985
10. *ST*, 3 November 1985
11. *Daily Express*, 8 November 1985
12. *Guardian*, 12 July 1984
13. *Guardian*, 16 April 1985
14. W. A. de Klerk, *The Puritans in Africa* (Penguin, 1976), pp. 270–72; *Star*, 14 July 1984
15. Official figures
16. *CT*, 13 February 1985
17. Parliamentary answer, 14 March 1984
18. *Star*, 14 July 1984
19. *Guardian*, 16 April 1985
20. ibid.
21. *Star*, 14 July 1984
22. *Guardian*, 16 April 1985
23. ibid.
24. *Laws* 1948–79, pp. 19–20

25. ibid.
26. Eric Walker, *A History of South Africa*, 3rd edn (Longman, 1962), p. 72.
27. De Klerk, *The Puritans in Africa*, pp. 270–72
28. CT, 4 February 1984
29. Leo Marquard, *The Peoples and Policies of South Afirca*, 3rd edn (OUP, 1962), p. 173
30. Julius Lewin, *Politics and Law in South Africa* (Merlin Press, 1963)
31. *Citizen*, 2 October 1985 and 18 November 1985

Group Areas

1. *Laws* 1948–79, pp. 39ff.
2. *WM*, 3 September 1985
3. *Laws* 1948–79, pp. 39ff.
4. *Express*, 9 December 1984
5. *RDM*, 26 February 1985
6. *CT*, 8 May 1984
7. *RDM*, 26 February 1985
8. *SAPA*, 2 October 1985
9. *FM*, 18 October 1985
10. SA Radio, 8 October 1985
11. *Sunday Star*, 6 October 1985
12. *Star*, 29 June 1984
13. AP, 30 May 1985
14. *SA Hansard*, 26 February 1985, Col. 292
15. AP, 8 February 1985
16. *CT*, 27 March 1985
17. *BD*, 28 August 1985
18. *Cape Herald*, 12 October 1985
19. *Guardian*, 2 September 1985
20. *CT*, 25 January 1985

National Government

1. This section based on government publications; *Survey* 1983, pp. 71–8; and press reports

Local Government

1. *Laws* 1948–79, p. 33
2. *Laws* 1948–79, pp. 33ff.; *Survey* 1983, pp. 246ff.

3. *Yearbook* 1983, pp. 157ff.
4. ibid.
5. *Guardian*, 10 May 1985
6. *Yearbook* 1983, p. 162
7. *Survey* 1983, p. 246; *Yearbook* 1983, p. 164
8. *Yearbook* 1983, p. 165
9. *Survey* 1983, pp. 248–50
10. SAPA, 8 November 1985
11. *Survey* 1983, pp. 248–50
12. *Argus*, 24 January 1983
13. *Survey* 1983, p. 248
14. *Pretoria News*, 27 October 1984
15. *Laws* 1948–79, p. 35
16. *Survey* 1983, pp. 252–61
17. ibid.
18. ibid.
19. ibid.
20. ibid.
21. ibid.
22. ibid.
23. *Guardian*, 23 May 1985
24. *Guardian*, 9 November 1985
25. *EPH*, 29 August 1985
26. *BD*, 21 October 1985
27. *Sowetan*, 12 August 1985
28. *Sash*, August 1985

Social Segregation

1. *Yearbook* 1985, p. 231
2. Reuter, 14 August 1985
3. *Laws* 1948–79, pp. 49ff.
4. ibid.
5. ibid.
6. *Survey* 1978, p. 362
7. *Laws* 1948–79, p. 50
8. *Laws* 1948–79, pp. 50–61
9. ibid.
10. *Survey* 1983, p. 224
11. *Survey* 1983, p. 225
12. *Laws* 1948–79, pp. 56–8
13. *Argus*, 13 March 1985
14. *Laws* 1948–79, pp. 63–4
15. *Guardian*, 8 October 1985; *Citizen*, 2 November 1985
16. *Survey* 1983, p. 220; *Survey* 1982, p. 352; *Laws* 1948–79, p. 62

17. *CT*, 27 March 1985
18. *Survey* 1984, p. 361
19. *Burger*, 18 January 1985
20. *Argus*, 9 September 1985; *EPH*, 3 October 1985
21. *Argus*, 14 March 1985
22. *Survey* 1983, pp. 51 and 65
23. *Guardian*, 25 October 1983; *Survey* 1983, p. 224
24. ibid.
25. *EPH*, 2 November 1984
26. *Sunday Star*, 18 December 1984
27. ibid.
28. *Witness*, 6 September 1984
29. *Star*, 18 August 1984
30. *EPH*, 22 November 1984
31. *Express*, 2 December 1984
32. *AP*, 15 February 1985
33. *AP*, 26 February 1985
34. *CT*, 26 February 1985
35. *Sowetan*, 8 August 1985
36. *Argus*, 3 August 1985
37. ibid.

Beach Apartheid

1. *Laws* 1948–79, pp. 49ff. and 64ff.
2. *Survey* 1982, p. 356
3. *AP*, 12 March 1984
4. *Survey* 1982, p. 356
5. *CT*, 14 September 1983
6. *ST*, 23 December 1984
7. *Tribune*, 30 December 1984
8. *CT*, 21 January 1985
9. *CT*, 17 January 1985
10. *CT*, 13 December 1984
11. *Deurbraak*, August 1985
12. *RDM*, 13 March 1985
13. *RDM*, 26 June 1984
14. *Deurbraak*, August 1984
15. ibid.
16. *Survey* 1984, p. 367
17. *Survey* 1984, p. 366
18. *Times*, 1 December 1983
19. *Laws* 1948–76, p. 49
20. *Guardian*, 27 September 1984
21. *Tribune*, 25 November 1984
22. Capital Radio, 4 October 1985
23. *DD*, 10 September 1984
24. *RDM*, 24 February 1983
25. *Survey* 1984, p. 367
26. *Guardian*, 27 August 1984

Transport

1. *Laws* 1948–79, p. 53; Reuter, 24 June 1985
2. *Times*, 1 December 1983
3. Reuter, 19 December 1984
4. *Laws* 1948–79, p. 52
5. *RDM*, 15 March 1984
6. *RDM*, 6 March 1985
7. *Laws* 1948–79, p. 53; *Survey* 1985, p. 368
8. *ST*, 3 March 1985
9. *Laws* 1948–79, p. 53
10. *ST*, 2 December 1984
11. *RDM*, 16 August 1983
12. *Laws* 1948–79, p. 53
13. *City Press*, 24 June 1984
14. *BD*, 16 August 1985
15. *Survey* 1984, p. 412
16. *Survey* 1984, pp. 414–6
17. ibid.
18. *Star*, 27 January 1983
19. *Survey* 1983, p. 404
20. *Tribune*, 2 March 1983
21. *Survey* 1983, pp. 401–2
22. ibid.
23. *Star*, 1 July 1984
24. *Survey* 1984, p. 431
25. *Survey* 1983, pp. 288–9
26. *Star*, 28 June 1983 and 1 July 1984
27. *CT*, 16 September 1985
28. *Yearbook* 1985, pp. 433–4

Sport

1. *Yearbook* 1985, p. 845
2. ibid.
3. *Survey* 1983, pp. 640–42
4. SA Radio, 13 September 1985
5. *Survey* 1983, p. 638
6. *Survey* 1984, pp. 923–4
7. *ST*, 27 May 1984

8. *Survey* 1982, p. 586
9. *Survey* 1983, p. 640
10. *Survey* 1984, p. 924
11. *Survey* 1983, pp. 642–9
12. *ST*, 14 October 1984

Social Welfare

1. *Yearbook* 1985, p. 649
2. *Laws* 1948–79, pp. 163–7
3. ibid.
4. *Survey* 1983, p. 509
5. *Argus*, 15 August 1985; *BD* 5 September 1985
6. *Survey* 1984, pp. 728 and 508ff.
7. *Survey* 1984, p. 729
8. ibid.
9. *Survey* 1984, p. 734
10. *Survey* 1983, pp. 514–15
11. *Survey* 1984, pp. 730
12. *CT*, 4 March 1984
13. *Witness*, 14 December 1984
14. *Express*, 16 September 1984
15. ibid.
16. *EPH*, 16 May 1985
17. *Tribune*, 22 January 1984
18. *WM*, 25 October 1985
19. *Survey* 1984, p. 734
20. *Survey* 1984, p. 735
21. *Survey* 1984, p. 717

Health

1. *Yearbook* 1985, p. 659
2. *Sowetan*, 12 July 1983
3. *Survey* 1984, p. 717
4. *CT*, 15 April 1984
5. *Survey* 1983, p. 485
6. ibid.
7. *Survey* 1983, p. 488
8. *Laws* 1948–79, p. 160
9. Reuter, 18 December 1984
10. *Argus*, 23 April 1983; *CT*, 20 April 1984
11. *Survey* 1983, p. 490
12. *Yearbook* 1985, p. 26
13. *SA Hansard*, 21 February 1985, col. 218

14. *Star*, 21 January 1985
15. *DD*, 18 April 1984
16. *RDM*, 13 April 1984
17. *Survey* 1983, pp. 503–4
18. *Survey* 1984, p. 724
19. *Survey* 1983, pp. 503–4
20. *Survey*, 1983, pp. 501–3
21. *CT*, 16 April 1984
22. *CT*, 7 April 1984
23. *FM*, 20 April 1984
24. *Survey* 1983, p. 501
25. *Yearbook* 1985, p. 26
26. *Survey* 1985, p. 721
27. *Yearbook* 1985, p. 26
28. *Yearbook* 1985, p. 666
29. *Survey* 1983, pp. 504–6
30. ibid.
31. ibid.
32. *RDM*, 22 March 1983
33. *Leader*, 18 October 1985
34. *Guardian*, 21 February 1985
35. *Guardian*, 31 January 1985
36. *Guardian*, 6 July 1985; SA Radio, 16 October 1985
37. *EPH*, 3 October 1985
38. SA Radio, 21 October 1985
39. Capital Radio, 22 October 1985
40. *Argus*, 3 August 1985; *WM*, 25 October 1985

Education

1. *ST*, 29 September 1985
2. *Survey* 1984, p. 648
3. *Survey* 1984, p. 650
4. *Guardian*, 23 April 1985
5. *Survey* 1984, p. 658
6. Official figures
7. ibid.
8. ibid.
9. ibid.
10. *Star*, 30 January 1985
11. *Survey* 1983, p. 439
12. Official figures
13. *Survey* 1983, pp. 436–7
14. Official figures
15. AP, 30 December 1985; SAPA, 29 December 1985

Higher Education

1. *Survey* 1984, p. 694
2. *Beeld*, 4 October 1985
3. *Argus*, 18 October 1985; SAPA, 17 October 1985
4. *ST*, 25 August 1985
5. *Survey* 1983, pp. 461–3
6. *Survey* 1983, p. 461
7. ibid.
8. *Survey* 1983, p. 460
9. SAPA, 25 October 1985; *CT*, 1 November 1985

Employment

1. *Laws* 1948–79, pp. 86–7
2. *Laws* 1948–79, pp. 84–93; *RDM*, 24 June 1983
3. Reuter, 24 May 1985
4. Reuter, 17 November 1985; SAPA, 18 November 1985
5. *FM*, 18 January 1985
6. *Laws* 1948–79, pp. 84–93; *RDM*, 24 June 1983
7. *BD*, 30 August 1985
8. *Argus*, 23 May 1984
9. *Survey* 1983, p. 125
10. *ST*, 22 July 1984
11. *Argus*, 11 February 1984
12. *RDM*, 29 October 1984
13. *Survey* 1983, p. 134; *RDM*, 29 October 1984
14. *Laws* 1948–79, p. 101
15. *Survey* 1984, p. 247
16. *Survey* 1983, p. 136
17. *Finance Week*, 23 June 1983
18. *WP*, 22 June 1985
19. *ST*, 4 August 1985
20. *FM*, 9 August 1985
21. *CP*, 25 August 1985
22. *Star*, 8 December 1983
23. *CT*, 21 October 1983
24. *Star*, 27 April 1983
25. *Argus*, 22 October 1985
26. *EPH*, 23 October 1985
27. *Witness*, 19 April 1984
28. Reuter, 25 October 1984
29. *Sowetan*, 19 April 1984

30. *RDM*, 17 April 1984
31. ibid.
32. *Argus*, 24, April 1984
33. *RDM*, 16 April 1984
34. SAPA, 26 September 1985; *SAD*, 11 October 1985
35. *Guardian*, 12 November 1985

Trade Unions

1. *Survey* 1983, p. 177
2. *RDM*, 2 March 1983
3. *RDM*, 25 March 1983
4. *FM*, 9 September 1983
5. *Survey* 1983, p. 177
6. *Laws* 1948–79, pp. 106–7
7. ibid.
8. *Laws* 1948–79, p. 108; *Yearbook* 1983, p. 474
9. *RDM*, 10 October 1983
10. ibid.
11. *Yearbook* 1983, p. 473
12. *Survey* 1983, pp. 190–93
13. *FM*, 18 January 1985
14. *Survey* 1983, pp. 190–93
15. *Survey* 1984, p. 324
16. *Argus*, 9 March 1983; *Survey* 1984, p. 313
17. *BD*, 21 September 1985
18. *Guardian*, 2 December 1985
19. *Survey* 1983, pp. 178–9
20. *Sowetan*, 29 September 1983
21. *Guardian*, 23 February 1985
22. *Survey* 1983, pp. 195–8
23. *Survey* 1983, pp. 200 and 206
24. *FT*, 10 May 1985; *Tribune*, 20 October 1985
25. *FM*, 9 September 1983
26. *Survey* 1983, pp. 205–6
27. *Yearbook* 1983, pp. 459 and 461
28. *Yearbook* 1983, p. 460
29. *Survey* 1983, pp. 188–90

The Homelands

1. *Yearbook* 1983, p. 195
2. *Yearbook* 1983, pp. 203–4
3. *Laws* 1948–79, pp. 3 and 16
4. *Survey* 1984, pp. 184–5

5. *Guardian*, 12 September 1985; SAPA, 11 September 1985; *BD*, 26 September 1985
6. *SA Hansard*, 26 June 1984, col. 9834
7. National Union of South African Students, *The Ciskei* (Cape Town, 1983)
8. *RDM*, 22 November 1983
9. *Yearbook* 1983, p. 205
10. *Survey* 1983, pp. 132ff.
11. *SA Hansard*, 26 June 1984, cols. 9832ff., and 5 July 1984, cols 10649ff.
12. ibid.
13. ibid.
14. ibid.
15. *Pace*, February 1983
16. *Argus*, 11 February 1983
17. John Dugard, *The Denationalization of Black South Africans in Pursuance of Apartheid*, Centre for Applied Legal Studies Occasional Papers 8 (University of the Witwatersrand, Johannesburg, 1984), pp. 6–7
18. *Laws* 1948–79, pp. 17ff.
19. *SA Hansard*, 7 February 1978, col. 579 (quoted in Dugard, *Denationalization*)
20. Dugard, *Denationalization*
21. *Guardian*, 26 January 1985
22. *Guardian*, 20 April 1985
23. SAPA, 11 September 1985; *SAD*, 20 September 1985
24. *EPH*, 29 September; *RDM*, 3 December 1983
25. *RDM*, 14 September 1983
26. *Laws* 1948–79, pp. 275ff.; Barry Streek and Richard Wicksteed, *Render Unto Kaiser: A Transkei Dossier* (Ravan Press, Johannesburg, 1981), chaps. 11–13
27. *Survey* 1983, pp. 354ff.
28. *Guardian*, 25 August 1984
29. SAPA, 21 July 1985
30. *Guardian*, 15 October 1985; *Sunday Star*, 13 October 1985
31. *Survey* 1983, p. 329
32. *Pace*, October 1983
33. *Guardian*, 27 February 1984
34. ibid.
35. *Tribune*, 23 January 1983
36. ibid.
37. ibid.
38. ibid.
39. *DD*, 2 September 1983
40. Nicholas Haysom, *Ruling with the Whip* (Centre for Applied Legal Studies, University of the Witwatersrand, Johannesburg, 1983)
41. *Pace*, July 1983
42. *City Press*, 7 August 1983; for a full account of Ciskei unrest see Haysom, *Ruling with the Whip*
43. *ST*, 20 January 1985; *CT*, 23 January 1985
44. *DD*, 4 August 1985; *CP*, 15 September 1985

The Pass Laws

1. SAPA, 21 May 1985
2. *ST*, 11 August 1985
3. Reuter, 10 September 1985
4. *Laws* 1948–79, p. 69
5. *Laws* 1948–79, p. 70
6. *Yearbook* 1983, p. 278
7. *Deurbraak*, August 1985
8. *Laws* 1948–79, pp. 69 ff.
9. *Laws* 1948–79, pp. 20 and 70
10. Official figures; AP, 13 February 1985
11. Official figures
12. *Survey* 1983, p. 264
13. ibid.
14. *RDM*, 1 May 1984
15. *Star*, 13 April 1984
16. *Mercury*, 23 October 1985
17. *Survey* 1984, p. 350
18. *RDM*, 12 March 1983
19. *CT*, 16 July 1983
20. *CT*, 24 and 25 June 1983
21. *FM*, 22 April 1983
22. *Guardian*, 7 June 1984
23. *Survey* 1984, p. 351
24. *Laws* 1948–79, p. 70; SAPA, 10 June 1985

25. ibid.
26. *RDM*, 31 May 1983
27. *RDM*, 31 May 1983; *Survey* 1983; *Survey* 1982
28. *WM*, 20 September 1985
29. *Argus*, 27 February 1985
30. *EPH*, 7 June 1984; *CT*, 9 June 1984; *Star*, 10 June 1984; *RDM*, 30 June 1984
31. *Survey* 1983, p. 267
32. *RDM*, 30 June 1984
33. *Survey* 1984, p. 348
34. *FM*, 15 March 1985
35. *Guardian*, 13 and 14 September 1985; *SAD*, 20 September 1985
36. *SAPA*, 25 September 1985
37. *FM*, 4 October 1985
38. *Daily Telegraph*, 2 December 1985

Removals

1. *Survey* 1983, pp. 298ff.; *Star*, 10 June 1983
2. *Star*, 10 June 1983
3. ibid.
4. *Star*, 15 June 1984
5. *Times*, 17 May 1984
6. *RDM*, 7 March 1985
7. *CT*, 6 March 1985
8. Cosmas Desmond, *The Discarded People* (Penguin, 1971), pp. 224ff.
9. *Survey* 1983, pp. 302ff.
10. *Times*, 17 May 1984
11. ibid.
12. *Survey* 1983, p. 299
13. *Sash*, May 1984; *Survey* 1983, pp. 306ff.
14. *Tribune*, 22 September 1985
15. *Survey* 1983, p. 300
16. *Survey* 1983, p. 309
17. *Star*, 10 June 1983
18. *DD*, 10 June 1983
19. *Times*, 2 February 1985; *Guardian*, 2 February 1985
20. *Guardian*, 10 May 1985
21. Reuter, 26 February 1985; *IHT*, 28 February 1985
22. *ST*, 7 April 1985
23. *WM*, 30 August 1985

Housing

1. E.g., *RDM*, 16 March 1983
2. *Star*, 16 July 1983
3. *Laws* 1948–79, pp. 44–5
4. *Guardian*, 26 January 1985; *SA Hansard*, 25 January 1985
5. SA Radio, 12 September 1985
6. AP, 4 December 1985
7. *Sowetan*, 31 July 1985
8. SAPA, 30 August 1985
9. *Laws* 1948–79, pp. 44–5
10. ibid.
11. *Star*, 7 March 1983
12. *CT*, 4 August 1983
13. *BD*, 11 September 1985
14. *Star*, 7 March 1983
15. *CT*, 24 June 1983
16. *Survey* 1983, p. 268
17. *Witness*, 11 July 1983
18. *FM*, 11 March 1984
19. *Survey* 1983, p. 231
20. *Argus*, 30 October 1985
21. *Citizen*, 12 July 1985
22. *Sowetan*, 31 July 1985
23. *Survey* 1983, p. 273
24. *Survey* 1983, p. 284
25. *Star*, 6 July 1983
26. *CT*, 30 March 1983

Squatting

1. *Survey* 1983, p. 231
2. *CT*, 24 February 1983
3. *Laws* 1948–79, pp. 46ff.
4. ibid.
5. *Laws* 1948–79, p. 47
6. *Guardian*, 20 November 1985
7. *Guardian*, 14 November 1985
8. *Survey* 1983, p. 487
9. *ST*, 7 April 1985
10. *FM*, 20 September 1985

Defence

1. *Times*, 19 March 1985
2. *Guardian*, 29 March 1984
3. *Resister*, no. 32, June/July 1984

4. *Sunday Star*, quoted in *West Africa*, 18 February 1985
5. *Guardian*, 19 May 1985
6. *CT*, 8 November 1984
7. ibid.
8. ibid.
9. *Yearbook* 1983, p. 317
10. ibid.
11. *Argus*, 18 January 1984
12. ibid.
13. *Times*, 2 August 1984
14. *RDM*, 29 September 1983
15. *Survey* 1983, pp. 575–7
16. *Citizen*, 13 August 1984
17. *Resister*, no. 35, December/January 1984–5
18. *CT*, 10 September 1985
19. *CT*, 2 September 1985
20. *IHT*, 19 August 1985
21. *Total War in South Africa* (Allies Press, 1984), p. 9
22. ibid., p. 8
23. *Survey* 1983, p. 578
24. *AP*, 27 August 1985
25. *EPH*, 16 August 1984
26. *CT*, 14 March 1985
27. *Tribune*, 18 August 1985
28. *CT*, 10 June 1983
29. *Mercury*, 4 September 1985
30. *Star*, 14 September 1985
31. *Citizen*, 22 September 1984
32. *Star*, 22 March 1983
33. *Star*, 4 August 1983
34. *Citizen*, 29 May 1985
35. *Guardian*, 18 March 1985; *FT*, 18 and 29 March 1985
36. *Guardian Weekly*, 27 October 1984
37. Capital Radio, 20 December 1985

Police

1. *ST*, 27 October 1985; SA Radio, 12 November 1985
2. *CT*, 29 March 1984; Budget figures
3. *Laws* 1948–79, pp. 199–200
4. ibid.
5. *Times*, 3 May 1985

6. *Survey* 1984, pp. 788–9; *Survey* 1983, p. 533
7. ibid.
8. *CT*, 16 February 1984
9. *SASPU Focus*, December 1982
10. *RDM*, 9 March 1983
11. *Survey* 1983, p. 534
12. *Times*, 22 February 1984
13. *City Press*, 10 November 1985
14. *Guardian*, 3 April 1984
15. *RDM*, 9 March 1983
16. *Survey* 1983, p. 535
17. *CT*, 12 September 1985
18. Reuter, 22 August 1985
19. *WM*, 20 September 1985
20. SA Radio, 21 August 1985
21. *IHT*, 13 February 1985
22. *Argus*, 26 September 1985
23. *Star*, 18 April 1985
24. *Survey* 1984, p. 792
25. *Star*, 18 April 1984
26. AP, 12 March 1985
27. *Star*, 18 October 1984; *Guardian*, 7 October 1985

Crime

1. *Survey* 1983, p. 525
2. *FM*, 23 November 1984
3. ibid.
4. *Sash*, May 1984
5. *Survey* 1984, p. 785
6. *FM*, 23 November 1984; *Guardian*, 4 January 1986
7. ibid.
8. AP, 24 July 1984; *RDM*, 27 December 1984
9. *RDM*, 27 December 1984
10. *Argus*, 3 February 1983
11. *Argus*, 12 August 1983
12. *EPH*, 18 December 1984
13. *Star*, 27 December 1984
14. *Survey* 1983, p. 526
15. *Sash*, May 1984

Punishment

1. *Laws* 1948–79, p. 193
2. Reuter, 26 February 1985

3. *Survey* 1983, pp. 528–9
4. *Guardian*, 31 January 1985
5. *Survey* 1984, p. 785
6. *Survey* 1981, p. 66
7. ibid.
8. *Survey* 1984, pp. 783–4
9. *Mercury*, 20 April 1984
10. *CT*, 25 October 1985
11. *Star*, 10 October 1985
12. *RDM*, 16 April 1985
13. *Survey* 1983, p. 524
14. *Survey* 1983, pp. 523–4
15. *Survey* 1983, p. 525
16. *Star*, 11 April 1983
17. ibid.
18. *Guardian*, 25 May 1984
19. *DD*, 2 March 1985
20. *Tribune*, 27 January 1985
21. *Deurbraak*, August 1985
22. *Survey* 1970, pp. 43–6
23. *Tribune*, 27 January 1985
24. *Guardian*, 20 September 1985
25. *RDM*, 24 April 1983
26. *Guardian*, 24 May 1984
27. ibid.
28. *Observer*, 11 December 1983
29. ibid.
30. *Guardian*, 6 February 1985
31. *Survey* 1982, p. 210
32. *Tribune*, 8 September 1985

Prisons

1. *Guardian*, 6 April 1984
2. *Sash*, May 1984; *Economist*, 8 October 1983
3. *Sash*, May 1984
4. *Star*, 14 October 1983
5. *SA Hansard*, 18 March 1985, col. 695
6. *Guardian*, 27 July 1985; *SA Hansard*, 18 March 1985, col. 695; *Survey* 1984, p. 797
7. *RDM*, 16 April 1985
8. *Guardian*, 6 June 1985
9. *Sash*, May 1984
10. *Star*, 12 May 1983
11. *Laws* 1948–79, p. 193

12. *Star*, 1 October 1983
13. *RDM*, 26 March 1983
14. *SA Hansard*, 21 May 1985
15. *City Press*, 27 February 1983
16. *Survey* 1984, p. 802
17. *Guardian*, 11 February 1985 and 25 November 1985
18. *Guardian*, 29 February 1985
19. ibid.
20. Reuter, 14 November 1985
21. *RDM*, 2 February 1985; *Guardian*, 25 November 1985
22. *Guardian*, 7 May 1985; *Survey* 1984, p. 747
23. *RDM*, 6 April 1984
24. *RDM*, 29 September 1980
25. *Survey* 1984, p. 805
26. SAPA, 21 and 22 August 1985

Security Services and Law

1. *CT*, 29 March 1984; *Survey* 1984, p. 770
2. *Laws* 1948–79, p. 245
3. *Laws* 1948–79, p. 247
4. *CT*, 25 January 1985
5. *Yearbook* 1983, p. 309
6. *Yearbook* 1983, p. 306
7. *Yearbook* 1983, p. 307
8. *RDM*, 4 February 1980
9. ibid.
10. *RDM*, 9 August 1979
11. *Argus*, 31 December 1979
12. ibid.
13. *Survey* 1970, p. 37
14. *Argus*, 5 January 1980
15. ibid.
16. *ST*, 24 July 1977
17. *RDM*, 4 May 1982
18. *RDM*, 6 June 1979
19. *FM*, 14 October 1983
20. T. R. H. Davenport, *South Africa: A Modern History*, 2nd edn (Macmillan, 1978), p. 280
21. *Guardian*, 10 April 1985
22. Raymond Suttner in *South African Review*, vol. II (Ravan Press, Johannesburg, 1984), pp. 63ff.

23. *Guardian*, 6 May 1985

Detention without Trial

1. *Laws* 1948–76, p. 467
2. *Laws* 1948–76, p. 440
3. *Laws* 1948–76, p. 468
4. ibid.
5. *Laws* 1948–76, pp. 469–70
6. *Laws* 1948–76, pp. 471–2
7. ibid.
8. *Laws* 1948–76, pp. 468–9
9. *Laws* 1948–76, p. 475
10. *Survey* 1983, p. 547
11. *Laws* 1948–76, p. 445
12. This answer is based on an article by John Dugard in *South African Law Journal*, vol. 99, 1982, pp. 589–604
13. Lawyers for Human Rights, *Bulletin*, no. 2, June 1983
14. *WM*, 20 September 1985; *Guardian*, 27 September 1985
15. Inquest records
16. *Laws* 1948–79, p. 242
17. ibid.
18. *Survey* 1983, p. 556
19. *CT*, 26 January 1985
20. *Star*, 29 January 1985; *WM*, 8 November 1985
21. Reuter, 3 January 1986; *WM*, 6 December 1985
22. SAPA, 2 December 1985
23. *CP*, 15 September 1985
24. *WM*, 8 November 1985
25. *Survey* 1982, p. 216
26. *DD*, 15 September 1977
27. *WM*, 13 September 1985
28. *Guardian*, 28 September 1985
29. *BD*, 17 October 1985
30. *CT*, 27 October 1985
31. *WM*, 25 October 1985

Banning orders

1. *Laws* 1948–76, pp. 423–9; *Survey* 1982, pp. 222–6
2. *Survey* 1982, pp. 222–6

3. *Laws* 1948–79, p. 217
4. *Star*, 5 December 1984; *WM*, 4 October 1985; AP, 15 November 1985
5. *Laws* 1948–76, pp. 429–31; *SA Hansard*, 5 March 1985
6. *Laws* 1948–76, p. 424
7. *Star*, 12 July 1983
8. *Observer*, 18 August 1985
9. *Times*, 22 August 1985
10. *Argus*, 21 October 1985
11. Reuter, 3 December 1985
12. SAPA, 21 December 1985; SA Radio, 22 December 1985; *IHT*, 23 December 1985; *Guardian*, 28 and 31 December 1985; *Guardian*, 6 January 1986

Banned Gatherings

1. *Laws* 1948–79, p. 208
2. *CT*, 23 March 1985
3. *CT*, 30 September 1985
4. *CT*, 28 October 1985
5. SAPA, 9 November 1985
6. SAPA, 29 November 1985
7. *Argus*, 31 October 1985
8. *Survey* 1982, pp. 224–5
9. *Laws* 1948–79, p. 211
10. *Laws* 1948–79, p. 209
11. ibid.
12. *Survey* 1984, p. 755
13. *Laws* 1948–79, p. 210
14. *Laws* 1948–79, pp. 418–23

Unlawful Organizations

1. *Laws* 1948–76, p. 27
2. ibid.
3. *Citizen*, 27 May 1985
4. *Sowetan*, 24 January 1985
5. *Deurbraak*, August 1985
6. Capital Radio, 30 August 1985
7. *Deurbraak*, August 1985
8. *Sunday Star*, 26 May 1985
9. *Laws* 1948–76, pp. 414–18
10. *Laws* 1948–76, pp. 412–13
11. *Laws* 1948–76, p. 415
12. *Laws* 1948–76, p. 400
13. *Laws* 1948–76, pp. 415–16

14. *Laws* 1948–76, p. 400
15. *Laws* 1948–76, p. 206
16. ibid.
17. *Laws* 1948–79, pp. 110, 166
18. *Laws* 1948–79, p. 205
19. *Laws* 1948–79, pp. 205–6

Passports and Visas

1. *Survey* 1983, pp. 546–7
2. *Survey* 1984, p. 757
3. ibid.
4. *Survey* 1983, p. 547; *Survey* 1982, p. 262
5. Capital Radio, 5 November 1985; *Times*, 20 December 1985
6. *CT*, 28 October 1985; *Argus*, 28 October 1985
7. *Yearbook* 1983, p. 280
8. *Laws* 1948–79, pp. 66–7
9. *Yearbook* 1983, p. 281
10. *Laws* 1948–76, p. 190
11. Reuter, 7 September 1985
12. Reuter, 24 October 1985; *WM*, 1 November 1985
13. *ST*, 20 January 1985
14. *RDM*, 17 September 1983
15. Capital Radio, 27 June 1985
16. *Citizen*, 10 July 1985

Right-wing Violence

1. *Tribune*, 4 August 1985
2. *Sunday Star*, 25 July 1985
3. *Guardian*, 8 August 1984
4. ibid.
5. ibid.
6. *CT*, 9 May 1983
7. ibid.
8. *Survey* 1982, pp. 231–2
9. *Survey* 1984, p. 82
10. *Guardian*, 14 August 1985
11. SAPA, 8 October 1985
12. *CT*, 16 October 1985
13. *CT*, 21 October 1985
14. SAPA, 16 November 1985
15. *CT*, 15 June 1983
16. *CT*, 25 June 1983

17. Reuter, 21 May 1984
18. *Times*, 2 May 1985
19. *Argus*, 15 April 1983
20. *RDM*, 21 April 1983
21. SAPA, 4 September 1985

Guerrilla Attacks

1. *Survey* 1983, p. 47
2. *FM*, 4 April 1983
3. *ST*, 29 September 1985
4. *FM*, 10 June 1983
5. *FM*, 18 March 1983
6. *Guardian*, 9 December 1985
7. Reuter, 8 March 1985
8. *Sunday Times* (London), 25 August 1985
9. *WM*, 11 October 1985
10. *Pretoria News*, 16 August 1985
11. *Sunday Times* (London), 25 August 1985
12. SAPA, 8 September 1985
13. ibid.
14. *Guardian*, 22 December 1984
15. AP, 10 March 1985
16. *Survey* 1983, pp. 45–6
17. *Observer*, 21 July 1985
18. *FM*, 15 November 1985; *WM*, 20 December 1985
19. SAPA, 9 September 1985
20. *Guardian*, 6 January 1986

The Churches

1. *Laws* 1948–79, pp. 50–51
2. *Survey* 1978, pp. 43–4
3. *Yearbook* 1985, pp. 783ff.
4. ibid.
5. *Survey* 1983, pp. 626ff.
6. *Argus*, 14 December 1984
7. *Star*, 31 July 1984
8. *Survey* 1983, pp. 626ff.
9. *Survey* 1983, p. 629
10. *Laws* 1948–79, p. 51
11. *Survey* 1984, pp. 485 and 910
12. *Guardian*, 19 February 1985
13. SA Radio, 14 October 1985
14. *Guardian*, 16 February 1984
15. *Times*, 21 March 1985
16. *Guardian*, 26 November 1985

The Press

1. *CT*, 1 December 1984
2. *Times*, 6 November 1985; *CT*, 14 November 1985
3. *CT*, 1 December 1984
4. *Fair Lady*, 6 March 1985
5. This section was written with the aid of Kelsey Stuart, *The Newspaperman's Guide to the Law*, 2nd edn (Butterworth, Durban, 1977)
6. *RDM*, 25 April 1983
7. *Journalist*, June 1983
8. AP, 26 October 1984
9. *Survey* 1984, p. 794
10. *Mercury*, 20 March 1985
11. *RDM*, 5 March 1983
12. *Star*, 24 February 1984
13. *Survey* 1983, pp. 211–13
14. Reuter, 31 August 1984
15. *Star*, 21 February 1983
16. Stuart, *Newspaperman's Guide*; *CT*, 24 November 1984
17. Interview with the author
18. *CT*, 29 August 1984
19. *WM*, 9 August 1985
20. *Argus*, 6 September 1985
21. *CT*, 30 October 1985
22. *Survey* 1984, pp. 886–7
23. ibid.
24. *EPH*, 13 February 1985 and 12 March 1985
25. Capital Radio, 30 August 1985; AP, 28 August 1985; AFP, 30 July 1985
26. Interview with the author
27. *WM*, 2 August 1985
28. *Tribune*, 6 May 1984
29. *Journalist*, December 1984
30. *South African Newsletter*, August 1984

Radio and Television

1. *Yearbook* 1985, p. 843
2. *Yearbook* 1985, pp. 841–4; *Citizen*, 22 June 1985
3. *Yearbook* 1983, p. 821
4. *RDM*, 5 May 1983

5. ibid.
6. *RDM*, 1 November 1983
7. SAPA, 4 September 1985
8. AP, 17 September 1985
9. SAPA, 2 November 1985; SAPA, 20 November 1985

Books

1. *Laws* 1948–79, p. 262
2. ibid.
3. *Yearbook* 1983, pp. 761–3
4. *Survey* 1982, p. 210
5. *Yearbook* 1983, p. 762
6. ibid.
7. *Laws* 1948–79, pp. 263–6
8. *Yearbook* 1983, p. 762
9. *Laws* 1948–79, pp. 263–6
10. *Survey* 1982, p. 266
11. *Yearbook* 1983, p. 762
12. *Laws* 1948–79, p. 266
13. *ST*, 30 December 1984
14. *Laws* 1948–79, p. 263
15. *Star*, 14 March 1983
16. *Tribune*, 17 February 1985
17. *RDM*, 27 April 1984
18. *Star*, 14 March 1983
19. *RDM*, 27 April 1984
20. *ST*, 30 December 1984
21. *Guardian*, 7 November 1983
22. *RDM*, 17 January 1983
23. *EPH*, 2 February 1983
24. *Argus*, 29 March 1983
25. *Tribune*, 17 February 1985
26. *Survey* 1984, pp. 883–4
27. *Laws* 1948–79, p. 264
28. *Laws* 1948–79, p. 265
29. *Star*, 25 February 1984
30. *Laws* 1948–79, p. 266
31. André Brink, *Mapmakers* (Faber & Faber, 1983)
32. Reuter, 14 December 1984
33. Brink, *Mapmakers*

Film and Theatre

1. *Laws* 1948–76, p. 264
2. ibid.
3. ibid.

4. *RDM*, 4 August 1984
5. *ST*, 20 January 1985
6. *Tribune*, 17 February 1985
7. *ST*, 17 February 1985
8. *Survey* 1984, pp. 882–3
9. *CT*, 1 November 1984
10. AP, 19 December 1984
11. *Survey* 1984, p. 882
12. *Argus*, 26 January 1983
13. *Index on Censorship*, 9 February 1984
14. *Star*, 30 July 1983
15. *Star*, 10 November 1983
16. *City Press*, 6 February 1983
17. *Tribune*, 17 February 1985
18. *CT*, 12 January 1985

State of Emergency

1. AP, 23 July 1985; *Sunday Times*, 21 July 1985
2. ibid.
3. ibid.
4. *Argus*, 20 October 1985; *Sash*, August 1985
5. *Sunday Times*, 21 July 1985
6. *Guardian*, 28 October 1985; SAPA, 26 October 1985
7. SAPA, 3 December 1985
8. *Sash*, August 1985
9. *Guardian*, 13 December 1985
10. SAPA, 4 November 1985
11. ibid.
12. *Guardian*, 16 November 1985
13. ibid.
14. *SAD*, 8 November 1985
15. AP, 15 August 1985
16. *WM*, 20 September 1985
17. SAPA, 26 October 1985
18. SAPA, 31 October 1985; *Guardian*, 7 December 1985
19. *CT*, 5 August 1985; AP, 29 October 1985
20. *ST*, 3 November 1985
21. *CT*, 25 October 1985
22. AP, 15 August 1985
23. AP, 23 July 1985
24. *Guardian*, 25 July 1985
25. ibid.
26. *Star*, 20 August 1985
27. ibid.
28. *Guardian*, 27 July 1985
29. *IH'''*, 19 November 1985
30. *BD*, 17 October 1985
31. SAPA, 10 and 13 November 1985
32. *WM*, 6 December 1985
33. *Sunday Star*, 16 September 1985
34. *WM*, 6 September 1985
35. SAPA, 25 September 1985
36. SAPA, 13 October 1985
37. AP, 23 August 1985
38. *Guardian*, 15 August 1985
39. SAPA, 15 November 1985
40. *Guardian*, 24 August 1985
41. *Guardian*, 17 October 1985; *Tribune*, 20 October 1985
42. *Times*, 29 August 1985
43. *Guardian*, 23 November 1985
44. *ST*, 13 October 1985
45. SAPA, 2 September 1985
46. SAPA, 25 October 1985
47. SA Radio, 4 December 1985
48. *CT*, 2 November 1985
49. *WM*, 6 December 1985
50. SAPA, 13 November 1985
51. *Star*, 25 October 1985
52. SAPA, 1 August 1985
53. *ST*, 25 August 1985
54. *FM*, 1 November 1985
55. *Guardian*, 1 August 1985
56. SAPA, 21 July 1985
57. Capital Radio, 22 July 1985; *DD*, 4 October 1985
58. *DD*, 4 August 1985
59. *Star*, 25 October 1985
60. *WM*, 6 December 1985
61. *FM*, 16 August 1985
62. *FM*, 11 October 1985
63. *FT*, 10 December 1985
64. *Argus*, 12 September 1985

Index of Legislation

Note: Bantu, Black and Native all refer to black Africans

General Index

A CHOICE OF PENGUINS

☐ **The Complete Penguin Stereo Record and Cassette Guide**
Greenfield, Layton and March £7.95

A new edition, now including information on compact discs. 'One of the few indispensables on the record collector's bookshelf' – *Gramophone*

☐ **Selected Letters of Malcolm Lowry**
Edited by Harvey Breit and Margerie Bonner Lowry £5.95

'Lowry emerges from these letters not only as an extremely interesting man, but also a lovable one' – Philip Toynbee

☐ **The First Day on the Somme**
Martin Middlebrook £3.95

1 July 1916 was the blackest day of slaughter in the history of the British Army. 'The soldiers receive the best service a historian can provide: their story told in their own words' – *Guardian*

☐ **A Better Class of Person** John Osborne £2.50

The playwright's autobiography, 1929–56. 'Splendidly enjoyable' – John Mortimer. 'One of the best, richest and most bitterly truthful autobiographies that I have ever read' – Melvyn Bragg

☐ **The Winning Streak** Goldsmith and Clutterbuck £2.95

Marks & Spencer, Saatchi & Saatchi, United Biscuits, GEC . . . The UK's top companies reveal their formulas for success, in an important and stimulating book that no British manager can afford to ignore.

☐ **The First World War** A. J. P. Taylor £4.95

'He manages in some 200 illustrated pages to say almost everything that is important . . . A special text . . . a remarkable collection of photographs' – *Observer*

A CHOICE OF PENGUINS

☐ *Man and the Natural World* **Keith Thomas** £4.95

Changing attitudes in England, 1500–1800. 'An encyclopedic study of man's relationship to animals and plants . . . a book to read again and again' – Paul Theroux, *Sunday Times* Books of the Year

☐ *Jean Rhys: Letters 1931–66*
   ·Edited by Francis Wyndham and Diana Melly £4.95

'Eloquent and invaluable . . . her life emerges, and with it a portrait of an unexpectedly indomitable figure' – Marina Warner in the *Sunday Times*

☐ *The French Revolution* **Christopher Hibbert** £4.95

'One of the best accounts of the Revolution that I know . . . Mr Hibbert is outstanding' – J. H. Plumb in the *Sunday Telegraph*

☐ *Isak Dinesen* **Judith Thurman** £4.95

The acclaimed life of Karen Blixen, 'beautiful bride, disappointed wife, radiant lover, bereft and widowed woman, writer, sibyl, Scheherazade, child of Lucifer, Baroness; always a unique human being . . . an assiduously researched and finely narrated biography' – *Books & Bookmen*

☐ *The Amateur Naturalist*
   Gerald Durrell with Lee Durrell £4.95

'Delight . . . on every page . . . packed with authoritative writing, learning without pomposity . . . it represents a real bargain' – *The Times Educational Supplement*. 'What treats are in store for the average British household' – *Daily Express*

☐ *When the Wind Blows* **Raymond Briggs** £2.95

'A visual parable against nuclear war: all the more chilling for being in the form of a strip cartoon' – *Sunday Times*. 'The most eloquent anti-Bomb statement you are likely to read' – *Daily Mail*

PENGUIN REFERENCE BOOKS

☐ **The Penguin Dictionary of Troublesome Words**   £2.50

A witty, straightforward guide to the pitfalls and hotly disputed issues in standard written English, illustrated with examples and including a glossary of grammatical terms and an appendix on punctuation.

☐ **The Penguin Guide to the Law**   £8.95

This acclaimed reference book is designed for everyday use, and forms the most comprehensive handbook ever published on the law as it affects the individual.

☐ **The Penguin Dictionary of Religions**   £4.95

The rites, beliefs, gods and holy books of all the major religions throughout the world are covered in this book, which is illustrated with charts, maps and line drawings.

☐ **The Penguin Medical Encyclopedia**   £4.95

Covers the body and mind in sickness and in health, including drugs, surgery, history, institutions, medical vocabulary and many other aspects. Second Edition. 'Highly commendable' – *Journal of the Institute of Health Education*

☐ **The Penguin Dictionary of Physical Geography**   £4.95

This book discusses all the main terms used, in over 5,000 entries illustrated with diagrams and meticulously cross-referenced.

☐ **Roget's Thesaurus**   £3.50

Specially adapted for Penguins, Sue Lloyd's acclaimed new version of Roget's original will help you find the right words for your purposes. 'As normal a part of an intelligent household's library as the Bible, Shakespeare or a dictionary' – *Daily Telegraph*